A. T.
JONES

Other books by George R. Knight (selected):

A Brief History of Seventh-day Adventists
A Search for Identity: The Development of the Seventh-day Adventist Beliefs
A User-friendly Guide to the 1888 Message
Ellen White's World
I Used to Be Perfect (Andrews University Press)
If I Were the Devil
Joseph Bates: The Real Founder of Seventh-day Adventism
Lest We Forget
Meeting Ellen White
Myths in Adventism
Organizing for Mission and Growth: The Development of Adventist Church Structure
Reading Ellen White
Sin and Salvation
The Apocalyptic Vision and the Neutering of Adventism
The Cross of Christ
Walking With Ellen White
William Miller and the Rise of Adventism (Pacific Press)

The Exploring Series
Exploring Ecclesiastes & Song of Solomon
Exploring Mark
Exploring Romans
Exploring Galatians & Ephesians
Exploring Hebrews
Exploring the Letters of John & Jude

To order, call 1-800-765-6955.

Visit us at
www.reviewandherald.com
for information on other Review and Herald® products.

A. T.
JONES

Point Man on
Adventism's Charismatic Frontier

GEORGE R. KNIGHT

REVIEW AND HERALD® PUBLISHING ASSOCIATION
Since 1861 | www.reviewandherald.com

Published by Review and Herald® Publishing Association, Hagerstown, MD 21741-1119

Review and Herald® titles may be purchased in bulk for educational, business, fund-raising, or sales promotional use. For information, e-mail SpecialMarkets@reviewandherald.com.

The Review and Herald® Publishing Association publishes biblically based materials for spiritual, physical, and mental growth and Christian discipleship.

The author assumes full responsibility for the accuracy of all facts and quotations as cited in this book.

This book was
Edited by Gerald Wheeler
Designed by Trent Truman
Typeset: 11/14 Berkeley Book

PRINTED IN U.S.A.

15 14 13 12 11   5 4 3 2 1

Library of Congress Cataloging-in-Publication Data

Knight, George R.
  A.T. Jones : point man on Adventism's charismatic frontier / George R. Knight.
    p. cm.
  Includes bibliographical references and index.
  1. Jones, Alonzo Trévier, 1850-1923. I. Title.
  BX6193.J64K58 2011
  286.7'32092--dc22
  [B]

ISBN 978-0-8280-2562-1

A. T. JONES

"Bro. Jones is a splendid man. Think he will make a stir worth something.
Give him a country and he will cut his own fodder."
—S. N. Haskell to J. S. White (1879)

"The Lord in his great mercy sent a most precious message to his
people through Elders Waggoner and Jones. This message was to bring
more prominently before the world the uplifted Saviour, the sacrifice
for the sins of the whole world. It presented justification through faith
in the surety, it invited the people to receive the righteousness of Christ,
which is made manifest in obedience to all the commandments of God. Many
had lost sight of Jesus. They needed to have their eyes directed to his divine
person, his merits, and his changeless love for the human family."
—E. G. White to O. A. Olsen (1895)

"Your work has been represented to me in figures. You were passing round
to a company a vessel filled with most beautified fruit. But as you offered
them this fruit, you spoke words so harsh, and your attitude was so forbidding,
that no one would accept it. Then another came to the same company, and
offered them the same fruit. And so courteous and pleasant were His words and
manner as He spoke of the desirability of the fruit, that the vessel was emptied."
—E. G. White to A. T. Jones (1902)

"Elder Jones will make a statement, and make it as strong as it will bear,
and then some of his disciples . . . will take his statement,
and make it ten times as strong as he did."
—F. M. Wilcox to M. C. Wilcox (1894)

IN APPRECIATION

of **Jeannette Johnson**,
to whom I owe more than I can ever express
for her unceasing encouragement and insight
as acquisitions editor at the Review and Herald.

CONTENTS

CONTENTS

A WORD TO THE READER

Controversial throughout his entire ministry, Alonzo T. Jones was one of the most fascinating personalities ever to grace a Seventh-day Adventist pulpit. Adventists have always had a curiosity regarding the powerful Jones, who meteorically rose to denominational prominence in 1888 and sank almost as rapidly into oblivion in the early twentieth century.

The primary purpose of *A. T. Jones: Point Man on Adventism's Charismatic Frontier* is to develop Jones's biography, with a special focus on his contributions to Adventism and its theology. As the subtitle indicates, an especially prominent aspect of the man and his contribution to Adventism centered on his charismatic personality and beliefs. A secondary purpose is to examine issues related to Jones's life and teachings that have become controversial since his death. It is, for example, impossible to comprehend his significance in twentieth-century Adventism without understanding such topics as the meaning of the 1888 experience and Jones's interpretation of the human nature of Christ. Chapters 5 and 11 have deviated somewhat from the strictly biographical format of the book to achieve its secondary goal.

To examine Jones's life is to study a cross section of Adventist history during one of its most formative and controversial periods. Because he was at the center of action, his biography, of necessity, must deal with such issues as the meaning of the 1888 General Conference session, the problem of 1893 and the delay of Christ's return, the nature of sanctification, the Adventist holiness movement, charismatic gifts, the role of Ellen White, the human nature of Christ, the Adventist crusade against a Christian America, church and state relationships, and the proper function of church organization. Those issues have been at the focal point of Adventist discussion for more than a century. As a result, the biography of A. T. Jones is not merely a fascinating story, but is pregnant with contemporary meaning.

Jones's life, of course, is of interest and value in its own right. How, we query, could one so blessed of God apostatize and fight the faith he spent so much of his adult life building up? After having studied Jones's life for three decades, I am haunted by two impressions. The first is that it seems incomprehensible that the mighty A. T. Jones of the 1890s ever could have fallen. The second is that his fall—given his character traits—was inevitable. The key to the paradox of Jones lies at the center of the message he preached so fervently—that the secret of salvation is through individual surrender of the self to Christ through faith, so that God can both justify and transform the human life. It was at that very point that Jones seems to have failed. He knew salvific truth, but he failed to internalize it and put it into practice. At this juncture, it is crucial for each reader to recognize that the seeds of A. T. Jones's potential for victory and failure lie within each of us. There is, therefore, existential meaning to be gleaned from his experience. That is particularly true because he was in many ways an archetype of the weaknesses and strengths of a large portion of the Adventist membership.

The reader will discover that Ellen White stands close to the center of Jones's Adventist experience. We can characterize his relationship to her as one of love and hate. The love came from the helpful, personal guidance and support she provided in his life. The hate stemmed from her stepping on his egotistic toes as well as his disillusionment when she failed to measure up to his human-made theory of inspiration. Once again, such feelings are not exactly unknown in late twentieth-century Adventism.

Seventh-day Adventists have published a large number of delightful stories about people's lives, but they have written little biography. Much of what has passed for biography has been hagiography (the writing of the lives of the saints), rather than histories of real people who desperately needed Jesus as their Saviour *after* becoming Christians. While the traditional stories are often helpful, they can be discouraging, since their readers' lives never seem to be quite so flawless. By way of contrast, A. T. Jones was a genuine human being in the same sense that the biblical Peter, David, and Judas were real persons. Jones had "warts" and problems that are quite similar to some of our characteristics and some of the experiences that we have to face. His struggles with pride, harshness, and so on are our struggles. On the other hand, his victories are similar to our victories. While we do not have to make his choices, we can certainly learn from them. I have attempted to paint the man Jones as a person who lived in the real world, which, as we know, is somewhat less than perfect. His world, unfortunately, may come across as even more imperfect than most of ours. If so, it is because he was embroiled in controversy for nearly his entire career. He seemed, in fact, to thrive in the midst of conflict.

In spite of Jones's importance in Adventist history, no extensive treatments of his life and work existed before my publishing of *From 1888 to Apostasy: The Case of A. T. Jones* in 1987. Subsequently I wrote two books on the 1888 experience that was so central to Jones's place in Adventist history—*Angry Saints* in 1989 and *A User-friendly Guide to the 1888 Message* in 1998.[1] Those books, along with the work of Gilbert Valentine on W. W. Prescott and Woodrow Whidden and Clinton Wahlen on E. J. Waggoner, have broadened and refined and at times transformed my understanding of Jones and his contribution to Adventism.[2]

Those new insights have helped me in the revising of my earlier biography of Jones. While the basic outline of that biography remains the same, the current version reflects changes in every chapter. The most radical are the addition of a chapter on Jones and faith healing, an almost total rewrite of the chapter dealing with the meaning of the Minneapolis event, major modifications in the chapter on the human nature of Christ, and lesser but significant additions and deletions from the sections dealing with Jones's bitter years and his views on church organization.

Readers need to keep my biographical focus in mind. While *A. T. Jones* has treated the man's theological, ecclesiological, and sociopolitical positions, it has not done so exhaustively. Of particular importance to aspiring scholars is the need to develop Jones's religious liberty contribution more fully, to carefully analyze his theology, and to write a history of the 1888 General Conference session that takes into account the massive data banks that have come to light in the past 35 years and the extensive secondary literature developed in that period.

I would expect that the majority of the readers of *A. T. Jones* will be Seventh-day Adventists, but its subject matter is of value to all who have an interest in the history of religion in America since it represents a cross section of Adventist history and it interrelates in significant ways with the larger culture—particularly in Jones's crusade against a Christian America and his advocacy of holiness and antimonopolistic principles. To some extent I have contextualized Jones within the larger religious issues of his time. I could have done more along that line, but ideas are long and space is short. Therefore, I had to limit contextual discussion more than might be desirable.

For help on my initial biography of Jones, I was indebted to many people for their inspiration, encouragement, insight, and hard work. Special thanks went to the archivists and librarians who provided invaluable aid in locating and obtaining documents. Among them were Donald Yost and Bert Haloviak, of the General Conference Archives; Louise Dederen, of the Adventist Heritage Center at Andrews University; Vida Lickey and Sandra Richardson, of the interlibrary loan division of the James White Library at Andrews University; Jim Nix, of the Loma Linda University Heritage Room; and Robert Olson and William Fagal and their staffs (especially Tim Poirier) at the Ellen G. White Estate offices in Washington, D.C., and Berrien Springs, Michigan. Without their help, I could never have completed my work.

Additional appreciation related to my early biographical work went to Lorena Bustos, who served as my research assistant for two years; to Patricia Saliba, who entered the manuscript into the computer while mastering the art of reading my handwriting; to Wilma Bing, who typed the footnotes; to Aldemar Hernandez, who computerized the index; to Bert Haloviak, C. Mervyn Maxwell, Richard W. Schwarz, Donald Yost, and Robert Olson, who offered helpful suggestions regarding content and format; to Richard Coffen, Penny Estes Wheeler, and Gerald Wheeler of the Review and Herald Publishing Association, who guided the book through the editorial process; and to the administration of Andrews University, for providing financial support and time to develop the manuscript.

For this revised biography I am in debt to my wife, Bonnie, who devoted countless hours to preparing the manuscript for publication; and to Jeannette Johnson, JoAlyce Waugh, and Gerald Wheeler, for shepherding it through the steps to publication.

My hope is that *A. T. Jones: Point Man on Adventism's Charismatic Frontier* will be helpful to its readers as it enables them to clarify issues in the realms of Christian belief and practice.

—George R. Knight
Rogue River, Oregon

---

[1] George R. Knight, *Angry Saints: Tensions and Possibilities in the Adventist Struggle Over*

Righteousness by Faith (Hagerstown, Md., 1989); George R. Knight, *A User-friendly Guide to the 1888 Message* (Hagerstown, Md., 1998).

 [2] Gilbert M. Valentine, *W. W. Prescott: Forgotten Giant of Adventism's Second Generation* (Hagerstown, Md., 2005); Woodrow Whidden II, *E. J. Waggoner: From the Physician of Good News to the Agent of Division* (Hagerstown, Md., 2008); Clinton L. Wahlen, "Selected Aspects of Ellet J. Waggoner's Eschatology and their Relationship to His Understanding of Righteousness by Faith" (M.Div. thesis, Andrews University, 1988).

A NOTE ON SOURCES AND ABBREVIATIONS

Space limitations have dictated making references as brief as possible. On the other hand, they must provide the essential information for those who desire to check the interpretation or extend the research. I have abbreviated names of people, organizations, and publications repeatedly used in order to achieve both brevity and completeness. References within each footnote generally follow the same order as employed in the text.

There is no existing collection of "Jones papers." The majority of the unpublished sources can be found in the Adventist Heritage Center at Andrews University, the General Conference Archives, and the offices of the Ellen G. White Estate. The need for brevity once again precluded listing the exact location of each document.

LIST OF ABBREVIATIONS

ACR	Anna C. Rice	EGW	Ellen G. White
Ad Her	*Adventist Heritage*	EJW	Ellet J. Waggoner
AFB	Albion Fox Ballenger	ESB	E. S. Ballenger
ALW	Arthur L. White	EWF	Eugene W. Farnsworth
AGD	Arthur G. Daniells	FEJ	Frances E. Jones
APVH	Adelia Patten Van Horn	FMB	Foreign Mission Board
AS	*American Sentinel*	FMW	Francis M. Wilcox
AS(2)	*American Sentinel* (ATJ's	GAI	George A. Irwin
	nondenominational	GC	General Conference
	journal, 1915-1923)	*GCB*	*General Conference Bulletin*
ATJ	Alonzo T. Jones	GCC	General Conference
ATR	Asa T. Robinson		Committee
BE	*Bible Echo*	*GCQB*	*General Conference*
CEH	Claude E. Holmes		*Quarterly Bulletin*
CHJ	Charles H. Jones	GIB	George I. Butler
CLT	Clifton L. Taylor	HHC	Harold H. Cobban
CPB	Calvin P. Bollman	*HM*	*Home Missionary*
DP	David Paulson	HWC	Hampton W. Cottrell
DTJ	Dan T. Jones	IDVH	Issac D. Van Horn

JHK	John Harvey Kellogg	SNH	Stephen N. Haskell
JNL	John N. Loughborough	*ST*	*Signs of the Times*
JSW	James S. White	TGB	Taylor G. Bunch
LEF	LeRoy E. Froom	US	Uriah Smith
LTN	Leroy T. Nicola	WAC	Willard A. Colcord
Min	Minutes	WAS	William A. Spicer
MM	*Medical Missionary*	WCW	William C. White
MS(S)	Manuscript(s)	WMH	William M. Healey
MW	Mary White	WTK	Walter T. Knox
OAO	Ole A. Olsen	WWP	William W. Prescott
RH	*Review and Herald*	*YI*	*Youth's Instructor*

A. T. Jones

CHAPTER I

CHARISMATIC FROM THE BEGINNING

Dead to the world, and alive to thee, O my God!" With those words and upraised hands Sergeant Alonzo T. Jones arose from his watery baptismal grave in Walla Walla, Washington Territory, August 8, 1874. For weeks he had been "earnestly seeking the Lord," and a few days earlier he had received "bright evidence of sins forgiven."[1]

Charismatic, forceful, handsome, and tending to extremes, A. T. Jones became a leading figure in the Adventist Church during the 1890s. In the first decade of the twentieth century, however, he would turn against the church he loved and develop into one of its most ardent foes. Throughout his career he was controversial, remaining so to this day.

Jones was proud of his military past. Any claim to military glory came from his participation in the Modoc war of northern California in 1873. "I was in and through," he writes, "the fight of three nights and days that drove the Modocs out of their stronghold. It was the good fortune of my squad to get between the stronghold and the lake, so as to shut them off from water and compel them to abandon the place."

Earlier in the "war" Jones's squad had been nearest the point where Lieutenant W. L. Sherwood had been treacherously shot while under a Modoc "flag-of-truce-trap." "It has always been one of the supremest satisfactions of my life," Jones commented, "that by pouring in a hail of bullets beyond where the wounded officer lay, my squad was able effectually to prevent any further savagery being perpetrated upon him; and so to protect him till he could be carried into camp." Though Sherwood soon died from his wounds, the rapid fire of Jones's squad, he claims, did provide cover for the escape of Lieutenant W. H. Boyle—the other unarmed peace negotiator.[2]

Born in Rockhill, Ohio, on April 21, 1850, Alonzo Trévier Jones enlisted as a private in the United States Army on November 2, 1870. He received his discharge as a sergeant five years later on the same day. Military records indicate that he was 5 feet 11 1/2 inches tall, had a fair complexion, hazel eyes, and light-brown hair.[3]

Descriptions of Jones at the peak of his career in the 1890s generally picture him as a large and dynamic person. Hjalmar Holand, for example, portrays "Mr. Jones" as "a big, powerful man and a good advertisement" of the value of certain theories on breathing he was proposing in the early nineties. Arthur Spalding, "one of his boys" in the nineties, writes that "Jones was a towering, angular man, with a loping gait and uncouth posturings and gestures. . . . Not only was he naturally abrupt, but he cultivated singularity of speech and manner, early discovering that it was an asset with his audiences."[4] Although comparatively tall in an era of poorer nutrition than that of the early twenty-first century, because of his personal forcefulness and aggressiveness Jones undoubtedly appeared even larger to his contemporaries than he actually was.

WORK IN THE NORTHWEST

Not being bashful, Jones delivered his first sermon soon after his baptism. It was a failure. Using Daniel 2 as his text, "he told all he knew in twenty minutes and Elder Van Horn [who had baptized him] had to take over and finish it." That was not an auspicious beginning for a preacher who would later deliver sermons that were printed as 60- to 100-page booklets. By 1894 Ellen White would write to him that his lengthy discourses were "a taxation to the hearers. . . . One half the matter presented would be more benefit to the hearer than the large mass poured forth." He regularly preached sermons that lasted between two and two and one-half hours.[5]

Between his discharge from the Army and 1878 Jones founded churches in Oregon and Washington and served as tentmaster and assistant to Isaac Van Horn. During the summer of 1877 Jones became convicted of his need for formal education, desiring to attend Battle Creek College. He also wanted to go east to preach the Adventist message to his family, whom he had not seen since joining the Army in 1870. At the forefront of his thoughts were his aging grandparents who had raised him and were "urging" him to come. The fact that they were "worth considerable property" and that "it would be for his financial interest to go there" also fueled his wish to visit Ohio. But he postponed such desire at the request of James White, president of the budding denomination, who asked Alonzo to continue his work in the Washington Territory.[6]

Those who met Jones during those early years went away impressed with his potential. S. N. Haskell wrote in 1879: "Bro. Jones is a splendid man. Think he will make a stir. Give him a country and he will cut his own fodder." Ellen White, who first encountered Jones in 1878, also recognized his possibilities. She noted to her husband on June 27 that "if Brother Jones could have the right starting in, he would make a promising young man." She pointed out that he was conscientious and deeply sensitive, but that he needed those traits to be "balanced aright." The problem was that he had no one to teach him or to be a good pastoral example in the Northwest. Appealing to James to reverse his decision to keep Jones in the West, she gently hinted that she wished "he could attend college this winter and next summer. . . . If Brother Jones could be instructed as some young men are being instructed at Battle Creek, it would be the making of him." A week later she reinforced her plea by writing: "Brother Jones is a promising young man, calls great congregations and is an acceptable speaker."[7]

Apparently James, who had to face a perpetual personnel shortage, did not respond to her suggestion. We find Jones still laboring in Oregon when Ellen White returned for the 1880 camp meeting season. During that visit the condition of the churches in the Northwest left her deeply depressed. "These poor souls have had no labor and yet they seem to cling to the truth, but are starving for food." She laid a great deal of the blame on Van Horn, who had accomplished little during the past year. He had spent most of his time building a home and caring for his family. "The only hope for Oregon," she despaired, "is for him to leave ."[8]

Ellen White was not nearly as discouraged with Jones, who, she claimed, had done the only work in that region during the past year. On the other hand, he had not managed in such discouraging circumstances to keep his record totally clean, as we see demonstrated by the fact that Stephen Haskell and Ellen White had not "dared" to let Van Horn or Jones preach at the camp meeting until they had "made as deep an impression as possible upon the people" in the hope of generating a spirit of reformation and genuine revival. By May 27 Mrs. White could gratefully write that advancement had taken place and that Van Horn and others had offered humble confession.[9]

Jones, to put it mildly, did not begin his work under favorable circumstances. To complicate matters, Van Horn was not only Jones's "teacher," immediate superior, and ministerial mentor, but had also been his brother-in-law since April 15, 1877, when Jones had married Mrs. Van Horn's sister, Frances E. Patten. For a time the two families had lived and worked together, but domestic difficulties soon drove them apart. After that, Jones mostly labored by himself. By August 1880 Van Horn was deeply concerned that Jones, who had not been replying to his letters, might "make shipwreck of his faith in the message." Ellen White must have shared his worry. She advised Alonzo to leave the Northwest as soon as he could, even if he had to borrow money. Apparently not sensing his danger, Jones thought it best not to go into debt and continued laboring in the Northwest.[10]

In 1880 the denomination split the work in the Northwest into two conferences, and Jones and his brother-in-law went their separate ways. Jones became the first secretary of the newly created Upper Columbia Conference. We should not inflate that honor beyond its actual importance, however, since the conference had only two ordained ministers. The other minister was the president.[11]

It was during this period that we find Jones's first recorded conflict with a Sunday law. A citizen of Dayton, Washington Territory, had contracted to supply the meals for the Upper Columbia Conference camp meeting. On Sunday they had a large number of diners, and the contractor did quite well. On Monday, however, the local authorities fined him $25 for violating the recently enacted, and very stringent, Sunday law of the territory. That incident undoubtedly heightened Jones's feelings concerning the justice of such legislation—legislation that he would devote most of his life to fighting.[12]

WIDER LABORS

Another concern that Jones would foster throughout the rest of the century also developed during the early 1880s. That was his interest in and support of the prophetic gift of Ellen White. In 1883 a man who had "great capacity for evil" and several others began a campaign against Mrs. White in Farmington, Washington, where Jones had made his home. Jones and his church sold several of James and Ellen White's *Life Sketches* and distributed *Signs of the Times* to combat the problem. As a result, he wrote to Ellen White, the people "now have a great desire to see you, and hear you, for themselves." A visit in the near future, he suggested, would do great good. "It is safe to say that if you shall come the whole community with one accord will turn out to hear you, because you have been so extensively advertised by our Enemies." Thus he early became an avid supporter of Ellen White. He not only promoted and defended her gifts, but he was also quite responsive to her personal counsel to him, suggesting that she was better acquainted with his true character than he was.[13]

While Jones wanted Ellen White to come to Farmington so that the community could evaluate her for itself, he also had ulterior motives. He hoped to add new members to his congregation, but, more important, he wanted her and her influential son to become better acquainted with his accomplishments. That is evident from a letter he wrote to W. C. White in April 1884.

In it he set forth his accomplishments in no uncertain terms. Jones utilized his role in the recent building of the Farmington church as a case in point. Not only had he raised the money for the materials, but—not having enough cash for labor—he constructed it with his "own hands." After the completion of the structure he still owed some for the material. In addition, he had some personal debts that he could not care for with his inadequate pay. As a result, he gladly accepted the invitation of the local public school board to teach for them. "This," he reported, "opened the way for me to pay off my debts without taxing the conference for anything, and gives a good church, and house, to the conference without costing it a cent." To top off his accomplishments, he had persuaded the local non-Adventist community to buy the bell for his church. Beyond that, he had recently doubled the church membership from 13 to 26 members.[14]

Undoubtedly Jones believed he was a success, and he was right. He was also quite sure that the time had come for him to leave the Northwest. "*I want to go East*," he wrote to W. C. White in his April 1884 letter. "I want to go to school. I want to see the workings of the cause there. And I want to learn how to do rightly, what may fall my lot. I want to learn everything." Next he reminded White that he had not left the Northwest when Ellen White had urged him to in 1880. Instead of going into debt, he had patiently waited and worked. As a result, Jones claimed that when he sold his property he would have enough cash to pay his expenses east, buy a house in his new location, go to school for a season, and give $1,000 or more to the cause. While his estimates of his possibilities appear to be quite inflated, they do suggest in quite certain terms that A. T. Jones was ready for a move.

Jones was telling White that the time had come for broader horizons. For 10 years Jones had quietly developed strength in ministerial skills and academic knowledge. Although he had been foiled in his desire to broaden his education in 1877 and had not felt free to leave in 1880, he now would not be denied the opportunity in 1884. His time had arrived. The young minister had demonstrated his credentials under the worst of circumstances, and now it was time to flex his muscles and utilize his talent in a larger sphere. From deep down in his being came the cry: "*Please let me go.*" With those words Jones ended his letter, suggesting that W. C. White could mention his desire to his mother if he thought it best.[15]

Jones's wish would be granted a few months later. The *Signs of the Times* for July 17, 1884, reported that the leadership was moving Elder Jones from the Northwest to give him broader experience and to further his education. Being transferred at the same time was Elder W. L. Raymond, who also needed greater exposure. Jones and Raymond had worked together in the Northwest for a number of years.

The latter individual is of vital interest in our effort to understand Jones because of his ecclesiastical aberrations. Raymond's difficulties lay mainly in "complaining of all the leaders and finding fault with the General Conference." By the early twentieth century Jones had imbibed that spirit and would be the foremost critic of the Seventh-day Adventist Church, particularly of the General Conference presidency. Coupled with Raymond's critical attitude were his "new light" and the belief that the denomination had no right to discipline wayward clergy. Citing the recent trials of liberal clergymen in the Presbyterian and Methodist churches, Joseph Harvey Waggoner, editor of the *Signs*, made it plain in responding to Raymond's ideas that denominations have both the right and the responsibility to discipline their ministers. Part of Raymond's problem was an inadequate doctrine of the church. While it is impossible to determine the amount of influence he had on Jones (or of Jones on Raymond), it seems to be more than coincidental that Jones later espoused Raymond's theories and attitudes toward the church and its leaders (see chapters 13 and 15).[16]

The ambitious young Jones did not get his opportunity to attend college in Battle Creek, Michigan—Adventism's power center—in 1884. Instead, he received a summons to the denomination's second most dynamic area—northern California. W. C. White, S. N. Haskell, and J. H. Waggoner, who had all met Jones several times in camp meeting tours of the Northwest, were not about to let that kind of talent drift east. Soon Jones was doing editorial work with Waggoner, who was editor of both the *Signs of the Times* and the *Sabbath Sentinel*. In his editorial activities Jones became acquainted with Waggoner's son, Ellet J. Waggoner. By 1887 Jones and E. J. Waggoner had become coeditors of both the *Signs* and the religious liberty journal.

Early in 1884, even before he left the Northwest, Jones's articles began to appear in the *Review and Herald*, the church's most important periodical. His first article, published in January, dealt with the little horn of Daniel 7:21, 22 and the proposed constitutional amendment put forth by the National Reform Association that would explicitly proclaim the United States to be a Christian nation. Four more hard-hitting contributions on prophecy and contemporary religious liberty issues followed in March, April, and May. The bluntness of his early articles, in which Jones claimed that the National Reform party was able to *"out-Jesuit* the Jesuits," is characteristic of his later writing style. His articles undoubtedly had helped influence J. H. Waggoner in his decision to take him on as an editorial assistant. Waggoner was impressed not only by Jones as a person, but also with him as a writer.[17]

By August 1884 Jones's material had become a regular feature in the *Signs*. He was soon doing public combat with Wilbur Crafts, the national champion of the Sunday law advocates.

The fall term of 1885 found Jones as the Bible teacher at Healdsburg College in northern California. His teaching, however, was in addition to his editorial duties, not in place of them. Although Jones taught several classes, the one that excited him most was his course on prophecy and history. He began with Genesis 10 and correlated the Bible story with history and prophecy. That led him into an in-depth study of the book of Daniel. By December 4, 1885, he and his students were deeply involved in tracing out the 10 kingdoms of Daniel 7—a topic that would eventually bring him into open conflict with Uriah Smith, editor of the *Review* and author of *Thoughts on Daniel and the Revelation.*[18]

Early in 1887, in addition to his other duties, Jones pastored the important Healdsburg church. According to one of his ministerial members, he was just the man for the job and "all the brethren love him."[19]

During the Healdsburg years the Jones family had its second child. Desi Jones was born on November 27, 1887. The first child, who had been born in the Northwest in 1883, was mentally incompetent and had to be cared for by others for her entire life. That unfortunate situation posed its own special problems for Jones and his wife—problems that strained their marriage relationship and brought distance between them.[20]

By 1887 A. T. Jones had developed into one of the denomination's most important workers on the West Coast. The next year would thrust him into the storm center of theological controversy within the church and into all-out war in the realm of religious liberty outside the denomination.

[1] *RH*, Aug. 25, 1874, p. 78; AS (2), July 1923, p. 3.

[2] ATJ to the Commissioner of Pensions, May 10, 1916. While Jones wrote this letter 43 years after the event, its contents are remarkably accurate according to the standard work on the topic. See Keith A. Murray, *The Modocs and Their War* (Norman, Okla., 1959), pp. 213-216, 192, 193. See also William H. Boyle, "Personal Observations on the Conduct of the Modoc War," in Peter Cozzens, ed., *Eyewitnesses to the Indian Wars, 1865-1890* (Mechanicsburg, Pa., 2002), vol. 2, pp. 148, 149; cf. pp. 107, 125, 237. Historian Frederick G. Hoyt, after extensive research on the topic, has challenged Jones's account, noting that he finds him nowhere mentioned by name in the contemporary records as having any significant part in the battle. And Hoyt may be correct. After all, Jones in applying for a military pension would want to make his part look as important as possible. On the other hand, it tended to be officers rather than enlisted men who got mentioned by name in such actions. That is definitely so in Boyle's own recounting of the incident and in other nineteenth century reports (see Cozzens above). Given the accuracy of Jones's account and the other facts of the case, we have no compelling reason to reject his general claim.

[3] The Adjutant General's Office to the Commissioner of Pensions, Nov. 19, 1917.

[4] Hjalmar Rued Holand in *Ad Her*, Spring 1986, p. 53; A. W. Spalding to R. Lukens, Aug. 3, 1952; A. W. Spalding, *Origin and History of Seventh-day Adventists* (Washington, D.C., 1961, 1962), vol. 2, p. 291.

[5] TGB to LEF, Nov. 1, 1961; TGB to ALW, Nov. 25, 1964; EGW to ATJ, November 1894; W. D. Emory to L. K. Dickson, c. April 1956; CLT to LEF, Nov. 9, 1960.

[6] IDVH to JSW, Apr. 16, Sept. 5, 1877; APVH to JSW, Aug. 5, 26, 1877; *RH*, Mar. 8, 22,

1877, pp. 80, 94; Mar. 7, Apr. 25, May 23, 1878, pp. 79, 135, 167; Sept. 22, 26, Nov. 21, 1878, pp. 95, 110, 166. For the context of Jones's work in Oregon and Washington, see Doug R. Johnson, *Adventism on the Northwestern Frontier* (Berrien Springs, Mich., 1996).

[7] SNH to JSW, June 4, 1879; EGW to JSW, June 27, July 3, 1878.

[8] EGW to JSW, May 16, 20, 1880; *ST*, June 17, 1880, pp. 272, 273.

[9] EGW to JSW, May 26, 1880.

[10] Marriage certificate, state of Oregon, county of Marion, recorded Apr. 16, 1877; IDVH to EGW, Apr. 1, 1884; Aug. 4, 1880; ATJ to WCW, Apr. 13, 1884.

[11] *ST*, June 17, 1880, pp. 272, 273; *RH*, July 19, 1881, pp. 59, 60; July 4, 1882, p. 427.

[12] *RH*, July 4, 1882, p. 427.

[13] ATJ to EGW, Nov. 5, 1883; cf. ATJ to WCW, Nov. 5, 1883; ATJ to EGW, Mar. 13, 1887.

[14] ATJ to EGW, Nov. 5, 1883; ATJ to WCW, Nov. 5, 1883; Apr. 13, 1884.

[15] ATJ to WCW, Apr. 13, 1884.

[16] EGW to SNH, c. June 10, 1884; *ST*, July 17, 1884, p. 424; cf. *ST*, July 3, 1884, p. 408.

[17] *RH*, Jan. 22, Mar. 25, Apr. 1, 8, May 13, 1884, pp. 49, 50, 202, 203, 209, 210, 226, 227, 306, 307.

[18] ATJ to WCW, Dec. 4, 1885.

[19] E. P. Daniels to EGW, Jan. 18, 1887.

[20] Application for death compensation or pension by widow and/or child, Sept. 20, 1940; W. O. Upson to Whom It May Concern, Sept. 16, 1940; A. B. Olsen to Whom It May Concern, Sept. 10, 1940; EGW to ATJ, Sept. 1902; EGW to ATJ, c. 1902 (J-207, 1901); EGW to ATJ et al., Mar. 23, 1906 (MS 34, 1906).

CHAPTER II

THE LOADED ATMOSPHERE OF 1888

W e have much reason to thank God and take courage as we enter the year 1888," wrote General Conference president George I. Butler in a circular letter to the Adventist ministry in January 1888. "Every incoming year adds, if possible, to the strength of our positions. Seventh-day Adventists have never taken a stand upon Bible exegesis which they have been compelled to surrender."[1]

Butler's letter was not merely a "state of the church" message. It was a notice to the opposition forces in Adventism's theological realm that they would not push any doctrinal changes past his administration. Also, in more subtle ways, it suggested that they had better not try.

The young editors of the *Signs of the Times* and the *American Sentinel*— Alonzo T. Jones and Ellet J. Waggoner (son of J. H. Waggoner)—headed the opposition forces. On Butler's side was Uriah Smith, widely respected as the editor of the *Review and Herald* and the denomination's authority on prophetic interpretation.

THE GALATIANS CONTROVERSY

At the dawn of 1888 Butler had good reasons to take an aggressive stance. For more than two years he and his church had felt themselves threatened by theological change regarding the denomination's teachings on the nature of the law in Galatians—particularly Galatians 3:24, which claims that "the law was our schoolmaster to bring us unto Christ."

For three decades Adventists had understood the text as talking about the ceremonial law. That interpretation, Adventist leaders held, was important in guarding the perpetuity of the Ten Commandments. After all, did not Galatians 3:25 plainly teach that once an individual had faith he was "no longer under a schoolmaster"?

The law in Galatians had become a controversial issue between 1884 and 1886 when Jones and Waggoner began to teach that the law in Galatians was the Ten Commandments rather than the ceremonial law. Waggoner explicitly set forth his view in the *Signs*. Butler regarded the "new" interpretation as a threat to the very heart of Adventist theology— the continuing sacredness of the seventh-day Sabbath embedded in the moral law. In order to defend their position on the Sabbath in a hostile religious context, Adventists had protected their theology by their interpretation of the law in Galatians as the ceremonial regulations. Thus the church leadership viewed Jones and Waggoner as threatening one of Adventism's central theological pillars.

The General Conference forces, led by Butler and Smith, felt quite confident in their viewpoint because they believed that the Adventist pioneers had settled the issue once and for all back in 1856. Before that time, many Adventists—including James White, J. N. Andrews, and Joseph Bates—had held that the law in Galatians was the Ten Commandments. The question came to a head in 1854 when J. H. Waggoner had published *The Law of God: An Examination of the Testimony of Both Testaments,* which took the Ten Commandments view on the law in Galatians. Stephen Pierce, who argued that the law in Galatians "was the law system 'including the ceremonial law,'" had publicly challenged J. H. Waggoner's position. Pierce won the participants in the discussion—including James and Ellen White—over to his viewpoint. Butler was convinced that after Ellen White's vision on the topic she had written to J. H. Waggoner that the law in Galatians was the ceremonial rather than the moral law. While Butler could never document his claim, it is a historical fact that after the conference James White removed Waggoner's book from the market. For the next 30 years the church harmoniously taught that the law in Galatians was the ceremonial one.[2]

It was into this settled theological atmosphere that E. J. Waggoner shot his articles on Galatians. As president of the General Conference and defender of the faith, Butler immediately felt concerned. His first tactic was to write several letters to Ellen White, then in Europe, to enlist her aid against a man who was bold enough to advocate in print a theological viewpoint contrary to the established Adventist position. When she failed to reply, Butler published *The Law in the Book of Galatians,* in which he argued that the ceremonial law was the only one referred to by Galatians 3:19, 24. The book was not particularly gentle with his opponents on the West Coast.[3]

Butler took his next step at the 1886 General Conference session. Before the session ended, the delegates had approved a resolution that "doctrinal views not held by a fair majority of our people" were not to be made a part of the instruction in Adventist schools or published in denominational periodicals until they had been "examined and approved by the leading brethren of experience." The regulation obviously had in mind Jones and Waggoner, their editing of the *Signs,* and their teaching at Healdsburg College. While that solution looked like the answer to Butler in 1886, we will soon see that Ellen White rejected it with forcefulness in 1888.[4]

Meanwhile, Jones and Waggoner continued to present their views in the *Signs* and to teach them at the college. Back in Battle Creek, the leaders of "the establishment" utilized the pages of the *Review* to get their position before the people. Beyond that, they began publishing the *Gospel Sickle* as a medium for their ideas.

On February 18, 1887, Ellen White wrote an important letter to Jones and E. J. Waggoner. In it she pointed out that she had been looking for the testimony she had written to J. H. Waggoner in the 1850s, but could not find it. She recalled that she had written "to him that I had been shown his position in regard to the law was incorrect," but that she could not recall exactly what was wrong about it, since "the matter does not lie clear and distinct in my mind." Of one thing, however, she was sure: that Seventh-day Adventists should present a united doctrinal front to the public. The various positions on the law in Galatians "are not vital points," and no one should make them an issue. It upset her to see the two leading Adventist papers in contention with each other. After congratulating Jones and Waggoner on the fact that the *Signs* was full of "precious articles" and "food for the people," she admitted that "a pain comes to my heart every time I see the *Sickle.* . . . If Satan can get in dissension among us as a people, he will only be too glad."

Advising the two young editors not to make their differences public, she pointed out that Waggoner needed humility and meekness, while Jones would be a power for good if he cultivated practical godliness. She then moved onto a topic that would become one of her major themes at the

1888 General Conference session and throughout the 1890s. "There is danger," she wrote, "of our ministers dwelling too much on doctrines, preaching altogether too many discourses on argumentative subjects when their own soul needs practical godliness. . . . There is danger of keeping the discourses and the articles in the paper like Cain's offering, Christless." Ellen White, as would soon become evident, was even more interested in practical Christianity as expressed in the lives of believers than she was in their doctrinal or exegetical concerns.[5]

Jones replied to her letter on March 13, thanking her for the testimony and noting that he had read it several times. Claiming that he knew nothing of the letter to J. H. Waggoner, he committed himself to avoiding controversy on the law in Galatians. He had been telling his students "to look for the gospel of Christ in Galatians," rather than the law. E. J. Waggoner replied two weeks later, also professing ignorance of her letter to his father. Assuring Ellen White that he would avoid controversy, he pointed out that his position on the Galatians law was in reality quite different from that of his father.[6]

A copy of the letter reproving Jones and Waggoner for their part in the controversy also went to Butler. He was ecstatic with its contents, mistakenly interpreting it to be a confirmation of his position on the law. In his euphoria, Butler wrote to Ellen White that he had really come to appreciate the two young men, and noted that he felt sorry for them: "I always pity those who suffer keen disappointment." Despite his "pity," Butler joyfully published an aggressive article in the *Review* of March 22 entitled "Laws Which Are 'Contrary to Us,' a 'Yoke of Bondage,' and 'Not Good.'" It was gratifying indeed for Butler and Smith to be on the winning side, especially with the prophet's approbation.[7]

The prophet, on the other hand, was not nearly as delighted with Butler's article as he was. On April 5 she fired off an epistle to Butler and Smith, claiming that she had not sent them a copy of the Jones-Waggoner rebuke so that they could use it as a weapon against the younger men, but that they would employ the same cautions in bringing disagreements into public. Now that Butler had reopened the battle publicly, she stated adamantly, Waggoner would have to have his chance to present his views. That demand for open discussion on the issue of the law in Galatians eventually led to its being a major item on the agenda at the 1888 General Conference meetings.

In her letter to Butler and Smith, Ellen White once again referred to the lost testimony to J. H. Waggoner, pointing out that the counsel might not have been on doctrine at all. "It may be it was a caution not to make his ideas prominent at that time, for there was great danger of disunion."[8]

Butler and Smith disagreed with her recollection, holding that she had seen in vision that J. H. Waggoner had been wrong theologically. Thus, as they understood it, the law in Galatians issue posed a double threat. After all, Smith would point out in 1892, if the law in Galatians is only the moral law, "*it overthrows the Testimonies and the Sabbath.*"[9] Smith's letter helps us see why the issue seemed so threatening: if he and Butler were wrong, he believed that two of Adventism's great doctrinal pillars would crumble—the Sabbath and the gift of prophecy through Ellen White. As a result, Smith, Butler, and their colleagues were ready to fight the law in Galatians issue to the bitter end. Part of the stage for the 1888 General Conference meetings had been set.

THE NATIONAL SUNDAY LAW

A second element in the background of the 1888 Minneapolis conference was the problem of an imminent national Sunday law. Since the early 1860s a move had been under way to create a "Christian America." Many organizations sponsored it. One of the most active was the National Reform Association, established to secure an amendment to the Constitution declaring that the United States was a Christian nation. By 1887 the Women's Christian Temperance Union had joined the National Reform Association in its drive for a national Sunday law.

Mainline Protestantism was in a state of panic as it viewed hordes of immigrants invading the United States. It found post-Civil War immigration to be much more objectionable than prewar immigration because it contained larger proportions of Roman Catholics from Southern and Eastern Europe. The new immigrants brought with them an "un-American" approach to alcoholic beverages and Sunday observance, having been raised in the tradition of the loose continental Sunday in contrast to the strict Puritan Sabbath (Sunday). Coupled with the new immigration were such problems as industrialization, urbanization, religious liberalism, and Darwinism.[10]

By the 1880s American Protestants were scared. In 1885 Josiah Strong in his best-selling *Our Country* summed up the perils of America as immigration, Romanism, Mormonism, intemperance, socialism, wealth, and the city. The National Reform Association in its campaign to develop a Christian America espoused a love-it-or-leave-it doctrine. A vice president of the association suggested that same year that "if the opponents of the Bible do not like our Government and its Christian features, let them go to some wild, desolate land, and in the name of the Devil, and for the sake of the Devil, subdue it, and set up a government of their own on infidel and atheistic ideas; and then if they can stand it, stay there till they die."[11]

The Adventists found such language to be far from comforting, especially since two of the major planks in the National Reform platform were the "Christianizing" of the public schools and a national Sunday law. The issue came to a head in the spring of 1888, when Senator H. W. Blair, of New Hampshire, introduced a bill in the United States Senate on May 21 for the promotion of the observance of "the Lord's day" "as a day of religious worship." Four days later Blair submitted a proposed amendment to the United States Constitution that would Christianize the nation's public school system.[12]

Seventh-day Adventists did not miss the prophetic significance of the bills. It was obvious to them that the forming of the image to the beast of Revelation 13, the giving of the mark of the beast, and the end of the world were close at hand. American freedom, Jones and his colleagues claimed, was on the verge of collapse. Arkansas alone, for example, had witnessed 21 prosecutions for desecrating Sunday since 1885 when the state had repealed the exemption clause for Sabbathkeepers from its 1883 Sunday ordinance. Other states also actively promoted Sunday legislation. Adventist eschatological excitement intensified when Cardinal Gibbons joined hands with the Protestants in 1888 by endorsing a petition to Congress on behalf of national Sunday legislation. The Protestants were more than willing to accept such help. "Whenever they [the Roman Catholics] are willing to co-operate in resisting the progress of political atheism," proclaimed *The Christian Statesman*, "we will gladly join hands with them."[13]

A. T. Jones, as editor of the *American Sentinel*, stood at the forefront of the religious liberty battle. With pen and voice he crusaded against Sunday laws and all other attempts to create a Christian America. That, as one might expect, won him the enmity of his opponents. The *Christian Nation*, for example, published an open letter to Jones: "You look for trouble in this land in the future, if these principles are applied. I think it will come to you, if you maintain your present position. The fool-hardy fellow who persists in standing on a railroad track, may well anticipate trouble when he hears the rumble of the coming train. If he shall read the signs of the times in the screaming whistle and flaming head-light, he may change his position and avoid the danger but if he won't be influenced by these, his most gloomy forebodings of trouble will be realized when the express strikes him. So you, neighbor, if . . . you have determined to oppose the progress of this nation in fulfilling its vocation as an instrument in the divine work of regenerating human society, may rightly expect trouble. It will be sure to come to you."[14]

Jones, however, was not one to be intimidated, nor would he back down from a good fight. Instead, he would continue to champion the cause of religious liberty, even in front of congressional committees before 1888 ended. One of his goals that year was to increase the yearly circulation of the *Sentinel* from 255,000 to 500,000 copies. He especially wanted to place it in the hands of "lawyers, legislators, and other men of public affairs." If the champion of Sunday legislation argued that Sunday laws were consistent with religious liberty, Jones took the opposing position and met Wilbur Crafts and other Sunday proponents at every turn in the road. In Jones they had a tireless enemy, a born publicist, and one who thrived in the midst of controversy.[15]

The religious liberty issue would take its place with the law in Galatians at the top of the agenda at the 1888 General Conference meetings. We should recognize that the two issues were not unrelated. *The pending Sunday legislation certainly did not make it look like an auspicious time for Adventists to begin wrangling with each other over a major change in their theology of the law.*

THE 10 KINGDOMS DEBATE

The third explosive factor that set the stage for the 1888 meetings was the ongoing debate between Jones and Smith over the identity of the 10 prophetic kingdoms of Daniel 7. Smith had been the acknowledged Adventist champion of prophetic interpretation for several decades. His *Thoughts on Daniel and the Revelation* was the standard Adventist work on the subject.

Uriah Smith's role seemed secure enough until Jones "found that the . . . traditional list of those kingdoms . . . was not correct." Jones informed the older man that he was "going to search that out." Smith replied that he was glad that Alonzo was willing to undertake the study, since the church had merely adopted the Millerite explanation of the 10 kingdoms without having verified it, and that the task was somewhat like "hunting the pieces of a building" after it had been "struck by a hundred pounds of dynamite." In 1886 Jones published his findings in the *Signs*. "But," he wrote, "when I brought out the truth that [his] list was not correct, Bro. Smith was not a bit glad; and opposed it, and defended the old list."[16]

Smith, in fact, held that if he was wrong then "we are yet ten percent short on the fulfillment of Dan. 2 & 7" and that if the denomination changed its position on one point its opponents would claim that, given enough time, the Adventists would "probably come to acknowledge finally, that" they "are mistaken on everything" in their prophetic understanding. He accused the younger man of a "ransacking of history" in an attempt to prove him wrong. Jones replied that Adventist tradition, "third rate names," and commentaries could not substitute for the "standard historians."[17]

The controversy brewed on throughout the period from 1886 through 1888, and it formed another agenda item for the 1888 General Conference session. It also provided a major source of ill-will between the old leaders in the East and the young upstarts in the West. Butler thundered on the eve of the meetings that Jones had proved himself to be a troublemaker by bringing up an interpretation "contrary to the long-established faith of our people taken forty years ago."[18]

THE CALIFORNIA CONSPIRACY

The "California conspiracy" is a fourth contextual element in the dynamics of the Minneapolis conference of 1888. It is impossible to comprehend the strength of emotion evidenced in that series of meetings without understanding this alleged conspiracy, partly rooted in fact and partly in rumor.

Its factual basis began with a meeting of C. H. Jones, W. C. White, E. J. Waggoner, A. T. Jones, and several others a few weeks before the beginning of the General Conference session. They assembled to study the Bible in relation to such issues as the 10 kingdoms, the law in Galatians, and prophetic events.[19]

William M. Healey, a pastor in California, took it upon himself to expose the gathering to the "old guard" in the East as a sinister plot by the Western leadership to force a change in the denomination's theology.

ATJ-2

Ellen White also got implicated in the conspiracy.[20]

Healey's letter found fertile ground in the emotionally exhausted mind of George I. Butler, who had been smarting for 18 months under the testimony Ellen White had sent him in April 1887 regarding his wrong attitude toward Jones and Waggoner in the Galatians controversy.

The "facts" set forth by Healey both aroused and enraged Butler. He fired off a 40-page letter to Ellen White on October 1, 1888, a few days before the General Conference meetings would begin. In his angry epistle the denomination's president blamed the Galatians controversy and Ellen White's "betrayal" of him for his broken mental and physical health. He raised the conspiracy issue when he pointed out that Waggoner was too astute to take such a bold stand on the Galatians issue by himself. Someone was behind him, and that someone, Butler suggested, must be W. C. White and perhaps even Ellen White herself. Merely bringing the Galatians issue into the meetings, he pontificated, "will tend to break the confidence of our people in the testimonies. . . . This whole matter I believe will do more to break down confidence in your work than anything which has occurred since this cause has had an existence. . . . There is no other possible result."

The General Conference president felt betrayed, his "nerve power" ground out, and, as he put it, "slaughtered in the house of my friends." His only regret was that he and Smith "did not just wade into" the arguments of Jones and Waggoner "and show them up in the widest channels possible" when the younger men had first put them into print. The only thing to do now, he proclaimed, was to halt such teachings and publicly rebuke Jones and Waggoner. Stating that because of his broken condition he would retire from the presidency of the church, Butler suggested that the shaking time had arrived.[21]

Not being one to keep his remarks to himself, he sent a telegram to the delegates of the soon-to-open General Conference meetings. "Stand by the old landmarks" was his message. As a result, his followers dug in for battle, desiring to protect both their president and the "old landmarks."

Jones, Waggoner, and the other California leaders were unaware that the Battle Creek forces viewed them as conspirators. "We did not know till after the . . . conference," Jones penned, "that the General Conference men . . . held these things concerning us. . . . In all innocence we came to the meeting expecting just nothing but plain Bible study to know the truth." In like manner, W. C. White claimed that he was "innocent as a goose" about the problem "while my old friends in B[attle] C[reek] . . . were saying the bitterest things against me."[22]

The results of the trumped-up California conspiracy were many, not the least of which was that it stirred up feelings of prejudice and "Pharisaism," so that those at the General Conference session could not evaluate the presentations of Jones and Waggoner with fairness or "anything like Christian feelings." It also resulted in a breakdown of confidence in Ellen White— even before the meetings began. "To men who suspected she was in 'the plot,'" Emmett K. Vande Vere wrote in 1974, "the next idea gulped had it that here was evidence that the Messenger sometimes acted as an uninspired person."[23] A third result was a great deal of emotional confusion over the identity of Adventism's doctrinal landmarks. In the end, a large portion of the participants in the General Conference session rejected basic Christian conduct in an effort to salvage their human opinions.

PERSONALITY CONFLICTS

A final contextual element in the eruptive atmosphere of the Minneapolis conference was the personalities of the participants. Butler and Smith were men accustomed to being in control. They had led the church without much resistance, especially since the death of James White in 1881. Certainly they did not take kindly to opposition, particularly from "young men fairly fledged in the editorial chair." Butler had a lofty view of the role of the General Conference president. Never, he wrote in 1873, in referring to James and Ellen White, was there a "great movement in this world without a leader." The members of a movement should "intelligently" follow "the counsels of those best qualified to guide." He adopted that management style for himself. Not only did he view himself as a strong leader who should rule from the top, but also as kind of a theological watchdog. After all, did not he hold "the highest position that our people could impose"?[24]

Ellen White, on the other hand, frankly told him that he had a wrong conception of the General Conference presidency. She condemned him for looking with suspicion on those who "do not feel obliged to receive their impressions and ideas from human beings, act[ing] only as they act, talk[ing] only as they talk, think[ing] only as they think, and in fact, mak[ing] themselves little less than machines." Soon after the 1888 meetings, she would write that Butler "thinks his position gives him such power that his voice is infallible."[25] Jones's run-in with the "kingly power" of Butler undoubtedly tilted him toward the antiorganization and freedom of individual conscience positions he would violently espouse after the beginning of the twentieth century.

The younger men did not help matters any. As W. C. White (a participant in the conference) put it, "the pomposity and egotism" of Jones and Waggoner "seemed out of place in such young men," and did much to develop prejudice and feeling against them. Jones, he noted, was especially pompous. Beyond that, his careless and harsh speech turned many against him. In 1902 Ellen White would write to him that unless he changed his careless way of speaking, his manners would "make fruitless the most precious truths."[26]

That counsel could have been uttered, and often was, at any time throughout Jones's career. Unfortunately, he never learned the lesson. A. T. Jones could preach the greatest truths of Christianity, but he never mastered the art of making Christian kindness a part of his repertoire. That problem, in part, would set the tone for conflict at the Minneapolis General Conference meetings of 1888.

---

[1] GIB, circular letter to all state conference committees and our brethren in the ministry, [January 1888]. (Ital. sup.)

[2] GIB to EGW, Oct. 1, 1888; Aug. 23, 1886; US to W. A. McCutchen, Aug. 8, 1901; US to EGW, Feb. 17, 1890; US to H. J. Adams, Oct. 30, 1900.

[3] GIB to EGW, Oct. 1, 1888; GIB, *The Law in the Book of Galatians: Is It the Moral Law or Does It Refer to That System of Laws Peculiarly Jewish?* (Battle Creek, 1886); WCW to DTJ, Apr. 8, 1890.

[4] *RH*, Dec. 14, 1886, p. 779; EGW, MS 8a, Oct. 21, 1888.

[5] EGW to EJW and ATJ, Feb. 18, 1887.

[6] ATJ to EGW, Mar. 13, 1887; EJW to EGW, Apr. 1, 1887.

[7] GIB to EGW, Mar. 31, 1887; *RH*, Mar. 22, 1887, pp. 182-184.

[8] EGW to GIB and US, Apr. 5, 1887.

[9] US to ATR, Sept. 21, 1892; cf. GIB to EGW, Oct. 1, 1888.

[10] On the rise of the NRA and the move to Christianize America, see Robert T. Handy, *A Christian America: Protestant Hopes and Historical Realities*, 2nd ed. (New York, 1984), pp, 64-87; W. H. Littlejohn, *The Coming Conflict: Or the United States to Become a Persecuting Power* (Battle Creek, 1883).

[11] Josiah Strong, *Our Country: Its Possible Future and Its Present Crisis* (New York, 1885), pp. ix, x; *Christian Statesman*, May 21, 1885, quoted in ATJ, *Civil Government and Religion*

(Battle Creek, 1889), p. 52.

[12] For the texts of the two Blair bills see ATJ, *Civil Government*, pp. 43, 44, 68, 69. See Handy, *Christian America*, pp. 87-90, for a discussion of the attempt to Christianize the public schools in the 1880s.

[13] A. H. Lewis, *A Critical History of Sunday Legislation From 321 to 1888 A.D.* (New York, 1888), pp. 209-256; ATJ, *Civil Government*, pp. 117-156; Francis P. Weisenburger, *Ordeal of Faith: The Crisis of Church-Going America, 1865-1900* (New York, 1959), p. 13; *Christian Statesman*, Dec. 11, 1884, quoted in ATJ, *Civil Government*, p. 56.

[14] *Christian Nation*, Dec. 14, 1887, quoted in ATJ, *Civil Government*, p. 109.

[15] 1887 *GCB*, No. 10, pp. 2, 3; Wilbur F. Crafts, *The Sabbath for Man* (New York, 1885), pp. 189-266.

[16] ATJ to CEH, May 12, 1921; WCW to TGB, Dec. 30, 1930.

[17] US to ATJ, Nov. 8, 1886; ATJ to US, Dec. 27, 3, 1886.

[18] GIB to EGW, Oct. 1, 1888.

[19] ATJ to CEH, May 12, 1921; WCW to DTJ, Apr. 8, 1890.

[20] EGW to WMH, Dec. 9, 1888.

[21] GIB to EGW, Oct. 1, 1888.

[22] EGW to WMH, Dec. 9, 1888; ATJ to CEH, May 12, 1921; WCW to DTJ, Apr. 8, 1890.

[23] EGW to WMH, Dec. 9, 1888; E. K. Vande Vere, "The Minneapolis Event," unpub. MS, 1974, p. 20.

[24] GIB to EGW, Oct. 1, 1888; GIB, *Leadership* (Battle Creek, Mich., 1873), p. 1.

[25] EGW to GIB, Oct. 14, 1888; EGW to MW, Nov, 4, 1888.

[26] WCW to TGB, Dec. 30, 1930; EGW to ATJ, May 7, 1902.

CRAPTER III

CONFLICT AT MINNEAPOLIS

"Elder Smith," A. T. Jones blurted early in the Minneapolis meetings, "has told you he does not know anything about this matter. I do, and I don't want you to blame me for what he does not know." Ellen White responded with "Not so sharp, brother Jones, not so sharp."[1] Unfortunately, such harsh words and pompous attitudes provided part of the backdrop for the conflict that characterized the 1888 General Conference session. They certainly did not win friends for the two young editors from California.

Jones and Smith had been debating the identity of the 10 horns of Daniel 7, with Jones contending for the Alamanni as the tenth and Smith for the Huns. While the topic was not all that significant, the discussion was "spirited." In a moment of honesty, Smith had modestly stated that he had not had the time to do original research into the historical documents, but had relied on Bible commentaries. It was that admission that had brought forth Jones's self-confident remark. He had done his homework, knew he was correct, and sought to drive his point home.[2]

Smith responded in kind, accusing Jones of "coming prepared with Libraries" and tearing up "established positions" with "ruthless hands." If, the *Review* editor proposed, the old view "has stood the test 40 years," why should not any new interpretation stand the same test before it was accepted? "If we have diversity of testimony[,] why change[?]" According to the Minneapolis *Tribune,* some of Smith's colleagues sought to force a vote on the issue, but E. J. Waggoner, who held that no vote should take place until the topic had been thoroughly investigated, blocked that ploy. "The matter was discussed in this manner," quipped the *Tribune,* "until it was high noon and time for adjournment."[3]

The once modest Smith, writing the next day, immodestly claimed victory for his view in an editorial in the *Review.* "The sentiment of the delegates appeared . . . ," he pontificated, "to be overwhelmingly on the side of established principles of interpretation, and the old view." Jones, for his part, was equally modest, suggesting that since none of the old guard "knew the history well enough," all they could do "was to appeal to tradition."[4]

Although the struggle over the identity of the 10 horns did much to set the tone for the 1888 meetings, it was only one item in a crowded agenda.

THE GENERAL CONFERENCE AGENDA

The 1888 General Conference session convened in the newly constructed Adventist church in Minneapolis, Minnesota, from October 17 through November 4. A ministerial institute lasting from the tenth of October through the nineteenth preceded the formal conference session. The agenda contained two categories of items: business matters and theological concerns. While official action on the business items was restricted to the General Conference session, action and reaction on the theological issues flowed from the institute into the regular session as if they were one meeting.

Writing near the beginning of the institute, Smith listed the topics proposed for discussion as "A historical view of the ten kingdoms, The divinity of Christ, The healing of the deadly wound, Justification by faith, How far we should go in trying to use the wisdom of the serpent, and Predestination."[5]

Because of the intensity of debate over three of the topics, however, not all the proposed items were studied or presented at Minneapolis. Near the close of the meetings, Waggoner noted that the subjects considered had been the 10 kingdoms of Daniel 7, the Papacy and the proposed National Reform Government, and "the law and the gospel in their various relations, coming under the general head of justification by faith."[6]

Several contemporary records verify Waggoner's report of the topics discussed. Among those records that have been known for some time are the *General Conference Bulletin,* the items in the *Review* and *Signs,* Jones's sermons on religious liberty, the sermons of Ellen White, and the incoming and outgoing correspondence files of the Whites. Noticeably absent from the list of existing documents are Waggoner's sermons. They have probably been permanently lost, despite claims to the contrary.[7]

Two important sources of information, discovered in the 1980s, however, have joined the records of the 1888 General Conference meetings: the diary of R. Dewitt Hottel, which gives a day-by-day report of the topics covered; and two booklets of notes that W. C. White took during the meetings. White's booklets are especially valuable, since he listed the Bible texts used in the studies. In addition, the General Conference Archives holds a fair amount of correspondence bearing on the 1888 General Conference agenda.

None of these records demonstrate that the divinity of Christ, the human nature of Christ, or "sinless living" were topics of emphasis at the 1888 meetings. Persons holding that those topics were central to the theology of the meetings generally read subsequent developments in Jones and Waggoner's treatment of righteousness by faith back into the 1888 meetings.

One nonagenda theological item did make its way into the discussions several times. On November 1, 2, and 4 a certain "crank on religion" claimed that Christ had already come. Ellen White made short work of his unscheduled presentations, relating them to the fanaticism that appeared in Adventism shortly after the great disappointment of 1844.[8]

RIGHTEOUSNESS BY FAITH

If the struggle between Jones and Smith over the 10 horns had been divisive, the battle over the law in Galatians was more so. Butler and Smith did not even want the topic on the agenda, but they felt that Ellen White had forced their hand with her call for fair play and equal time for both sides on the Galatians issue. Her forthright stand undoubtedly did nothing to lessen their fears of her supposed part in the "California conspiracy."[9]

To make things worse, Butler—the champion of traditional orthodoxy on the Galatians question—became ill and could not attend the Minneapolis meetings. That prompted R. M. Kilgore (president of the Illinois Conference) to argue from the floor of the General Conference that the Galatians issue should not come up. "It was," he accused, "a cowardly thing to broach this matter when Elder Butler could not be present." Once again Ellen White squared off with the Eastern forces, noting that Kilgore's position "was not of God."[10] As a result of her stand, the law in Galatians became a major item in the proceedings of the conference.

J. H. Morrison, president of the Iowa Conference and an expert debater, represented the Butlerites. Morrison claimed that Seventh-day Adventists had always believed in justification by faith. He feared, however, that the subject had been "overstressed" and was concerned that the law might lose its important place in Adventist theology. Morrison made several presentations on the topic during the meetings.[11]

Opposing him was E. J. Waggoner, who approached the Galatians issue as "the gospel" in the book of Galatians. According to Waggoner's theology, the ten-commandment/schoolmaster law brings us "unto Christ, *that we might be justified by faith.*" Waggoner made at least 9 presentations on the law/gospel theme during the Minneapolis meetings.[12]

Jones, on the other hand, did not directly present that topic at Minneapolis, although he would become a foremost speaker on righteousness by faith soon after the close of the conference. His part of the action at the 1888 General Conference meetings had to do with the 10 horns and religious liberty. He did, however, couch his religious liberty messages in the context of the freedom of the gospel. Beyond that, he supported Waggoner and his position throughout the meetings. For the rest of his ministry Jones would emphasize the "gospel" rather than the law in Galatians, a position he had taken in 1887 as a teacher at Healdsburg College.[13]

Another participant in the conference who stood behind Waggoner was Ellen White. On November 1 she appealed to the delegates to listen to him with unbiased minds. Some of the things he was teaching on the Galatians issue did "not harmonize with" her understanding "of this subject; but," she claimed, "truth is truth, and will lose nothing by investigation." While she did not agree with some of his interpretations of Scripture, yet, she asserted, that did not mean that she (or anyone else) had a right to denounce him or treat him as anything but a Christian brother. "I see," she noted, "the beauty of truth in the presentations of the *righteousness of Christ in relation to the law* as the Doctor has placed it before us. It harmonizes perfectly with the light which God has been pleased to give me during all the years of my experience. If our ministering brethren would accept the doctrine which has been presented so clearly,—*the righteousness of Christ in connection with the law,*—and I know they need to accept this, their prejudices would not have a controlling power, and the people would be fed with their portion of meat in due season."[14]

In the above passage Ellen White highlights what she considered to be Waggoner's central contribution to Adventist theology. *He had built a bridge between law and gospel by making explicit the gospel function of the ten-commandment law (i.e., to lead individuals to Christ for forgiveness and justification).*

With an understanding of that truth, Adventists would be better able to be both preachers of the law and believers in Christ. The connection between law and gospel should have been obvious, but Adventists—as Sabbath observers—had found themselves forced into a defensive position, and had tended to emphasize the law instead of the gospel. As a result, over time they largely had lost sight of the gospel and had become more obsessed with their relation to the rules and regulations of the law than with their relationship to Christ.

In her November 1 message, Ellen White, being unaware of the "California conspiracy" rumor, told the delegates that she saw no excuse for the "wrought-up state of feeling" that they had demonstrated at the meeting. It was the first time, she claimed, that she had heard Waggoner's explanation of his position on the Galatians question. Sensing the delegates' hostility to her, she noted that she had never discussed the issue with W. C. White, Jones, or Waggoner. She admonished them to close their ears to the messages Butler was sending from Battle Creek.[15]

Ellen White had several functions at Minneapolis. One of them was to act as a mediator between the two sides. In that, however, she was somewhat frustrated, because the Eastern forces distrusted her because of her purported implication in the "California conspiracy." On the other hand, she was not intimidated by the innuendos related to that subject that were now reaching her. She clearly recognized that Jones and Waggoner had gospel truth, that they were in a numerically lopsided battle, and that they had a right to be heard. Furthermore, she came to believe that God had selected them to revive the Adventist Church because of their responsiveness to Him.[16] As a result, she threw her weight firmly behind them. They certainly needed it. Without her aid they would never have had a hearing. Their case would have been crushed out of court.

Ellen White also participated as a major speaker at the 1888 meetings. Unlike Waggoner, however, *she had no concern for the law in Galatians. To her that issue was a "mere mote." "My burden during the meeting was to present Jesus and his love before my brethren, for I saw marked evidences that many had not the spirit of Christ.*" Her message dovetailed with Waggoner's. Looking back at the meetings later that year, she uplifted the "faith of Jesus." "The third angel's message," she wrote, "is the proclamation of the commandments of God and the faith of Jesus Christ. *The commandments of God have been proclaimed, but the faith of Jesus Christ has not been proclaimed by Seventh-day Adventists as of equal importance, the law and the gospel going hand in hand.*"[17]

Her messages startled some. While she noted that it was "strangely new to many," it was not new light to her. It was "old light placed where it should be in the third angel's message." She had, she claimed, been preaching it for 45 years, but Waggoner's Minneapolis sermons were the "first clear teaching on this subject" that she had heard outside of conversations with her husband. She clearly explained what she meant by old light being placed in its proper context when she wrote that the "holiness people" were correct in their understanding of justification by faith, but had separated it from the law. By way of contrast, Waggoner and Jones were preaching the same Reformation view of righteousness by faith but had related it to the Ten Commandments in their treatment of Revelation 14:12.[18]

Although righteousness by faith may not have been a new teaching, the amount of emphasis it received at the 1888 General Conference meetings threatened many. Its presentation in the context of the Galatians and 10 kingdoms controversies, the personality conflicts, and the alleged California conspiracy hindered their acceptance of it.

After Waggoner's final discourse on justification by faith, Smith inaccurately reported that all were agreed on the foundation principles, "but there are some differences in regard to the interpretation of several passages. . . . It is hoped that the unity of the faith will be reached on this important question."[19]

The forces aligned with Smith, unfortunately, were willing to achieve "unity of the faith" by coercion. As at the 1886 General Conference session and in the earlier conflict at the 1888 meetings over the 10 horns, the old guard attempted to establish a creedal statement by majority vote without impartial and thorough Bible study. "Willie and I," Ellen White wrote, "have had to watch at every point lest there should be moves made, resolutions passed, that would prove detrimental to the future work." She had condemned the 1886 resolution restricting editors and teachers to presenting the views held by the majority, and she reinforced that stand at Minneapolis. "Instructors in our schools," she told the audience on

October 21, "should never be bound about by being told that they are to teach only what has been taught hitherto. Away with these restrictions. . . . That which God gives His servants [i.e., Waggoner and Jones] to speak today would not perhaps have been present truth twenty years ago, but it is God's message for this time." She was not ready to give the Holy Spirit's direction of the church over to the Battle Creek establishment with its desire to control Jones and Waggoner.[20]

The struggle over righteousness by faith did not end with the closing of the conference session. Jones, Waggoner, and Ellen White would aggressively take the offensive in bringing that message to the church from November 1888 through the early nineties.

RELIGIOUS LIBERTY

Unlike the battles over Galatians and the 10 horns of Daniel 7, religious liberty did not divide the Adventist leadership at Minneapolis. All agreed that the proposed amendment to the United States Constitution advocating the teaching of Christianity in the public schools and the Blair national Sunday bill represented ominous signs in prophetic history—a vindication in fact of the Adventist interpretation of Revelation 13 and 14. Given such events, the delegates voted that every Adventist should be aroused "to such earnestness as never before"—even to "such diligence and earnestness as the fearful importance of the third angel's message demands."[21]

Jones was the major speaker on religious liberty issues. He had rapidly risen to an undisputed leadership position in that area. In harmony with the themes of Waggoner and Ellen White, Jones presented his religious liberty messages in the context of "Jesus Christ," who "came into the world to set men free." He covered such topics as (1) "Christianity in the Roman Empire"—an empire that confounded civil and religious obligations, thus creating martyrs; (2) "What Is Due to God, and What to Caesar?"; (3) "The Powers that Be"—an exposition of the correct role of civil government according to Romans 13; (4) "The Religious Attack upon the United States Constitution, and Those Who Are Making It"—a discussion of the public school issue and the National Reform Association and its confederates; (5) "Religious Legislation"—an examination of the current move to create a national Sunday law; (6) "The Sunday-Law Movement in the Fourth Century, and Its Parallel in the Nineteenth"; and

(7) "The Workings of a Sunday Law"—a revealing discussion of the discriminatory enforcement of the 1883 Arkansas Sunday law.[22]

His presentations were in his usual style—confrontational and factual. He was particularly eager to demonstrate that the formulation of the Sunday law as "a bill to secure to the people the privileges of rest and of religious worship, free from disturbance by others, on the first day of the week" was a thinly veiled subterfuge by its sponsors to give Sunday legislation a civic rather than a religious guise. There is no one in the land, he pointed out, who has not "the privileges of rest and religious worship free from disturbance by anybody, on the first day of the week, and all other days and nights of the week." Jones concluded that "the object of the Blair Sunday-rest bill is the enforcement of THE RELIGIOUS OBSERVANCE OF A DAY."[23]

He also spent a considerable amount of time demonstrating how Sunday laws worked in the real world of nineteenth-century America, using as his example Arkansas, which had had such a law since 1883. Originally it had had an exemption for Sabbath observers. The state legislature had repealed the exemption in 1885, allegedly to close certain saloons operated on Sunday in Little Rock by Jews. Since the repeal the state had had 21 cases related to Sunday desecration. All but two had involved seventh-day Sabbathkeepers, and the authorities had released the defendants in those two instances without bail and dismissed their cases. For the Seventh-day Adventists, however, bail ranged from $110 to $500 (the latter figure being roughly equivalent to a year's salary for a laborer) each. Meanwhile, the authorities had not arrested a single saloonkeeper. In addition, many of the accusing witnesses and informers also had been working on Sunday—sometimes with the arrested Sabbath observers—yet no one molested them, even though the courts found the Saturdaykeepers guilty. Jones concluded that "there could be no clearer demonstration that the law was used only as a means to vent religious spite against a class of citizens guiltless of any crime"—a class that could be accused "only of professing a religion different from that of the majority."[24]

Those were portentous times for the members of the Adventist Church. The prophecies that they had preached for four decades appeared to be fulfilling before their very eyes. Unfortunately, some of the leadership, Ellen White noted, were so wrought up over minor points of doctrine (i.e., the Galatians and 10 kingdoms controversies) that "the great question of the nation's religious liberty" was to them "a matter of little consequence."[25]

In spite of foot-dragging by some, Jones's presentations, coupled with the realities facing the denomination, moved the delegates to action. Three of their most important decisions involved him. First, the denomination would publish his General Conference sermons on religious liberty. They came off the press, with some editing, in 1889 as *Civil Government and Religion, or Christianity and the American Constitution.* Second, Jones was to visit Boston, Chicago, and other places to lecture on the topic of religious liberty. And, third, he was to lead a delegation of three to testify against the two Blair bills before the United States Senate Committee on Education and Labor.[26] Thus by the end of the Minneapolis conference Jones was well on his way to becoming a full-time religious liberty advocate—a position in which he would make some of his most important contributions to the Adventist Church.

THE SPIRIT OF MINNEAPOLIS

As a result of the doctrinal controversies, the personality conflicts, and the alleged California conspiracy, there developed an unchristian spirit among the Butler-Smith faction at Minneapolis. An understanding of the "spirit of Minneapolis," as Ellen White would later call it, is essential if we are to fully grasp the dynamics of the 1888 conference.

Ellen White claimed that she sensed an attitude among the delegates that she had not previously discerned, one that "burdened" her, being "*so unlike the spirit of Jesus.*" It was, in fact, the opposite of the spirit of Jesus. Calling it the spirit of the Pharisees, the spirit of the very ones who crucified Christ, she described the spirit of Minneapolis with many descriptive phrases. First, sarcasm and jesting characterized it. On one occasion she reported a vision that took her into one of the houses that boarded some of the delegates. "Sarcastic remarks," she reported, "were passed from one to another, ridiculing their brethren A. T. Jones, E. J. Waggoner, Willie C. White, and myself." Another example was that some referred to Waggoner as "Sister White's pet." Second, criticism dominated the spirit of Minneapolis. Third, it manifested envy, evil surmisings, hatred, and jealousy in the hearts of its possessors. Fourth, it prompted "sharp, hard feelings" and attitudes. Fifth, its possessors were "intoxicated with the spirit of resistance" to the voice of the Holy Spirit. Sixth, the spirit of Minneapolis drove those having it to speak in a manner calculated to inflame one another regarding those who held opposing doctrinal views. Seventh, it bred contention and doctrinal debate. As Ellen White put it, it stirred up "human passions" and "bitterness of spirit, because some of their brethren had ventured to entertain some ideas contrary to the ideas that some others . . . had entertained, which were thought . . . to be inroads upon ancient doctrines." Eighth, it followed the lead of the Pharisees in their relation to Christ, who were blinded by spiritual pride, self-righteousness, and self-sufficiency. Ninth, the spirit of Minneapolis generated an attitude that led to "playing upon words" and "quibbling upon words" in doctrinal discussions. In short, the mindset displayed at Minneapolis "was uncourteous, ungentlemanly, and not Christlike."[27]

One of the great tragedies of Minneapolis was that in seeking to protect Adventism's doctrinal purity and its traditional scriptural interpretations, the Battle Creek leadership had lost its Christianity. That is an ever-present danger among the defenders of orthodoxy. It was in this context that Jones, Waggoner, and Ellen White began to preach Jesus Christ and His merits. For Ellen White the theme of her writings throughout the nineties would be Jesus, His righteousness, His loving character, and our need of His Holy Spirit.

One spin-off of the spirit of Minneapolis was the rejection of not only Jones and Waggoner, but of Ellen White herself. The Minneapolis *Tribune* might report that "Mrs. White is a sort of prophetess, and everything she says is listened to by the Seventh Day [sic] Adventists with awe," but she knew better. She recognized that something had changed in the response of her listeners. To her daughter-in-law she reported that her testimony "has made the least impression upon many minds than at any period before in my history."[28]

Accused of having changed her theology on the Galatians issue, and having been openly doubted in her denials of any involvement in a conspiracy with Jones, Waggoner, and her son, Ellen White had reached the nadir of her influence.[29] It is no wonder that she would always look back on the 1888 General Conference session with feelings of dismay. She had seen its promise, but she had experienced its failure.

In spite of the rejection of herself, Jones, Waggoner, and their message, she did not give up. They left Minneapolis to begin a campaign to take Christ, His love, and His righteousness to the Adventist Church.

[1] ATR, "Did the Seventh-day Adventist Denomination Reject the Doctrine of Righteousness by Faith?" unpub. MS, Jan. 30, 1931; "An Interview with J. S. Washburn" by R. J. Wieland and D. K. Short, June 4, 1950. (ATR and Washburn both attended the 1888 conference.)

[2] ATR, "Did the Seventh-day Adventist Denomination"; 1888 *GCB*, No. 1, pp. 1, 2.

[3] WCW, handwritten notes on the 1888 GC, book 1, [pp. 27, 41]; Minneapolis *Tribune*, Oct. 18, 1888, p. 5.

[4] *RH*, Oct. 23, 1888, p. 664; ATJ to CEH, May 12, 1921. It is of interest to note that the denomination eventually adopted Jones's list of the 10 kingdoms.

[5] *RH*, Oct. 16, 1888, p. 648.

[6] *ST*, Nov. 2, 1888, p. 662.

[7] Several attempts have been made to establish EJW's "exact" message at the 1888 meetings, but all of them fall short. His "exact" message is probably lost forever, but, as I shall point out later, the loss is not all that crucial in understanding 1888, since we have other records. Furthermore, we also know that not all he taught, according to Ellen White, was theologically correct. For four varying attempts to identify EJW's message, see: (1) LEF, *Movement of Destiny* (Washington, D.C., 1971), p. 189; (2) David P. McMahon, *Ellet Joseph Waggoner: The Myth and the Man* (Fallbrook, Calif., 1979), pp. 74, 75; (3) EJW, *The Glad Tidings: Studies in Galatians,* reprinted., ed. Robert J. Wieland (Mountain View, Calif., 1972), [p. 6]; (We should note that Wieland's editing falls short of being a true reflection of Waggoner's original book, since Wieland took the liberty of deleting those sections teaching pantheism, apparently in an attempt to purify Waggoner.); (4) Clinton L. Wahlen, "Selected Aspects of Ellet J. Waggoner's Eschatology and Their Relation to His Understanding of Righteousness by Faith, 1882-1895," M.Div. Thesis, Andrews University, 1988. See also, Whidden, *E. J. Waggoner*, pp. 116-138.

[8] R. Dewitt Hottel, diary, Nov. 1, 2, 4, 1888.

[9] EGW to MW, Oct. 9, 1888; WCW to DTJ, Apr. 8, 1890; EGW to GIB and US, Apr. 5, 1887.

[10] EGW, MS 24, Nov. or Dec. 1888; EGW, MS 9, Oct. 24, 1888; WCW, handwritten notes on the 1888 GC, book 1, [p. 55.]

[11] R. T. Nash, *An Eyewitness Report of the 1888 General Conference* (privately pub., n.d.), p. 4; C. McReynolds, "Experiences While at the General Conference in Minneapolis, Minnesota, in 1888," unpub. MS, c. 1931.

[12] R. D. Hottel, diary, Oct. 16, 1888; Whidden, *E. J. Waggoner*, p. 135, n. 2; EJW, *The Gospel in the Book of Galatians* (Oakland, 1888), p. 45. While this book does not necessarily represent the words, or even the argument, used by EJW at Minneapolis, it can be said that it reflects the general approach he employed to link the law in Galatians to righteousness by faith.

[13] ATJ, *Civil Government*, p. 5; *RH,* July 25, Aug. 1, 8, 1899, pp. 476, 492, 508; Feb. 5, 1901, p. 89; ATJ to EGW, Mar, 13, 1887.

[14] EGW, MS 15, Nov. 1, 1888. (Ital. sup.)

[15] *Ibid.*

[16] EGW to SNH, June 1, 1894.

[17] EGW, MS 24, Nov. or Dec. 1888. (Ital. sup.) The sermons EGW preached at the 1888 GC have been published in A. V. Olson, *Thirteen Crisis Years, 1888-1901* (Washington, D.C., 1981), pp. 248-311 and in *The Ellen G. White 1888 Materials*, vol. 1.

[18] EGW, MS 8a, Oct. 21, 1888; EGW, MS 24, Nov. or Dec. 1888; EGW, MS 5, June 17, 1889; cf. *RH,* Aug. 13, 1889, p. 514; Knight, *Angry Saints*, pp. 54-57, 40-43.

[19] 1888 *GCB*, No. 7, p. 3; Knight, *Angry Saints*, pp. 45-49.

[20] EGW to Brethren, c. April 1889 (letter 85, 1889); EGW, MS 15, Nov. 1, 1888; EGW to MW, Nov. 4, 1888; EGW, MS 8a, Oct. 21, 1888; EGW to R. A. Underwood, Jan. 18, 1889; cf. WCW to MW, Nov. 3, 1888.

[21] 1888 *GCB*, No. 12, p. 1.

[22] ATJ, *Civil Government*, pp. 4, 5.

[23] *Ibid.*, 1890 ed., pp. 70, 71, 80.

[24] *Ibid.*, 1889 ed., pp. 112, 114-137.

[25] EGW, MS 24, Nov. or Dec. 1888.

[26] 1888 *GCB*, No. 6, pp. 1, 2; No. 10, p. 1; No. 12, p. 1.

[27] EGW, MS 24, Nov. or Dec. 1888 (Ital. sup.); EGW, MS 15, Nov. 1, 1888; EGW, MS 13, 1889, n.d.; EGW to Brethren, c. April 1889, (letter 85, 1889); EGW to Children, May 12, 1889; WCW to TGB, Dec. 30, 1930; McReynolds, "Experiences," c. 1931.

[28] Minneapolis *Tribune*, Oct. 21, 1888, p. 5; EGW to MW, Nov. 4, 1888; cf. EGW, MS 24, Nov. or Dec. 1888.

[29] EGW, MS 24, Nov. or Dec. 1888.

CHAPTER IV

EXPANDING THE BATTLE ZONE

Looking back at the 1888 General Conference session, Ellen White pictured it as the "most incomprehensible tug-of-war we have ever had among our people" and as "one of the saddest chapters in the history of the believers in present truth." That ministers could utilize unchristian methods and harsh attitudes to defend Christian orthodoxy was hard to grasp. If their doctrines, she exclaimed, produced such a pharisaic spirit in them, she wanted to be "as far from" their "understanding and interpretation of the Scriptures as . . . is possible."[1]

TAKING THE MESSAGE TO THE PEOPLE

The ministry, however, was not the church. On the morning of October 24, 1888, Ellen White had some straight talk for the assembled clergy. "What was the use," she chided, ". . . for our ministering brethren to come" to this conference "if they are here only to shut out the Spirit of God from the people? . . . If the ministers will not receive the light, I want to give the people a chance; perhaps they may receive it." They certainly needed it. In September 1889 she remarked that "there is not one in a hundred" who really understood what it meant to be justified by faith, what it meant that "Christ should be . . . the only hope and salvation."[2] Up through the fall of 1891 she, Jones, and Waggoner would tour the nation, preaching righteousness by faith to "the people" as well as to the ministry. After she left for Australia in 1891 and Waggoner had gone to England, Jones continued to carry out the battle in the United States. All through this period, and beyond it, she emphasized that God had chosen Jones and Waggoner to bear a special message to the Adventist Church.[3] That was a heady endorsement in a denomination that believed Ellen White was God's prophet.

Prophetic endorsement, however, did not mean that Jones had an open door to "the people." The first challenge took place when his name came up to assist Smith as a Bible teacher at Battle Creek College. The General Conference Committee had suggested the appointment in April 1888, but the board of trustees, apparently under Smith's influence, had refused to act. The topic surfaced again in late November. This time the college reluctantly appointed Jones, but it had taken a joint session of the board and the full General Conference Committee to break the deadlock. Furthermore, a specially chosen committee had had a "long conference with Eld. Jones and he had assured them in a very positive manner that if he should be employed to assist in the Lectures he would not knowingly teach any opinions contrary to those which the Board desired to be taught." In other words, Smith and Butler (two of the three committee members) had forced Jones to accept the essence of the "creedal" resolutions that some had wanted to pass at the recent General Conference session, but which Ellen White had blocked and would continue to protest.[4]

That administrative leash, however, would soon lose its effectiveness, especially after college president W. W. Prescott became a thorough convert to righteousness by faith and Jones's ally and follower. That was quite a turnaround for the sophisticated Prescott who had earlier, according to W. C. White, been put off by Jones's provocative and "uncouth" speaking style. Thus the college classroom eventually provided Jones with one avenue to reach the people.

More important than the classroom was access to the churches. But it would not be obtained without a struggle. The real test came in November 1888 when Jones accompanied Ellen White to Battle Creek—the headquarters of the denomination and a stronghold of theological conservatism. She had received an invitation to preach the Sabbath sermon. That morning two local elders called on her to inquire what her subject would be. Understanding their fear that she might teach some of the Minneapolis ideas, she suggested that they leave the selection of the topic to "the Lord and Sister White." Then she went on to request that they also invite Jones to the Tabernacle pulpit. The elders replied that they would have to check with Uriah Smith. Smith refused, deciding "it would not be best to ask him because he took strong positions, and carried the subject of National Reform too far."[5]

Jones, meanwhile, was not an easy man to ignore after December 1888. On the thirteenth of the month he had testified before the United States Senate Committee on Education and Labor against the Blair Sunday Bill. In the preceding weeks the Battle Creek *Daily Journal* had headlined his religious liberty presentations in three issues and had devoted the bulk of the December 11 issue to a reprinting of all of his lectures.[6] A. T. Jones, as the first Adventist to testify before a congressional body, was rapidly becoming a folk hero to the Adventist people, and a man to contend with for the religious and political forces crusading for a Christian America. That made it doubly difficult for Smith and his associates to keep him out of the Battle Creek pulpit. They soon found themselves forced to give up their opposition to his preaching there.

As a result, Jones led, along with Ellen White and J. O. Corliss, in a revival in the Tabernacle scheduled to last a week, but extended to nearly a month. The main topic was justification by faith. Also presented was the white-hot "Religious Amendment" issue and its place in prophecy. Thus their appeal to get right with God had an eschatological emphasis. The revival soon spread to the college and the sanitarium. Many, noted the *Review*, "testified that they were free in the Lord." Ellen White reported that a "good work has been done in Battle Creek. . . . We have gained a measure of victory." She also noted that she had had to "fight for every inch of ground" that they had advanced in Battle Creek. Then she went on to call for a "spiritual revolution throughout the churches that fruits unto righteousness may be seen in our daily life."[7]

From Battle Creek the Jones-Waggoner-White trio took the message of righteousness by faith to camp meetings, ministerial institutes, and churches across the Midwest and eastern part of the nation. Sometimes all three worked together, while at other times they labored separately.

Ellen White frequently commented on Jones's presentations. The following selections are typical. On January 19, 1889, at South Lancaster, Massachusetts, she wrote: "Elder Jones spoke in the forenoon with great power. It was meat in due season." She talked next. Then came a testimony service in which many spoke of sins forgiven. "Light and happiness," Ellen White wrote, "had come to their souls and they never knew what it was to love Jesus as they did now." In April she described their Chicago meetings: "Brother Jones is giving precious instruction. All are waking up to appreciate it. Brother Kilgore's [a Butler-Smith supporter at Minneapolis] face fairly shines. He talks and cries and praises God. I believe he is really converted." "Many testimonies," she penned two days later, "were borne by the ministering brethren to the effect that they could now see how little of the righteousness of Christ they had brought into their discourses, how ignorant they had been of the Scriptures and of the power of God!" Again, at the Wexford, Michigan, camp meeting in June 1889 she reported: "Elder Jones spoke with great freedom upon the righteousness of Christ. The people drink in this heaven-sent message as the earth drinks in the rain."[8]

From time to time Jones made similar reports. A letter written to W. A. Colcord from Mount Vernon, Ohio, in August 1891 shows him at his charismatic best: "We are having a great meeting here. The power of the Lord is present to forgive, to cleanse, and to *heal*. The early morning meeting this morning, was one of the most powerfully impressive I ever saw. The large tent was nearly full, and the whole congregation was weeping, many of them aloud, and praising God, and praying for mercy and grace. Oh, it was wonderful. . . . And it is going to continue and grow more powerful and more precious."[9]

Not everyone, of course, was happy with Jones and his associates and their "new theology." A hard-core resistance continued in Iowa and Battle Creek in particular. Others just did not seem to like Jones. The Indiana Conference president, for example, claimed that his conference did not want Jones's labors because he preached too long and ate three meals a day instead of two. Dr. John Harvey Kellogg was also crosswise with Jones, Waggoner, and Prescott for a number of years because of their lack of conformity to and concern for health reform principles and their fanaticism on faith healing. Kellogg felt particularly incensed at their declarations of unconditionally accomplished healing based totally on the faith of the sick individual, irrespective of God's will or remaining symptoms of disease.[10] (See chapter 7 for a fuller treatment of Jones and the faith healing movement.)

A third important avenue that helped Jones and his colleagues bring the message of 1888 to the church were the ministers' schools held in Battle Creek between the 1889 and 1891 General Conference sessions. The first, hosting some 50 students, lasted from November 5, 1889, to March 25,

1890. The second ministers' school, building upon the success of the first, had more than 130 students. It convened during the fall of 1890. The schools would continue until the mid-nineties, at which time Ellen White suggested that the light on righteousness had been "presented and accepted" and that the ministerial institutes were no longer needed and that the denomination should put more of its energies into evangelism and mission.[11]

The General Conference, under the presidency of O. A. Olsen since October 1888, sought to calm riled theological feelings by having both sides of the 1888 controversy represented on the instructional staff of the ministers' schools. Thus Jones, Waggoner, and Smith were the main teachers at the sessions in the early nineties. The schools did much to break down prejudice in the ministerial force. Beyond that accomplishment, Olsen, W. C. White, and others hoped they would help the clergy remedy their deplorable educational deficiencies. Many of them had only a proof-text knowledge of Adventist doctrines, whereas they needed a "general understanding of the Bible."[12] The underlying thought seemed to be that ministerial ignorance had contributed largely to the 1888 debacle.

Jones and Waggoner had several other channels open to them, besides those examined above, to reach the church in the nineties. First, the reform forces dominated the important Bible study hours at the General Conference sessions throughout the decade. Jones's influence reached a peak during the 1893 and 1895 sessions, when he preached 50 times on the meaning of the third angel's message. Second, Waggoner prepared a series of Sabbath school lessons on the covenants that the church studied during 1890. Third, both men held important editorial posts for Adventist periodicals. Jones's influence for his theories of righteousness and holiness became especially powerful after he became editor of the *Review* in 1897. Last, the two men had a large number of pamphlets and books published by the Review and Herald, Pacific Press, and the Religious Liberty Association throughout the nineties. In addition, Ellen White added to their literary contribution on Christ and His righteousness. It is important to note that *Steps to Christ, The Desire of Ages, Thoughts From the Mount of Blessing, Christ's Object Lessons,* and the Christ-centered opening chapters of *The Ministry of Healing* all appeared after 1888. That conference had created a definite shift in her literary output. Her burden was to present Jesus, His loving character, and His righteousness to the Adventist people.

BREAKTHROUGH ON THE CALIFORNIA CONSPIRACY

The months following the Minneapolis meetings were strenuous for Jones and his allies as they sought to depict Jesus and His gracious forgiveness to the church at large. While they achieved victories, they also had disappointments.

One of the most important turning points in the prolonged struggle took place near the end of the first ministers' school in March 1890. Up through that time, Smith, Butler, Dan T. Jones (secretary of the General Conference), and others had continued to claim that the California conspiracy, with its master plan of pushing through a new theology at Minneapolis, had been a reality. Smith, in fact, held that the combined work of Jones, Waggoner, and Ellen White in presenting their views in the post-1888 camp meetings, institutes, and ministers' meetings confirmed his suspicion of conspiracy. One spin-off of the widespread belief was the idea that Ellen White was unreliable since the young upstarts had influenced her. Her opinions were merely her own, "and her opinions," ran the criticism, "are no better than our opinions, unless it is something she has seen in vision."[13]

In that atmosphere of controversy and doubt, the ministers' school struggled through the winter, the major bone of contention being the nature of the covenants. On March 10, however, Ellen White wrote to W. C. White that "the current is changing." That same day she exclaimed to W. A. Colcord that "victory has come." The next day she penned that "the back bone of the rebellion is broken in those who came in from other places" (i.e., outside of Battle Creek). A series of confessions by ministers had begun to clear the air.[14]

On March 13 Ellen White called a special meeting of the leading ministers. At it she and Waggoner explained their side of some explosive issues and openly confronted the myth of the California conspiracy.[15] That was the first of several such meetings. By Sunday A. T. Jones had arrived and began to take part in the explanations and cross-examinations as the denomination's leaders sought to reach an understanding with each other.

As early as March 13 D. T. Jones, a leader in the opposition to the Jones-White-Waggoner team, admitted that they had been unjust in their suspicions and criticisms related to the alleged California conspiracy.[16] A great deal of animosity, however, still existed over the covenants, the law in Galatians, and other doctrinal issues.

In a subsequent meeting, Ellen White came to grips with the obsession over doctrinal issues. "She says," reported D. T. Jones, "*it is not what we believe that she feels exercised about;* it is not that we should all hold just the same view in reference to the covenants, in reference to the law in Galatians, *or in reference to any other point of doctrine; but that we should all have the spirit of Christ,* and should all be united in building up and pushing forward the third angel's message."[17]

The next day, after noting that all "theoretically agreed" on the doctrine of righteousness by faith, D. T. Jones wrote to W. C. White. His letter once again highlights the nature of the Minneapolis conflict. "Your mother and Dr. Waggoner both say that *the points of doctrine are not the matters at issue at all, but it is the spirit shown by our people in opposition to these questions which they object to. I am perfectly free to acknowledge that the spirit has not been the Spirit of Christ.* It has not been so in my case, and I think I can discern enough to be safe in saying that it has not been so in the case of others. *I have often thought over the matter and wondered why it was that such unimportant matters, practically, should cause such a disturbance, such a division,* and such a state of feeling as has existed for the last year and a half. . . . *The point in your mother's mind and in the mind of Dr. Waggoner, was not to bring in these questions and force them upon all, but to bring in the doctrine of justification by faith and the Spirit of Christ, and try to get the people converted to God.*"[18]

Such explanations proved to be a major turning point in the post-Minneapolis conflict. Church president O. A. Olsen, a supporter of Jones and Waggoner, was overjoyed with the breakthrough. "I think," he claimed on March 20, "I can say now that the prospects for a better understanding and greater unity were never so good for several years. Many that have felt greatly perplexed, are feeling much relieved, and light is coming in, where darkness has previously existed." From that time on, the heat of the controversy subsided, even though the battle over the law in Galatians and animosity toward Jones, Waggoner, and Ellen White continued to simmer in the minds of a portion of the denomination's leaders.[19]

CONFLICT OVER A. T. JONES'S TEACHING ON RIGHTEOUSNESS BY FAITH

Jones's confrontational style and his habit of publicly belittling those who disagreed with him never did much to win over the opposition. That was undoubtedly true regarding his presentations on righteousness by faith in the post-Minneapolis years. Adequate treatment of the development of his teachings on the topic would take a book in itself, and is beyond the scope of this study. The current discussion will have only enough space for the high points of his views and for a brief outlining of some of the problems that arose from his teachings or what people perceived to be his teachings. Additional examination of his views on sanctification will appear in chapter 8.

Jones's 1889 sermons indicate that he definitely held an objective (i.e., forensic) doctrine of justification. Preaching at the Ottawa, Kansas, camp meeting in May, he pointed out that "to be justified is to be accounted righteous." A few days later he claimed that Christ's righteousness is made to count for "our unrighteousness."[20]

Faith in Christ, Jones asserted, is the secret to victory—not only in justification but in Christian living after a person is justified. Such faith, he declared, does not do away with works. Rather, it is the only thing that allows us to do the good deeds for which God created us. Good works, however, do not make us good. To the contrary, "we must be made good, be made righteous [through forensic justification], before we can do good or do righteousness." We do not keep the commandments "to become righteous, but because we are righteous [justified]." It is the power of Christ within a person that allows the righteous (justified) Christian to obey the law. "*Where, then, do our works come in? Nowhere.*" All our works are Christ working in us. All our righteous deeds are as "*filthy rags.*" Salvation—both justification and sanctification—is totally by faith.[21]

Jones unalterably opposed those who put too much emphasis on the observance of the law. We often, he pointed out, look for righteousness in the wrong place. A person will never find it "in the law of God, and through keeping it. . . . That is not the place to seek for it." At the 1893 General Conference session *he chided those Adventists who "had worn out their souls almost, trying to manufacture a sufficient degree of righteousness to stand through the time of trouble,*" but had not accomplished it. What they needed was Christ's "free gift" of righteousness. He went on to point out that many Adventists had a Roman Catholic view of righteousness in which they believed in God to forgive them, and then did their best to do what was right instead of resting totally by faith in God.

His remarks on Roman Catholic views of justification undoubtedly had in mind Uriah Smith and his friends. Back in May 1889 when Jones was waxing eloquent on our righteousness as "filthy rags," he had suggested that "the more righteousness of the law a man has the worse he is off—the more ragged is he."[22]

Such sentiments did not go unheard and unanswered. On June 11, 1889, Smith fired off a broadside at Jones in the *Review* entitled "Our Righteousness." He noted that some of the correspondents of the *Review* were playing into the hands of those who would do away with the law with their remarks on our righteousness being "filthy rags." Smith went on to assert that "perfect obedience to it [the law] will develop perfect righteousness, and that is the only way any one can attain to righteousness. . . . We are not to rest on the stool of do-nothing, as a mass of inertia in the hands of the Redeemer. . . . 'Our righteousness' comes from being in harmony with the law of God. . . . And 'our righteousness' cannot in this case be filthy rags."[23]

The *Review* editor's article inspired Ellen White to jump into the fray in a sermon on June 17 at the Rome, New York, camp meeting. Faith must come before works, she asserted in backing up Jones's position at Ottawa. "'Well,' you say, 'What does Brother Smith's piece in the *Review* mean?' He doesn't know what he is talking about; he sees trees as men walking." She pointed out that just because Jesus and His righteousness are central in our salvation, that does not mean that we are discarding God's law. To Smith she wrote that he was on a path that would shortly bring him to the brink of a precipice, that he was "walking like a blind man," and that he had placed Jones in a false position.[24]

The *Review* editor replied in the July 2 issue with "Our Righteousness Again." In his article Smith more fully explained that he had not meant to suggest that human beings could obey the law without Christ's help. He, however, was not ready to surrender on the issue, as we see evidenced, for example, by the two sermons he allowed J. F. Ballenger to publish in the *Review* in 1891 entitled "Justification by Works."[25]

G. I. Butler, meanwhile, had also attacked Jones's teachings at Ottawa, Kansas, and other places. On May 14, 1889, Butler had published an article in the *Review* with a title that was quite expressive of his viewpoint: "The Righteousness of the Law Fulfilled by Us." "There is a sentiment prevailing almost everywhere," Butler thundered, that is pleasant but dangerous: "'Only believe in Christ, and you are all right.' . . . Jesus does it all." That teaching, he proclaimed, "is one of the most dangerous heresies in the world." The whole point of the third angel's message, he emphasized, is "the necessity of obedience to the law of God. 'Here are they that *keep the commandments of God*, and the faith of Jesus.'" The Christian world was rapidly losing that truth and Adventists needed to uplift it.[26]

Two things are certain so far: (1) Jones was not teaching that the Christian's obligation to the law had been abrogated, but (2) some believed that he was advocating exactly that. D. T. Jones, for example, found some of the ministers confused on the point during his visit to Kansas in April 1890. Elders Chaffee and Allee had apparently understood A. T. Jones as saying that "justification by faith practically did away with the law." His use of language certainly left him open to such misinterpretation. After all, he had remarked at the 1889 Kansas meetings: "Where . . . do our works come in? Nowhere." He interspersed such statements throughout his sermons.[27]

In February 1890 Ellen White cautioned Jones, suggesting that he should never imply that there were no conditions involved in a person's receiving the righteousness of Christ. She pointed out that his enemies made capital out of such incautious remarks.[28]

He failed to learn the lesson. In 1893 she again counseled him on that topic, explicitly telling him not to say that "works amounted to nothing, that there were no conditions. . . . While good works will not save even one soul[,] yet it is impossible for even one soul to be saved without good works." She admitted that she looked upon righteousness by faith as it related to the law as he did, but noted that his expressions confused minds. Knowing his weakness, she ominously advised him not to go "to any extreme in anything," pointing out to him that his enemies had their eyes "intently fixed" upon him, expecting that he would "over-reach the mark, and stumble, and fall." Thus she put her finger on Jones's greatest weakness—he was an extremist who had never mastered the Christian virtue of temperance.[29]

If some Adventists misunderstood him on the relation of the law to salvation, his expressions on Christian holiness misled others. In his Ottawa, Kansas, sermons of May 1889, for example, Jones pointed out that the indwelling of Christ's divine nature and power would enable individuals eventually to keep God's commandments. "It is only through being one with Him that we can be Christians, and only through Christ within us that we keep the commandments—it being all by faith in Christ that we do and say these things. *When the day comes that we actually keep the commandments of God, we will never die,* because keeping the commandments is righteousness, and righteousness and life are inseparable—so, 'Here are they that keep the commandments of God and [the] faith of Jesus,' and what is the result? *These people are translated.* Life, then, and keeping the commandments go together. If we die now, Christ's righteousness will be imputed to us and we will be raised, but *those who live to the end are made sinless before He comes, having so much of Christ's being in them that they 'hit the mark' every time,* and stand blameless without an intercessor, because Christ leaves the sanctuary sometime before He comes to earth."[30]

This teaching (although it is capable of more than one interpretation) became a major root for the spread of sinless perfectionism among Seventh-day Adventists—a root that produced some prolific branches in the 1890s. We find, for example, a fairly direct line from Jones in the post-Minneapolis period to the holy flesh movement in Indiana in 1900. Again, D. T. Jones encountered confusion over sinlessness in Kansas during his visit there in 1890. Some of the ministers, he reported, had become bewildered over the "exaggerated ideas they had received of what our brethren taught on the subject of justification by faith; they had got the idea that the position is now taken that we should stand in a position where we do not sin . . . , and that if we are not in that position we are not converted."[31]

A. T. Jones's expressions in Kansas in 1889 had found fertile soil.

The people were also excited about "new light" related to his teaching in California in 1890. J. H. Durland wrote to the General Conference president that several of the ministers were claiming that the people of God were "actually in possession of *eternal life* and would never die." The California ministers, upon being questioned, replied that A. T. Jones was in harmony with their view. When Durland approached Jones on the issue, he was noncommittal—he would not affirm it, "nor would he say he did not believe it."[32]

Then, in 1896 we find R. S. Donnell—the future leader of the holy flesh movement—agitating for the latter rain and the putting away of sin, claiming that Jones was with him in belief and action. September of 1897 found A. F. Ballenger preaching the "Receive Ye the Holy Ghost" message in Indiana, noting to a holiness minister that Adventists had just begun to receive the Spirit, but that it was spreading rapidly. Within two months Jones—as the newly appointed editor of the *Review*—would begin a one-year series of editorials that regularly closed with the admonition "Receive Ye the Holy Ghost." In those editorials he explicitly taught that "*perfect holiness embraces the flesh as well as the spirit.*"[33]

The "outpouring" was soon to come. The holy flesh excitement erupted in Indiana in 1899. While Jones was not in sympathy with the Indiana movement, many of its holy flesh ideas were extensions of his teachings on righteousness by faith. The key Indiana doctrines of "translation faith" and "the power to overcome every tendency to sin," for example, he had preached beginning at least as early as 1889 and 1895, respectively. One can conjecture that Jones's rejection of the holy flesh movement probably rested more on differing interpretations of the nature of Christ than on the movement's views on sinless flesh or Pentecostal-style worship (see chapter 12 for more on this topic). In connection with the last point, it is significant that in 1922 one of his last religious ministries was with a group of tongues-speaking, Sabbathkeeping Pentecostals.[34]

Although the focal point of the holy flesh movement was in Indiana, the doctrinal aberrations related to it were quite widespread. A new variety of Adventist theology had sprouted up during the 1890s.

Stephen N. Haskell, who had spent most of the 1890s overseas, expressed shock at many of the theological ideas he found upon his return to the United States. "Since I have come over to this country," he wrote in October 1899, I "find such queer doctrines preached by some of the leading ministers of the rising generation. . . . Some of the strangest doctrines I have heard is [sic] the Seal of God cannot be placed on any person of grey hairs, or any deformed person, for in the closing work we would reach a state of perfection both physically and spiritually, where we would be healed from all physically [sic] deformity and then could not die. . . . One woman said how convincing it would be to her friends to see her return home with her hairs all restored [in color] and believed it would be soon." Like many of the other Adventist fanaticisms of the decade, Adventists shared those teachings with the holiness believers and the developing pentecostal movement.[35]

The next day Haskell read a testimony to the disoriented believers that

Ellen White had sent to Jones and Waggoner in the early 1890s when they had carried "the praying for the sick to an extreme and it fully described the meeting of the sick we had the night before." Haskell explained to his audience the nature of the testimony and how it had come to "correct errors and suppress fanaticisms." At that point "one cried out as an unanswerable argument, what color would have been the color of the hair if man had not sinned[?] I at once," Haskell reported, "answered 'WHITE' as that was the color of Christ's and God the Father's." That answer, he noted, removed the pressure on many. He then explained to them that they could be sealed even if they were not physically perfect.[36]

That whole experience, along with other aberrations, Haskell claimed, was "a perversion of the doctrine of righteousness by faith." In September 1900 he went to Indiana to face off with Donnell. Mrs. Haskell wrote on September 22 that the holy flesh group had been preaching "'translating faith,' that if one became 'holy flesh' like Christ they could not see corruption any more than he did, that they would live to see him come."[37] Thus the focus of the holy flesh movement was not on the nature of Christ, but upon the concept of what a candidate for translation had to become.

Three days later, Haskell described the essence of the problem to Ellen White. "One of their great burdens is *moral purity* (which you know all about), and 'holy flesh,' and 'translating faith,' and all such terms, which carry the idea that there are two kinds of 'sons of God'—the 'adopted' sons of God, and the 'born' sons of God. The adopted are those who die, because they will not have the '*translating faith.*' Those who are born, get 'holy flesh,' and *there is no sin inside of them, and they are the ones that will live and be translated.*"[38]

Ellen White was not at all impressed with these particular versions of the doctrines of "translation faith" and "Holy flesh." "'Holy flesh,'" she expostulated, "is an error. *All may now obtain holy hearts, but it is not correct to claim in this life to have holy flesh. . . .* If those who speak so freely of perfection in the flesh, could see things in the true light, they would recoil with horror from their presumptuous ideas. . . . *While we can not claim perfection of the flesh, we may have Christian perfection of the soul. Through the sacrifice made in our behalf, sins may be perfectly forgiven.* Our dependence is not in what man can do; it is in what God can do for man through Christ. When we surrender ourselves wholly to God, and fully believe, *the blood of Christ cleanses from all sin. Through faith in His blood, all may be made perfect in Christ Jesus. . . . Thank God we are not dealing with impossibilities. We may claim sanctification. . . . We are not to be anxious about what Christ and God think of us, but about what God thinks of Christ, our Substitute."* She went on to say that no one would have holy flesh until the second coming of Christ. Ellen White's evaluation of the holy flesh perfectionism agrees with what she had written on the topic in early 1888: *"We cannot say, 'I am sinless,' till this vile body is changed and fashioned like unto His glorious body."*[39]

In conclusion, we can acknowledge that A. T. Jones was a champion of righteousness by faith during the post-Minneapolis period, but that his use of extreme verbal expressions often led to accusations of antinomianism on the one hand and exaggerated and misleading ideas of sinless perfectionism on the other. Those two issues still plague the Seventh-day Adventist Church as its members seek both to live the Christian life in the everyday world and to prepare for the world to come.

---

[1] EGW to MW, Nov. 4, 1888; EGW to CPB, Nov. 19, 1902; EGW to WCW and MW, Mar. 13, 1890.

[2] EGW, MS 9, Oct. 24, 1888; *RH*, Sept. 3, 1889, pp. 545, 546.

[3] E.g., EGW to US, Sept. 19, 1892.

[4] GCC Min, Apr. 5, 1888; Battle Creek College Board Min, Nov. 22, 25, 1888; EGW to R. A. Underwood, Jan. 18, 1889.

[5] EGW, MS 30, late June 1889; EGW, MS 16, c. January 1889.

[6] Battle Creek *Daily Journal*, Nov. 28, Dec. 5, 11, 1888. All of these were front-page articles. The first article was apparently published on November 25, but as of yet, I have found no extant copy.

[7] *RH*, Jan. 8, Feb. 12, 1889, pp. 25, 106, 107; EGW to R. A. Underwood, Jan. 18, 1889.

[8] EGW, diary, Jan. 19, June 28, 1889; EGW to WCW, Apr. 5, 7, 1889.

[9] ATJ to WAC, Aug. 21, 1891.

[10] OAO to F. D. Starr, Aug. 14, 1891; JHK to OAO, Jan. 10, 1892; JNL to OAO, Aug. 25, 1891; JHK to WCW, Oct. 2, 21, 1891, Sept. 9, 1892; OAO to WCW, Oct. 9, 1891; EGW, MS 26a, Aug. 5, 1892.

[11] 1891 *GCB*, p. 4; EGW to ATJ, June 7, 1894; EGW, *Testimonies for the Church* (Mountain View, Calif., 1948), vol. 6, p. 89; WCW to DAR, Sept. 10, 1895.

[12] OAO, WWP, and DTJ to GCC, Sept. 18, 1889; OAO to CHJ, Aug. 7, 1890; WCW to OAO, June 10, 1889; WCW to JNL, Mar. 31, 1890; DTJ to N. W. Allee, May 7, 1890.

[13] US to EGW, Feb. 17, 1890; EGW to WCW and MW, Mar. 13, 1890.

[14] EGW to WCW and MW, Mar. 10, 1890; EGW to WAC, Mar. 10, 1890; EGW to WCW, Mar. 7, 11, 1890.

[15] EGW to WCW and MW, Mar. 13, 1890.

[16] DTJ to HWC, Mar. 13, 1890; cf. DTJ to GIB, Mar. 27, 1890.

[17] DTJ to J. D. Pegg, Mar. 17, 1890, cf. DTJ to J. H. Morrison, Mar. 17, 1890. (Ital. sup.)

[18] DTJ to WCW, Mar. 18, 1890; cf. DTJ to J. H. Morrison, Mar. 17, 1890. (Ital. sup.)

[19] OAO to G. C. Tenney, Mar. 20, 1890; US to ATR, Sept. 21, 1892; DTJ to GIB, Apr. 14, 1890.

[20] Topeka *Daily Capital*, May 16, 1889, p. 3; May 18, 1889, p. 5. A General Conference reporter stenographically recorded the Ottawa, Kan., meetings and had them published in the *Capital*. See *RH,* Apr. 9, 1889, p. 240. The sermon published on May 18 was incorrectly attributed to WCW, but it is clearly ATJ's sermon. It is his style and it is part of the series of sermons that he presented on righteousness by faith at Ottawa. The May 17 *Daily Capital* (p. 3) indicates that ATJ was the speaker for the entire series. WCW, by contrast, was not a featured speaker on that topic at Ottawa or elsewhere.

[21] Topeka *Daily Capital*, May 18, 1889, p. 5 (see note 20); May 14, 1889, p. 7. (Ital. sup.)

[22] Topeka *Daily Capital*, May 14, 1889, p. 7; 1893 *GCB*, pp. 244, 257-266.

[23] *RH,* June 11, 1889, pp. 376, 377.

[24] EGW, MS 5, June 17, 1889; EGW to US, June 14, 1889.

[25] *RH,* July 2, 1889, p. 424; Oct. 13, 20, 1891, pp. 626, 642.

[26] *RH,* May 14, 1889, pp. 313, 314.

[27] DTJ to OAO, Apr. 27, 1890; Topeka *Daily Capital*, May 18, 1889, p. 5, see note 20.

[28] EGW to ATJ, Feb. 17, 1890.

[29] EGW to ATJ, Apr. 9, 1893.

[30] Topeka *Daily Capital*, May 18, 1889, p. 5, see note 20. (Ital. sup.)

[31] DTJ to OAO, Apr. 21, 1890.

[32] J. H. Durland to OAO, Nov. 7, 1890; cf. J. S. Washburn to EGW, Apr. 17, 1890.

[33] R. S. Donnell to OAO, June 2, 1896; AFB to GAI, Sept. 6, 1897; *RH,* Nov. 2, 1897, pp. 696, 697; Nov. 22, 1898, p. 752. (Ital, sup.) For more on the "Receive Ye the Holy Ghost" movement, see Calvin W. Edwards and Gary Land, *Seeker After Light: A. F. Ballenger, Adventism, and American Christianity* (Berrien Springs, Mich., 2000).

[34] Topeka *Daily Capital*, May 18, 1889, p. 5, see note 20; 1895 *GCB*, p. 267; O. S. Hadley to EGW, June 1, 1900; *AS* (2), September 1922, pp. 7, 8.

[35] SNH to EGW, Oct. 3, 1899; Virginia Lieson Brereton, *Training God's Army: The American Bible School, 1880-1940* (Bloomington, Ind., 1990), p. 11.

[36] SNH to EGW, Oct. 3, 1899.

[37] SNH to WCW, May 25, 1900 (cf. SNH to EGW, July 27, 1900); H. H. Haskell to EGW, Sept. 22, 1900.

[38] SNH to EGW, Sept. 25, 1900. (Ital. sup.)

[39] 1901 *GCB*, pp. 419, 420; *ST,* Mar. 23, 1888, p. 178. (Ital. sup.)

CHAPTER V

THE MEANING OF MINNEAPOLIS

For more than a hundred years Seventh-day Adventists have looked back at the 1888 General Conference session as a milestone in their history, a foremost turning point in their theological development. Some regard Minneapolis as a major victory, while others view it as the denomination's greatest tragedy. This chapter will examine three issues related to the 1888 meetings: (1) the acceptance or rejection of the "1888 message," (2) the nature of that message, and (3) the extent of Ellen White's theological endorsement of Jones and Waggoner. Since the source material for this chapter is extensive, the discussion will be introductory to its topic rather than comprehensive.

The present chapter differs from the others in the book in that it deals more with the 1888 experience than it does with Jones as an individual. I have included it because he has become inextricably related to the message, meaning, and controversy that has surrounded the 1888 General Conference session. In other words, if we are to comprehend Jones's role in Adventist history, we need to understand the issues treated in this chapter. The information set forth here also provides the groundwork for explanations in subsequent chapters.

ACCEPTED OR REJECTED?

The question of whether the church accepted or rejected the "message of 1888" has been periodically at the forefront of discussion ever since the event. Without doubt many refused to take part in the revival of righteousness by faith at the Minneapolis conference itself. That rejection was

ATJ-3

complicated by the spurning of other theological positions propounded by Jones and Waggoner and the repudiation of the men themselves and Ellen White. It is a messy picture.

A second point on which we can have certainty is that a large number of those involved admitted their error on some or all of these various rejections during the early nineties. Included in this list are the leaders of the opposition forces: Uriah Smith, who confessed in January 1891; J. H. Morrison, who acknowledged his error by July 1892; and George I. Butler, who belatedly published his admission of waywardness regarding justification by faith in the *Review* of June 13, 1893. That does not mean that they ever accepted everything taught at Minneapolis or that they ever learned to appreciate Jones and Waggoner. Smith and Butler, for example, let the law in Galatians issue grate upon them until their deaths.[1]

ˏ A third point that we can feel assured of is that no "official" action of the General Conference ever repudiated righteousness by faith. Some would have liked such an action, but, as we have seen, Ellen White aggressively blocked their moves. The rejection, as well as the acceptance, involved individuals.

A fourth item that we can document is that Jones and Waggoner received wide exposure to the church during the General Conference administrations of O. A. Olsen (1888-1897) and G. A. Irwin (1897-1901). They were, as seen in chapter 4, the major Bible teachers at the General Conference sessions, with Jones preaching a series on righteousness by faith at the 1889 session, Waggoner giving 16 sermons uplifting Christ and the everlasting gospel in 1891 (after 1889 the sessions convened every other year), Jones providing 24 and 26 sermons on the third angel's message in the 1893 and 1895 sessions respectively, and Waggoner speaking 18 times on the book of Hebrews and Jones making 11 presentations at the 1899 session. Beyond that, they were leading speakers at the ministers' schools and camp meetings and continued to have access to the Adventist press, Jones even becoming editor of the *Review* in 1897 with Smith being his assistant.

A fifth point beyond doubt is that some never did respond to the 1888 message. The most prominent members of this group were some of the leading financial officers of the General Conference and the Review and Herald Publishing Association, who formed a powerful clique in the

Adventist Church of the 1890s. Many of that group eventually left the church. Such was the case of Harmon Lindsay (treasurer of the General Conference who died as a Christian Scientist), Clement Eldridge (manager of the Review and Herald Publishing Association), Frank Belden, and others. Before abandoning the church, these influential men (and others who remained in Adventism) represented continuing sectors of rejection. Acceptance, even at an intellectual level, has never been universal, just as rejection at the 1888 meetings had not been universal. Thus, as we will see below, Ellen White not only indicated that the denomination had generally accepted the message by 1895-1896, but she could write "in warning to those who have stood for years resisting light and cherishing the spirit of opposition." How long, she asked in 1895, would such individuals reject the 1888 message? "Many," she said in the same letter, "have listened to the truth [of the 1888 message] spoken in demonstration of the Spirit, and they have not only refused to accept the message, but they have hated the light."[2]

Sixth, we should recognize that all parties not only accepted but agreed on the *doctrine* of righteousness by faith. None of the Adventist leaders ever denied it to be a central pillar of New Testament Christianity. Smith, for example, asserted his belief in righteousness by faith several times, and Butler had published an article uplifting the topic in the *Review* in 1884. As revealing as anything, however, was a meeting called by J. H. Kellogg, Smith, and Jones on February 18, 1893, to specifically discuss the issue in Kellogg's home. Those present were Olsen, D. T. Jones, Smith, Prescott, A. T. Jones, and Kellogg—certainly a strong-minded group that represented the various strands of the struggle. The participants unanimously voted the following resolution: "That, in view of the facts and explanations elicited by this conference, *there is no ground whatever for controversy or disagreement respecting the doctrine of righteousness by faith or concerning the relation of faith and works.*" Their resolution, Kellogg noted a few months later, did not mean that all the problems were cleared up, but it did indicate that all the participants in the discussion agreed on the doctrine of righteousness by faith.[3]

Last, by the second half of the 1890s Waggoner, Jones, and Ellen White agreed that the denomination had largely accepted the message. Waggoner, for example, told the delegates to the 1899 General Conference session that the principles that he and Jones had preached at Minneapolis "have been *accepted to a considerable extent, since that time.*"[4]

Jones reflected a similar position. Four days after Waggoner's remark on the topic he told the assembled delegates that "we used to preach the commandments of God as we thought. But we were not preaching them, indeed, as they must be. The Lord sent a message, and sent his word by that message, saying that the faith of Jesus, righteousness by faith, must be preached. He says that he sent the message of righteousness by faith because the people had lost sight of Christ, in the righteousness of Christ as he is. I am afraid that there has been a tendency to go over to the other end now, and preach the faith of Jesus without the commandments." Jones went on to argue that Adventists needed to present the commandments and the faith of Jesus in combination and in proper balance.[5]

A third witness to the theological acceptance of the 1888 message is Ellen White. On February 6, 1896, she addressed a letter to "My brethren in America," advising the discontinuance of the three- to five-month-long ministerial institutes set up in the wake of the Minneapolis crisis to educate the ministry, because they were no longer necessary. "Men," she penned, "are called from the fields, where they should have continued working in the love and fear of God, seeking to save the lost, to spend weeks in attending a ministerial institute. *There was a time when this work was made necessary, because our own people opposed the work of God by refusing the light of truth on the righteousness of Christ by faith.*"[6]

In her statement Ellen White recognized that in the seven years since Minneapolis, the situation had changed so much that it was no longer necessary to summon ministers together for institutes to instruct them on the topic of righteousness by faith.

W. C. White highlights and reinforces that point: "Mother tells me that some of our people are making a mistake in planning institutes for the benefit of ministers and laborers. . . . *She says that after the Minneapolis conference there was much need of ministerial institutes, but now that the light has been presented and accepted, that it is the duty of those workers to gather about them younger laborers and lay helpers, and to go into the mission fields* working, and teaching as they work."[7]

But did they really accept it? Jones held to the negative on this point to the end of his life. At the 1893 General Conference session he pointed out that some had accepted righteousness by faith, some had rejected it, while others held to some kind of middle ground. Later in the same conference he would suggest that the church had definitely rejected it along with the loud cry of the third angel (see chapter 8).[8]

His last word on the topic came in 1921. In reiterating his post-Minneapolis tours with Ellen White and E. J. Waggoner, he pointed out that "this turned the tide *with the people,* and *apparently* with most of the leading men. But this latter was only apparent; it was never real, for all the time in the General Conference Committee and amongst others there was a secret antagonism always carried on."[9] Of course, how much of that antagonism concerned righteousness by faith and how much involved such issues as the law in Galatians and Jones's abrasive and cocksure personality is impossible to determine.

W. C. White, who certainly did not have much common ground with Jones by 1930, basically agreed with him in evaluating the post-Minneapolis experience. White wrote Taylor G. Bunch that "one by one, those who had been among the opposition at Minneapolis, made confession, accepted and rejoiced in the new found light, and preached it, *at least theoretically.*" After pointing out that the message was not "generally rejected," White granted "that there was not that entering into the *experience* either by ministers or people, to the extent that God was calling for, and after a few years, without any open rejection or repudiation of the doctrine, a formalism and apathy prevailed."[10]

Perhaps White's remarks hold the answer to our unsolved question. It is one thing to accept a doctrine theoretically—quite another to apply it to daily experience. And that is a crucial point since experiential application of Christ's righteousness in daily life is at the heart of the 1888 message of righteousness by faith. Jones himself may be a case in point here—at least Ellen White thought so. While she often in the early nineties commended his gospel message, later in her life she would write that he had "*never yet been thoroughly converted. You have seen the strait gate,*" she told him, "*but you have not passed through it* to the narrow way."[11] Certainly many of his character traits in the 1890s tend to validate a lack of experimental application of his own teachings. That problem will become more evident as our study progresses.

At this point we should say a word about corporate acceptance and corporate rejection of the 1888 message of Jones and Waggoner. Recent years have seen a call for corporate or denominational repentance on the part of the Adventist Church.[12] The most serious fallacy for that theory is that there was no such thing as corporate or denominational rejection. To the contrary, as we noted above, the post-1888 General Conference administration supported the 1888 messengers and did much to make them the theological spokespersons for the church for the next decade. Beyond that, Waggoner, Jones, and Ellen White agreed that by the late 1890s the church had generally accepted the 1888 message.

A second flaw in the call for corporate repentance is that we have not even one quotation from Ellen White on the topic, even though the theory's modern proponents argue as if it were a major concern in her mind. One can read the four volumes of *The Ellen G. White 1888 Materials* and not find her once explicitly urging general denominational repentance for rejecting the 1888 message. What we do find are calls of repentance for those *individuals* who opposed the 1888 message of Christ's righteousness. Thus she could write to F. E. Belden that "never before have I seen among our people such firm self-complacency and unwillingness to accept and acknowledge light as was manifested at Minneapolis. I have been shown that not one of the company who cherished the spirit manifested at that meeting would again have clear light to discern the preciousness of the truth sent them from heaven until they humbled their pride and confessed that they were not actuated by the Spirit of God, but that their minds and hearts were filled with prejudice. The Lord desired to come near to them, to bless them and heal them of their backslidings, but they would not hearken."[13]

That quotation is typical of many urging *individuals* to repent over their rejection of the 1888 message. But it goes against the historical facts to say that Ellen White called for general denominational repentance for corporate or denominational guilt for any such repudiation. By way of contrast, the many calls for individual repentance indicate the problem as she saw it. She is clear on those points. And in that clarity she is quite in harmony with the New Testament view of salvation that Jones and Waggoner did so much to promote. Waggoner is in agreement with her on individual responsibility for accepting and rejecting the gospel message. "There can be no Christian experience," he wrote, "no faith, no justification, no righteousness, that is not an individual matter. People are saved as individuals, and not as nations."[14]

THE ESSENCE OF THE 1888 MESSAGE

Seventh-day Adventists have had a deep concern over the meaning of the 1888 experience and message. Ellen White's repeated endorsements of Jones and Waggoner have sustained that interest. Without her support they would never have received a hearing in 1888 or achieved responsible positions of influence in the church during the 1890s. Because of her centrality and the fact that all theological positions related to 1888 flow out of her endorsement of Jones and Waggoner, it is important to examine what she saw as of central importance in their presentations. The best way to understand what she perceived to be the essence of their teaching is by examining what she had to say about their message and those who opposed it. Her remarks center on two related issues: theology and spiritual attitude.

Ellen White set forth her most thorough analysis of what Jones and Waggoner presented in a letter she penned to General Conference president O. A. Olsen on May 1, 1895. "The Lord in His great mercy," she wrote, "sent a most precious message to His people through Elders Waggoner and Jones. This message was to bring more prominently before the world the uplifted Saviour, the sacrifice for the sins of the whole world. It presented justification through faith in the Surety; it invited the people to receive the righteousness of Christ, which is made manifest in obedience to all the commandments of God. Many had lost sight of Jesus. They needed to have their eyes directed to His divine person, His merits, and His changeless love for the human family. All power is given into His hands, that He may dispense rich gifts unto men, imparting the priceless gift of His own righteousness to the helpless human agent. This is the message that God commanded to be given to the world. It is the third angel's message, which is to be proclaimed with a loud voice, and attended with the outpouring of His Spirit in a large measure.

"The uplifted Saviour is to appear in His efficacious work as the Lamb slain, sitting upon the throne, to dispense the priceless covenant blessings, the benefits He died to purchase for every soul who should believe on Him. . . . The message of the gospel of His grace was to be given to the church in clear and distinct lines, that the world should no longer say that Seventh-day Adventists talk the law, the law, but do not teach or believe Christ.

"The efficacy of the blood of Christ was to be presented to the people with freshness and power, that their faith might lay hold upon its merits. . . .

"For years the church has been looking to man and expecting much from man, but not looking to Jesus, in whom our hopes of eternal life are centered. Therefore God gave to His servants a testimony that presented the truth as it is in Jesus, which is the third angel's message, in clear, distinct lines."[15]

Of particular note in the letter to Olsen is Ellen White's uplifting of Christ, justification by faith, and the intimate relationship between righteousness by faith and the third angel's message. It is of the utmost importance to grasp the fact that the Adventist theological struggle in the Minneapolis era centered around one verse in the third angel's message— Revelation 14:12 ("Here is the patience of the saints: here are they that keep the commandments of God, and the faith of Jesus."). The Butler-Smith coalition focused their attention on the keeping the commandments part of the verse, while Jones and Waggoner were more interested in "the faith of Jesus" portion.

Along that line, Waggoner asserted in his book on the gospel in Galatians, which he circulated at the 1888 meetings, that his understanding of the law and the gospel "would simply be a step nearer to the faith of the great Reformers from the days of Paul to the days of Luther and Wesley. It would be a step closer to the heart of the Third Angel's Message." He did not regard his view as "a new idea at all," but the one held by "all the eminent reformers."[16]

Jones backed Waggoner on the centrality of the third angel's message to their understanding of righteousness by faith. In December 1887 he wrote that "the only way in which they can ever attain to harmony with the righteous law of God is through the righteousness of God, which is by *faith of Jesus Christ*. . . . In the Third Angel's Message is embodied the supreme truth and the supreme righteousness." In that quotation he equated "the supreme truth" with "the commandments of God" and "the supreme righteousness" with "the faith of Jesus."[17]

Ellen White would expand upon Jones's insight in 1888 and beyond. The message given in Minneapolis, she asserted, was "not alone the commandments of God—a part of the third angel's message—but the faith of Jesus, which comprehends more than is generally supposed." The third angel's message needed "to be proclaimed in all its parts. . . . If we proclaim the commandments of God and leave the other half scarcely touched the message is marred in our hands." What Jones and Waggoner presented, she noted, was not anything "new or novel." Rather, "it is an old truth that has been lost sight of." Adventists needed "to bring the faith of Jesus into the right place where it belongs—in the third angel's message. The law has its important position but is powerless unless the righteousness of Christ is placed beside the law to give its glory to the whole royal standard of righteousness. . . . A thorough and complete trust in Jesus will give the right quality to religious experience. Aside from this the experience is nothing. The service is like the offering of Cain—Christless." She went on to talk about Christ's substitutionary death and His blood as the sinner's only hope.[18]

Soon after the Minneapolis meetings, Ellen White made one of her most powerful statements on Revelation 14:12 and the core meaning of Minneapolis. "The third angel's message," she penned, "is the proclamation of the commandments of God and the faith of Jesus Christ. The commandments of God have been proclaimed, but the faith of Jesus Christ has not been proclaimed by Seventh-day Adventists as of equal importance, the law and the gospel going hand in hand." She went on to discuss the meaning of the faith of Jesus, which "is talked of, but not understood." The faith of Jesus, she claimed, means "Jesus becoming our sin-bearer that He might become our sin-pardoning Saviour. . . . He came to our world and took our sins that we might take His righteousness. And faith in the ability of Christ to save us amply and fully and entirely is the faith of Jesus." Adventists, therefore, needed to apply His blood to their lives. By faith they must lay "hold of the righteousness of Christ." "Faith in Christ as the sinner's only hope" had been "largely left out, not only of the discourses given but of the religious experience of very many who claim to believe the third angel's message."[19]

Of particular interest to those seeking to comprehend Ellen White's understanding of Revelation 14:12 and justification by faith and Jones and Waggoner's contribution in linking the two is an article she published in the *Review* during August 1889. In it she wrote that there are "grand truths," including the "doctrine of justification by faith," that many Seventh-day Adventists had lost sight of. At this point in her argument she indicated most vividly what kind of justification by faith had been lost: "The Holiness people have gone to great extremes on this point. With great zeal they have

taught, 'Only believe in Christ, and be saved; but away with the law of God.'"
She went on to imply that although those people were correct in lifting up
faith, they were wrong in demeaning the law. Because of the imbalance, she
wrote, "God has raised up men [Jones and Waggoner] to meet the necessity
of this time . . . who will . . . lift up their voice like a trumpet, and show my
people their transgressions. . . . *Their work is not only to proclaim the law, but
to preach the truth for this time—the Lord our righteousness.*"[20]

That conclusion lines up with her earlier statement regarding her appreciation of Waggoner's uplifting of "the righteousness of Christ in connection with the law." We need to view all of these statements from the
perspective of her emphasis that the teaching of Jones and Waggoner on
righteousness by faith was "not new light" but "old light" that had "been
lost sight of by many" Adventists. "God" through them, she asserted, "has
rescued these truths from the companionship of error, and has placed
them in their proper framework."[21]

The content of those statements clearly indicates she is stating that the
old truth that Adventists had lost sight of was the same belief in justification by faith as that held by the holiness people. But they had bound it to
"the companionship of error" in their degrading of the law. Thus from her
perspective, Jones and Waggoner had rescued justification by faith from
its companionship with antinomian error and put it in the context of the
third angel's message.

Ellen White made the connection explicit when she reflected upon the
topic about a month after the Minneapolis meetings. "Elder E. J.
Waggoner," she wrote, "had the privilege granted him of speaking plainly
and presenting his views upon justification by faith and the righteousness
of Christ in relation to the law. This was no new light, but it was old light,
placed where it should be in the third angel's message."[22]

In summary, the major contribution of Jones and Waggoner from Ellen
White's perspective was putting Christ and His saving righteousness at the
center of Adventist theology through their uniting of the law ("the commandments of God") and the gospel ("the faith of Jesus") in Revelation
14:12. In the process the two reformers had captured the essence of the
meaning of the central text in Adventism.

If theological concerns related to righteousness by faith were important
at Minneapolis, so also were people's attitudes. In fact, the two are directly

related. We noted in chapter 3 that the wrong spirit ruled those who opposed righteousness by faith in 1888. The spirit of Minneapolis, among other things, consisted of a critical attitude toward those who differed theologically, was contentious, centered on doctrinal debate, and stirred up "human passions" and "bitterness of spirit" toward anyone who ventured to suggest ideas "which were thought . . . to be inroads upon ancient doctrines." Also it was characterized by "playing" and "quibbling upon words" and their meanings. Beyond that, the spirit of Minneapolis prompted "sharp, hard feelings" and attitudes and overemphasized the law and a concern with human righteousness. It was the inquisitional spirit that had put Christ on the cross and had excommunicated the Millerites during the 1844 movement.[23]

Contrasted to the spirit of Minneapolis is the spirit of Christianity, which Ellen White advocated in 1888 and throughout her ministry. That spirit was the attitude of Christian courtesy that would have treated Jones and Waggoner as Jesus would have done, even if some believed that the two men were wrong on certain doctrinal issues. In contrast to the hostility of the old guard, Ellen White was pleased with the "right spirit," the "Christlike spirit," manifested by Waggoner throughout the presentation of his views at Minneapolis.[24]

The attitude of the participants at the 1888 General Conference session stood near the forefront of Ellen White's concern. She feared, with a great deal of justification, that they had departed from the path of Christianity at the same time that they were fighting to maintain Adventist orthodoxy. Therefore she was overjoyed to be able to report that things had begun to change by the 1889 General Conference session. "We are having," she reported, "most excellent meetings. The spirit that was in the meeting at Minneapolis is not here."[25]

Ellen White highlighted the relationship between a correct spiritual attitude and doctrinal differences in December 1888 when she wrote that some were worried because "A. T. Jones and Dr. Waggoner hold views upon some doctrinal points[,] which all admit are not vital questions, different from those which some of the leading ones of our people have held. But it is a vital question whether we are Christians, whether we have a Christian spirit, and are true, open, and frank with one another." Again, in May 1889 she wrote: "The different views in regard to the law in

Galatians need not have produced any such exhibitions. I have not the slightest burden upon that subject. God has not inspired all this intense feeling over that subject. I have not a particle of burden on that subject. My only trouble is the position of those ministers who were at that conference who manifested so little of the spirit of Christ and possessed more largely the spirit which controlled the scribes and Pharisees." If partaking of their zeal for doctrinal purity would make her as "unchristian" as them, she said, "God deliver me from your ideas." Any such "pet theory" that overcomes our Christian attitude toward others is as "sacred as an idol."[26]

The experiential side of Christianity deeply concerned her during the 1888 era. In January 1889 she wrote that "there must be a spiritual revolution throughout the churches that fruits unto righteousness may be seen in our *daily life*." Her burden was that Seventh-day Adventists "individually know Him" as their Savior.[27]

That sentiment was nothing new. It had been her conviction before the Minneapolis conference. Back in 1887, when she saw the doctrinal battles of the next year on the horizon, she had written to A. T. Jones that "*there is danger of our ministers dwelling too much on doctrines, . . . when their own soul needs practical godliness.*"[28] But that was a hard message to grasp in a denomination that had prided itself on its distinctive theological positions. Its ministers were willing to fight to the death to preserve what they believed was traditional Adventism.

Early in 1891 Ellen White confided to her diary sentiments that tie the experiential to the doctrinal in the 1888 message. She noted that some feared that the church was "carrying the subject of justification by faith altogether too far, and not dwelling enough on the law." Then she complained that many Adventist ministers presented their "subjects in an argumentative way, . . . scarcely mentioning the saving power of the Redeemer." They and their messages were "destitute of the saving blood of Jesus Christ." "Of all professed Christians, Seventh-day Adventists should be foremost in uplifting Christ before the world." Adventists should preach both the law and the gospel—"blended, [they] will convict of sin." "God's law," she asserted (as she did when supporting Waggoner at Minneapolis), "while condemning sin, points to the gospel. . . . In no discourse are they to be divorced." Too many Adventists had not seen that "Jesus Christ is the glory of the law."

She went on to emphasize her central concern with both the 1888 message and the Adventist Church. "Why, then," she queried, "is there manifested in the church so great a lack of love . . . ? It is because Christ is not constantly brought before the people. *His attributes of character are not brought into the practical life. . . . A correct theory of the truth may be presented, and yet there may not be manifested the warmth of affection that the God of truth requires. . . . The religion of many is very much like an icicle— freezingly cold. . . .* They can not touch the hearts of others, because their own hearts are not surcharged with the blessed love that flows from the heart of Christ. *There are others who speak of religion as a matter of the will. They dwell upon stern duty as if it were a master ruling with a scepter of iron— a master stern, inflexible, all-powerful, devoid of the sweet, melting love and tender compassion of Christ.*"[29]

In conclusion, the essence of the 1888 message is both doctrinal and experiential. The two, from Ellen White's perspective, are united in believers who accept the saving merits of Jesus in relation to the law as found in the third angel's message and who let the love and character of Jesus flow out of their hearts to others—even to those who disagree with them.

THE EXTENT OF ELLEN WHITE'S ENDORSEMENT OF JONES AND WAGGONER

The extent of her approval of Jones and Waggoner is an important issue, since for the better part of a decade she drove home the idea that God had chosen them as special messengers because "many had lost sight of Jesus" and "justification through faith" in Him.[30] Because of Ellen White's endorsement, some interpreters have acted as if she had given Jones and Waggoner a kind of blank check in theological matters—especially in relation to issues involving righteousness by faith. That, however, had never been her intent, and such an approach fails to line up with the historical record.

Early in the Minneapolis meetings, for example, she wrote of her angelic "guide" who "stretched out his arms toward Dr. Waggoner and to you, Elder Butler, and said in substance as follows: Neither have [sic] all the light upon the law, neither position is perfect." While the context of that statement is the 1886 General Conference session, she still held the same position in 1888. In early November she told the delegates at Minneapolis that some things that Waggoner had presented on the law in Galatians "do not harmonize with the understanding I have had of this subject." Later in the same talk she claimed that "some interpretations of Scripture, given by Dr. Waggoner, I do not regard as correct."[31]

W. C. White substantiates his mother's position. He wrote to his wife from Minneapolis that "much that Dr. W. teaches is in line with what" his mother had "seen in vision." That had led some to jump to the conclusion "that she endorses all his views, an[d that no] part of his teaching disagrees wi[th Mother] and with her Testimonies. . . . I could prove all this to be f[alse]."[32]

Ellen White never indicated on what points she disagreed with Jones and Waggoner, but we do know that during this period they promoted several teachings out of harmony with her views. For instance, in January 1889 Waggoner argued in the *Signs* that Christ could not sin. Again, in *Christ and His Righteousness* (1890) he put forth semi-Arian views of the divinity of Christ when he wrote that "there was a time when Christ proceeded forth and came from God, . . . but that time was so far back in the days of eternity that to finite comprehension it is practically without beginning."[33] Ellen White would subsequently come out against both positions.

In like manner, she disagreed with Jones on many of his religious liberty ideas (see chapter 10) and in his teaching that "there were no conditions" in salvation. To her way of thinking "the Bible is full of conditions." "The *provisions* of redemption," she wrote in 1890, "are free to all; the *results* of redemption will be enjoyed by those who have complied with the conditions." "Faith," she noted in another connection the same month she rebuked him on the topic, "is the only condition upon which justification can be obtained."[34]

Again and again she validated Jones and Waggoner's uplifting of Christ and His righteousness, but she never regarded them as beyond theological error. In February 1890 she faced that very issue with the attendees assembled for the inservice ministers' school. "I believe," she told them, "without a doubt that God has given precious truth at the right time to Bro. Jones and Bro. Waggoner. Do I place them as infallible? Do I say that they will not make a statement, nor have an idea that can not be questioned? or that can not be error? Do I say so?—No, I do not say any such thing; . . . I do not say that of any man in the world. But I do say God has sent light, and do . . . be careful how you treat it. We want the truth as it is in Jesus."[35]

Despite such limitations, people began treating Jones and Waggoner's pronouncements as if they possessed divine authority. We can clearly see that in the case of Anna Rice, who felt called to the prophetic office in 1892 (see chapter 9). Presumably Anna would have sought counsel with Ellen White, but the latter was in Australia. The next best thing, Anna reasoned, would be an endorsement from Jones. After all, had not Ellen White said that he and Waggoner had advanced light? So Anna traveled from Salt Lake City to Chicago to visit Jones. If he said she was a prophet, then she must be one, since he had Ellen White's approval. Anna was overjoyed when Jones sanctioned her messages.[36]

Thus by late 1892 some were treating Jones as a kind of prophetic extension of Ellen White. People were beginning to validate truth by his words. Along that line, by 1894 S. N. Haskell complained to her that he realized that she had had to endorse Jones and Waggoner in the years right after 1888 because so many of the denominational leaders had been against them, but now "the whole country has been silenced against criticizing them to any extent." He claimed that many now regarded Jones as "almost inspired of God." F. M. Wilcox was of the same mind. Writing from Battle Creek, he noted that "there was a time when many of the principles that Brother Jones has brought out were opposed, but lately the great mass of our people have hung on his words almost as though they were the words of God." General Conference president O. A. Olsen also recognized Jones's power, claiming that a word from him ends all dispute in Battle Creek.[37]

Ellen White replied to Haskell that while she was in general agreement with Jones's work, she could not approve of his mistakes. She warned the Battle Creek congregation that they were "placing the servant where God should be. The Lord has given Brother Jones a message to prepare a people to stand in the day of God; but when the people shall look to Elder Jones instead of to God, they will become weak instead of strong."[38]

Adventists in the twenty-first century need to study carefully the lessons of the extent of Ellen White's endorsement of Jones and Waggoner, especially since they have been prone to repeat the mistake of their forebears on that point. In fact, one influential book in 1987 linked Jones and Waggoner with Ellen White as "the inspired trio."[39]

CONCLUDING REMARKS

In closing our discussion of the issues of 1888, it is important to realize that the Minneapolis General Conference session was one of Adventism's great turning points. In a sense it started a revolution still in process. The post-1888 period saw a great effort to put Christ and His righteousness into the center of Adventism and Adventist theology. Not that it had been absent before, but it had a magnitude after Minneapolis that it never had previous to that time.

One of Jones and Waggoner's greatest contributions was to give righteousness by faith eschatological meaning as they placed it in the context of the three angels' messages of Revelation 14. The 1888 conference was merely the beginning of that emphasis. The continued agitation for Sunday legislation in the early nineties led Jones to emphasize increasingly the link between the faith of Jesus and the commandments of God (Rev. 14:12) as he stressed two great themes of Minneapolis—righteousness by faith and religious liberty.[40]

Perhaps the greatest tragedy of the 1888 conference and its aftermath was the estrangement between the old guard denominational leadership and Jones and Waggoner. The insights of the latter would have been greatly enriched and stabilized if they could have united with the Smith-Butler forces. In June 1894 Ellen White indicated to Jones that he needed to appreciate and respect the older "warriors" who were also God's channels for truth. Jones, she claimed, was to be silent concerning what he might think was a defection, and let God alone specify their mistakes.[41]

Meanwhile, six days earlier, she had written to Haskell that "the Lord's work needed every jot and tittle of experience that He had given Eld. Butler and Eld. Smith," but that they and others had not respected the younger men. Their experience would have kept Jones, Prescott, and Waggoner from making some serious mistakes.[42]

Bert Haloviak has suggested that one of the great lessons of the period from 1888 to 1901 is that "we need each other." Both sides in the controversy that racked Adventism during the nineties "had a theological perspective that the church desperately needed—and one that they could have contributed were it not for the disunity they generated." As a result of its lack of unity, the denomination drifted toward the theological aberrations that resulted in the holy flesh movement, Kellogg's "pantheism," inadequate views on church organization (see chapter 13), and Ballenger's rejection of the sanctuary doctrine. Ellen White sought to mediate between the opposing sides by "creating an atmosphere for truth to flourish, rather than to emphasize the points of difference or to resolve the theological differences herself."[43] In her attempt, however, she largely failed. The results would become evident early in the twentieth century.

---

[1] DTJ to R. M. Kilgore, Jan. 9, 1891; OAO to J. H. Morrison, July 10, 1892; WAC to EJW, July 27, 1892; RH, June 13, 1893, p. 377; AGD to WCW, Jan. 21, 1910; US to W. A. McCutchen, Aug. 8, 1901.

[2] EGW, *Testimonies to Ministers and Gospel Workers* (Mountain View, Calif., 1962), pp. 401, 96, 97, 91.

[3] US to EGW, Feb. 17, 1890; RH, Sept, 23, 1884, pp. 616, 617; "Report of Conference for the Consideration of the Subjects of Righteousness by Faith and the Relation of Faith and Works, Held in Dr. Kellogg's Parlor on the Evening After the Sabbath, Feb. 18, 1893," unpub. MS; JHK to WCW, July 17, 1993. (Ital. sup.)

[4] 1899 *GCB*, p. 94. (Ital. sup.)

[5] *RH*, June 20, 1899, p. 392.

[6] EGW, *Testimonies to Ministers*, p. 401; cf. EGW, *Testimonies*, vol. 6, p. 89. (Ital. sup.)

[7] WCW to D. A. Robinson, Sept. 10, 1895. (Ital. sup.)

[8] 1893 *GCB*, pp. 183, 244.

[9] ATJ to CEH, May 12, 1921.

[10] WCW to TGB, Dec. 30, 1930. (Ital. sup.)

[11] EGW to ATJ, Nov. 19, 1911. (Ital. sup.)

[12] R. J. Wieland and D. K. Short, *1888 Re-Examined*, rev. ed. (Meadow Vista, Calif., 1987), p. 19; R. J. Wieland, *Corporate Repentance: Plea of the True Witness* (Paris, Ohio, 1992), pp. 39-41.

[13] EGW to Frank and Hattie Belden, Nov. 5, 1892.

[14] EJW, *The Gospel in the Book of Galatians*, p. 45.

[15] EGW to OAO, May 1, 1895.

[16] EJW, *The Gospel in the Book of Galatians*, p. 70.

[17] ATJ, *ST*, Dec. 8, 1887, p. 743.

[18] EGW, MS 30, late June 1889.

[19] EGW, MS 24, Nov. or Dec. 1888.

[20] EGW, *RH*, Aug. 13, 1889, p. 514. (Ital. sup.)

[21] EGW, MS 15, Nov. 1888; EGW, MS 8a, Oct. 21, 1888.

[22] EGW, MS 24, Nov. or Dec. 1888.

[23] EGW to Children, May 12, 1889; see chapter 3 for a discussion of the spirit of Minneapolis.

[24] EGW to R. A. Underwood, Jan. 18, 1889; EGW, MS 24, Nov. or Dec. 1888.

[25] EGW, MS 10, cir. Oct. 1889.

[26] EGW to WMH, Dec. 9, 1888; EGW to Brother Fargo, May 2, 1889; EGW, MS 55, 1890, n.d.

[27] EGW to R. A. Underwood, Jan. 18, 1889; EGW, MS 24, Nov. or Dec. 1888. (Ital. sup.)

[28] EGW to EJW and ATJ, Feb. 18, 1887. (Ital. sup.)

[29] EGW, diary, Feb. 27, 1891. (Ital. sup.)

[30] EGW to OAO, May 1, 1895.

[31] EGW to GIB, Oct. 14, 1888; EGW, MS 15, Nov. 1888.

[32] WCW to MW, Oct. 27, 1888. The torn sections of this letter have been reconstructed from the handwritten original. While some words are missing, the sense is clear.

[33] EJW, *ST*, Jan. 21, 1889, p. 39; EJW, *Christ and His Righteousness* (Oakland, 1890), pp. 21, 22, 9.

[34] EGW to ATJ, Apr. 9, 1893; EGW, *Patriarchs and Prophets* (Mountain View, Calif., 1958), p. 208; EGW, *Selected Messages* (Washington, D.C., 1958), book 1, p. 389. For more on the divergent theological ideas of ATJ and EJW from those of EGW, see Knight, *The 1888 Message*, pp. 73-77 and the various chapters of this biography.

[35] EGW, MS 56, Feb. 7, 1890, n.d.

[36] SNH to EGW, Jan. 4, 189[3]. This letter is dated 1892, but internal and external evidence point to 1893 as the only possible date.

[37] SNH to EGW, Apr. 22, 1894; FMW to SNH, Mar. 5, 1894.

[38] EGW to SNH, June 1, 1894; EGW to Brethren and Sisters, Mar. 16, 1894.

[39] R. Wieland and D. Short, *1888 Re-examined*, rev. ed., p. 75.

[40] For more on this topic, see Roy Israel McGarrell, "The Historical Development of Seventh-day Adventist Eschatology, 1884-1895," Ph.D. dissertation, Andrews University, 1989.

[41] EGW to ATJ, June 7, 1894.

[42] EGW to SNH, June 1, 1894.

[43] Bert Haloviak, "Why We Need Each Other: Ellen White and Theological Crises, 1844 and 1888," unpub. MS, Dec. 19, 1981.

CHAPTER VI

THE NATIONAL SUNDAY LAW AND THE IMAGE TO THE BEAST

"W e are certainly on the eve of a great conflict. We can see the forces gathering and can almost hear the distant rumbling of thunder." So spoke O. A. Olsen, president of the General Conference, in July 1890.[1]

SUNDAY LAWS ON EVERY HAND

Olsen had good reason for his apprehensions. The move to create a Christian America had been under way since the early 1860s, and the National Reform Association and its allies were keeping up, and even increasing, the pressure for national Sunday legislation.

Many states, especially in the South, had already deeply committed themselves to enforcing their Sunday laws. As noted in chapter 3, in the 1880s Arkansas led in Sunday law prosecutions, especially singling out Adventists for their legal favors. By the early nineties the locus of action had shifted to the state of Tennessee, where Adventists regularly faced arrest for violation of Sunday laws, and where some even served time on chain gangs.[2]

The most important of the Tennessee cases was that of R. M. King, a Seventh-day Adventist arrested on June 23, 1889, for plowing corn in his own field and in June 1890 "for hoeing in his potato patch on Sunday." Through a series of legal maneuvers made possible by his refusal to pay his fine and some questionable procedures on the part of the state, the case was appealed to the United States Supreme Court. The denomination's lawyers, using a strategy that the Jehovah's Witnesses would successfully utilize in the 1940s, took the position that the due process clause of the Fourteenth Amendment to the Constitution made the Bill of Rights—including the religion clauses of the First Amendment—applicable to the states.[3]

The King case, however, never reached the nation's highest court, because he died in November 1891. Some Adventist leaders held his death to be providential. After all, if the Court had ruled against him, it would have been viewed as open season for the persecution of Adventists. We can assume that Jones, given his heroic and abrasive stand against Sunday laws, would not have agreed with such "fearful" and "cowardly" thinking. From his perspective the stubborn resistance by Adventists and the frustration of the state to control them were good things. The unbending resistance that he consistently advocated would soon escalate the issue to where the exasperated state would find itself forced to issue the death decree. King, of course, did not live to cooperate fully with such a program, but his case had attracted a great deal of attention across the nation to the plight of Sabbatarians.[4]

The agitation for Sunday legislation went beyond the various states. The 1880s and early 1890s also saw several attempts to establish a national Sunday law. Jones found himself at the center of controversy over each attempt. The first proposed national Sunday legislation since 1830 was the national Sunday rest bill, sponsored by Senator H. W. Blair, chairman of the Senate Committee on Education and Labor, in the spring of 1888. Entitled "A Bill to Secure to the People the Enjoyment of the First Day of the Week, Commonly Known as the Lord's Day, as a Day of Rest, and to Promote Its Observance as a Day of Religious Worship," the Blair bill left few doubts regarding its religious implications. The Senate Committee on Education and Labor heard arguments for and against the bill on December 13, 1888. Jones championed the Sabbatarian cause, his testimony taking the largest portion of time by far. Blair later characterized Jones as "a man whom I shall always remember with respect on account of his great ability and the evident sincerity with which he presented his views to the committee."[5]

A. T. Jones's part in the hearing and his lecturing on the topic across the nation got him and his cause a great deal of publicity in the public press. Not only did various newspapers publish his lectures on religious liberty, but they also often printed his sermons regarding the seventh-day Sabbath.[6]

February 22, 1889, found Jones once again before the Senate Committee on Education and Labor, this time to testify against Blair's proposed amendment to the Constitution that would Christianize the nation's public school system. Both of Blair's measures failed to get enacted into law. Blair, however, was not one to give up.[7]

Late in 1889 he submitted a second national Sunday bill. This time, to appease Jones and his allies, it was phrased in more secular terms and provided an exemption for Sabbathkeepers. But the changes, Jones pointed out, were merely cosmetic. "The modification in the title is simply to disarm suspicion," he wrote, "and the exemption of those who conscientiously observe another day . . . is put into the bill for no other purpose than to checkmate the opposition." Once again the Adventists and their allies fought hard, and once again the national Sunday bill went down to defeat.[8]

The next major attempt to enact a federal Sunday law came on January 6, 1890, when W.C.P. Breckenridge of Kentucky introduced into the House of Representatives a bill designed to prevent anyone from working on Sunday in the federally controlled District of Columbia. The proposed legislation was entitled "A Bill to Prevent Persons From Being Forced to Labor on Sunday." The Adventists, understandably, held that the Breckenridge bill was deceptive since no one was being compelled to labor on Sunday. Its actual purpose, they pointed out, was to force people to rest on Sunday, and they viewed it as an entering wedge for stronger legislation.[9]

The House Committee on the District of Columbia heard the Breckenridge bill on February 18, 1890. Once again, Jones was a key witness, not only in arguing the bill's unconstitutionality, but also in using its religious arguments against its authors. Always at his best when under pressure, he later claimed that "it seemed as though the sentences he should speak were written on the wall, or suspended in the air before him."[10]

The Breckenridge bill also failed to pass, but the Sunday forces could not be held at bay indefinitely. August 5, 1892, saw President Benjamin Harrison sign the first national Sunday law in the United States. It stipulated that federal appropriations for the Chicago World's Fair would not be forthcoming unless the fair closed on Sundays. According to W. A. Spicer (secretary of Adventism's Foreign Mission Board), Jones had had an interview with President Harrison before the signing of the bill to see if he could veto it. That proved to be impossible since "all the running expenses of the government for the whole year were in the bill, and he" could not "veto a part without vetoing all."[11]

The enforcement of the law had a stormy history. From January 10 to 13, 1893, the House Committee on the Columbian Exposition held hearings on whether Congress should repeal the Sunday-closing law. Jones once again stood at the forefront of those who testified.[12]

The Sunday law problem was not merely an issue in the United States in the late 1880s and early 1890s. Australia, Switzerland, Norway, and England also had passed Sunday laws and had arrested Adventists for breaking them. Even China faced the issue of Sunday legislation.[13] It was truly a worldwide crisis for the Adventist Church. The denomination did not intend to meet it passively.

ADVENTISTS ORGANIZE FOR ACTION

In reaction to pending legislation on the Blair Sunday bill and the Blair educational amendment, in December 1888 the General Conference Committee organized a Press Committee to publicize the religious liberty issue. The Press Committee evolved into the National Religious Liberty Association in July, with Jones serving on its executive and editorial committees.[14] By 1893 the organization carried the title of International Religious Liberty Association.

Closely aligned to the association in purpose was the *American Sentinel,* edited by Jones. Though not officially connected with the association, the *Sentinel* had the same general aims—namely, to combat "anything and everything that had a tendency toward uniting Church and State," to preserve the Constitution "as it now stands," and to educate the people of the United States on the subject of religious and civil liberty.[15]

One of the most energetic activities of the Adventists in combating the Blair Sunday bills of 1888 and 1889 was the circulation of petitions against the proposals. By October 1889 they had secured nearly 500,000 signatures for their petition to Congress. That aggressive activity inspired Wilbur Crafts, secretary of the National Reform Association, to chide America's 26,000,000 Sundaykeeping Christians because they had been outworked by some 25,000 Adventists. The petition campaign not only gave Adventists much national publicity, but it seemed to put "new life and vitality into many of our people."[16]

Jones, as we might expect, was at the center of the petition campaign. He, however, unlike many of his colleagues, saw beyond the mere defeat of the Blair Sunday legislation. Religious legislation, he claimed, could not ultimately be defeated. Adventists could only delay it. "The principal object" of the petition drive, he noted, "is to spread the third angel's message, and to warn everybody against the making of the image of the beast," so that people would be left without excuse. As a result, he held that Adventists should continue to circulate the petitions until the image to the beast had been formed. Only then would the denomination's stupendous public relations work be finished.[17]

Undoubtedly Jones was the most aggressive Adventist in religious liberty in the nation between 1888 and 1895. A steady flow of articles, pamphlets, and books came from his pen. In addition, he was constantly on the campaign trail, often speaking before large non-Adventist audiences and several times testifying before congressional and legislative committees.

At times he even managed to speak in the camp of the enemy, a tactic well illustrated by his actions at a convention sponsored by Sunday law advocates in Washington, D.C., early in 1890. Several, including congressmen, spoke in favor of the pending legislation and against Adventists and their "deceptive" petition campaign. Then a "large, burly man" who represented the Knights of Labor arose. He held up an *American Sentinel* and noted that Alonzo T. Jones edited it. "I wish he was here in the congregation," he thundered. "I would like to talk straight to him." A voice from the audience replied, "He's here." That threw the man into shock, but he soon recovered, "pouring out his vial of wrath upon the editor of the *Sentinel*." When he had finished, Jones arose and said that since "his name had been publicly called, and his course criticized, he would like the privilege of saying a few words." On this particular occasion he did not manage to get a hearing, but that was not always the case.[18]

Jones was much more successful at the fourth annual convention of the American Sabbath Union in December 1892. The meeting convened to protest the possibility of opening the Chicago World's Fair on Sunday. It offered a resolution to that effect, then called for a vote. The motion, to the shock of the convention organizers, got voted down. When the stupefied chairman—still ignorant of the fact that Adventists organized for action had packed the meeting—called for an explanation as to why the majority had voted against the resolution, A. T. Jones arose. As was his style when presented an opportunity, he gave a lengthy speech that "ventilated" the remarks of the Sunday-closing proponents. The Chicago *Tribune,* overjoyed with this bit of news, published it under the heading "It Was Voted Down."[19]

MANHANDLING OPPONENTS

The combat between Jones and W. F. Crafts—opposing champions in the legal battle over Sunday—was vigorous, even brutal at times. In the July 1889 issues of the *Sentinel,* for example, Jones accused Crafts of being dishonest on July 3; of being an unrepentant liar who compared unfavorably to a dishonest politician on July 10; and of being blatantly contemptible of minorities on July 17. The National Reform Association itself was nothing but the leading edge of the "American Papacy."[20]

Crafts, for his part, was not particularly mild in his speech. In 1889 his opinion of Adventists (even though he later came to appreciate their sincerity) was that they "were a little 'insignificant set of hair-brained, woolly-headed fanatics.'" He also publicly attacked the denomination for "mixing in with liquor dealers" in their warfare against Sunday legislation. Jones shot back that Crafts was no one to talk since he was aligned with the Catholics, who had no qualms about saloonkeeping.[21]

The Adventists, of course, must have been a terrible irritant to Crafts. A constant tactic employed against him was to get a copy of his itinerary, then to go to the area he planned to visit and saturate it with religious liberty publications before he arrived. Jones, meanwhile, went around the country to "camp on Crafts' trail."[22]

The high point of the Jones-Crafts conflict came during the spring and summer of 1889. On March 6 Crafts challenged Jones to a public debate in Chicago. A series of quite cordial letters followed between the two men. Jones announced in April, according to the Chicago *Daily Inter Ocean,* that the debate would take place from June 12 to 14. As time went on, however, the once-cordial letters became acrimonious, and Jones's and Crafts' public utterances became more negative toward each other. Crafts reached the boiling point during his Colorado speaking tour in June. The Adventists had preceded him at every point of his itinerary and distributed books and periodicals. On this occasion they had even printed a special edition of the *Sentinel* for specific use against him in Colorado. In addition, they had also aligned some of the newspapers against him.[23]

Their tactics proved to be too much for Crafts. On June 28 he opened fire on Jones with a public affidavit against him and Waggoner, as editors of the *Sentinel,* in the Colorado Springs *Republic.* He accused them of "wholesale slander and falsehood, for which they might properly be called to answer either in civil or church courts."[24]

Crafts' prime example was the special issue of the *Sentinel* of June 19, 1889, which sported "seven falsehoods per square foot." The editors, he charged, had "put into one issue of their paper sixty-seven false statements, thirty-seven of them gross slanders, bolstered up by thirty petty slanders." He sent copies of his affidavit to Dr. J. H. Kellogg to pass on to the local churches where Jones and Waggoner were members so that the congregations could discipline them.[25]

August found Crafts in California facing the same Adventist tactics that he had met in Colorado, with the added problem of having Jones at some of his meetings. At one in San Francisco, Jones personally invited him to his trial across the bay in the Adventist church in Oakland where he was a member. Crafts agreed that it might be well to present his charges in person, but never did show for the hearing. The church, as one might expect, found Jones to be not guilty. A General Conference examining team came to a similar conclusion. Both investigating committees, however, faulted the editors of the *Sentinel* for "unnecessary sharpness," for "harshness of expression and tone," and for some of their overly explicit personal allusions. Such things were not, they indicated, the mark of Christian gentlemen.[26]

Unfortunately, Jones found that problem impossible to overcome. Not only did he continue to attack Protestants publicly as being "cowardly" and often "blinded by Romish gloom," but he also thrust at the Catholics, referring to the pope, for example, as "His Craftiness." His colleagues and publisher had labored with him long and hard, but with few results. Dan T. Jones and W. C. White believed they had him reformed in 1890, but he soon reverted to his old ways. Kellogg was quite convinced that "the sarcastic and savage manner in which Elders Jones and Waggoner . . . have been in the habit of treating our opponents, has been laying up for us a tremendous retribution."[27]

Ellen White felt constrained to write to Jones in 1894 that "Christianity is not manifested in pugilistic accusations and condemnations." "Stormy times will come rapidly enough upon us, without our taking any special course . . . that will hasten them." Again in 1895 she would caution him (and his editorial subordinates on the *Sentinel*) not to go out of his way "to make hard thrusts at the Catholics." She also pleaded with him and his associates not to ridicule, condemn, or censure those who differed from them. Instead, they should point them to Jesus. "We grieve the Lord . . . by our harshness, by our unchristlike thrusts."[28]

The occasion for the last-mentioned testimony had been the harsh words that Jones and C. P. Bollman had published against Adventist missionaries who, they claimed, had "sold themselves for a mess of African pottage" because they differed from the editors on accepting governmental financial aid. Thus Jones could aim his harshness at his coreligionists as well as at Catholics and the National Reformers. He himself, apparently, had imbibed of the spirit of Minneapolis and needed to be, Ellen White claimed, filled by the spirit of Jesus. In 1899 she would warn him that his harsh words were especially dangerous because some of his readers were following his example and speaking "just as A. T. Jones talks. Thus the evil is multiplied. Make it your aim to speak the truth in love."[29]

His editorial policy also caused difficulties between him and the leaders of the denomination's National Religious Liberty Association. The association wanted the *Sentinel* to be its official organ in 1891, but it could not tolerate the paper's sharp thrusts and sectarianism. However, if Jones is to be censured for his failure to overcome on the first point of their demand, he is to be commended for not giving in to the association officials on the second. During a closed-door meeting in March 1891 that lasted until 3:00 in the morning they had demanded that the *Sentinel* would have to drop the terms "Seventh-day Adventist" and "Sabbath" from its columns so that it could reach a wider audience. Jones and his associates, however, would not budge. The *Sentinel* would continue to preach the third angel's message in its fullness. He would not submit to the "nonsectarian" error. The trumpet of the *Sentinel* would continue to give a distinctive Adventist message.[30]

EXTREMISM ON SUNDAY LABOR

Jones's rigid inflexibility was not always helpful, though. A case in point was his position on obeying Sunday laws. Operating on the interpretation that the fourth commandment called for six days of labor and one of rest, he took an uncompromising stand. To stop work on Sunday because the civil law commands it, he told the delegates to the 1893 General Conference session, is to "put Satan above Christ." Of course, he pointed out, Adventists would be fined for working on Sunday. Then, since they would not pay their fines (another position he supported), they would have to go to jail. As soon as they were released, however, they would work on Sunday again and repeat the process of penalty. "But none of it stops the Sunday work. . . . Therefore don't you see, that as heavier penalties are laid on without reaching whatever the government is after, *it will simply have to reach the heaviest penalty at last, and that is death.*" His stand on Sunday-law disobedience was common among those Adventists who followed his lead in the 1890s, but few, if any besides Jones, had the courage to push it to its logical conclusion.[31]

The problem with obeying a Sunday law, Jones indicated in October 1895, was that to do so complied with the beast power of Revelation 14:9-11, and was therefore an act of worshipping the beast. In early November he justified his stand on the basis of Daniel 3, the story of Shadrach, Meshach, and Abednego, Nebuchadnezzar's image, and the fiery furnace. The three Hebrew exiles had resisted the king's decree to worship the government's image, and, Jones interpreted, so should Adventists, even if it meant death.[32]

His logic seemed sound enough, and it had been hallowed by practice in Tennessee, Arkansas, and even in Switzerland. Ellen White, however, vigorously objected to his determined stand. Writing in response to tensions created by his position, she declared that "refraining from work on Sunday is not receiving the mark of the beast." "Never," she counseled him, "encourage the spirit of defiance and resistance." "Our policy is, do not make prominent the objectionable features of our faith." The Christian's place is to have the meekness of Christ. A time will come, she claimed, when the fiery furnace illustration will be meaningful, but that will be when church members find themselves forced to make decisions against the commandments of God. That had not yet happened. Her suggestion was for Adventists not to work on Sunday where prejudice existed. "If work is done on Sunday, let our brethren make that day an occasion to do genuine missionary work."[33]

Despite the clarity of Ellen White's counsel, Jones never really changed his attitude toward the necessity of Sunday labor, even though he did not make it as prominent in his writings as before. At the 1899 General Conference session Jones once again presented his case from Daniel. The real explosion, however, came in 1909 upon the publication of volume 9 of *Testimonies for the Church*. In response to Ellen White's position on Sunday work in volume 9 (essentially her 1895 counsel), he wrote a pamphlet entitled *The Ten Commandments for Sunday Observance*, in which he flatly accused Ellen White of advocating that Adventists accept the mark of the beast.[34]

THE IMAGE TO THE BEAST IS FORMED

February 29, 1892, passed without any special recognition by Adventists, but it was a day fraught with great meaning for their interpretation of prophecy. On that date, notes Anson Phelps Stokes in his monumental *Church and State in the United States,* the Supreme Court in *Holy Trinity v. The United States* issued "one of the most authoritative statements of the fundamental importance of . . . Christianity . . . to the American State." *The United States, asserted the Court, "is a Christian nation."* As a part of its argument for its interpretation the Court supplied evidence from "its laws, its business, its customs and its society." *That evidence included "the laws respecting the observance of the Sabbath [Sunday]."* The Court's ruling, significantly, was unanimous.[35]

It did not take long for the religious world to wake up to the meaning of *Holy Trinity* with its "Christian nation" endorsement. The National Reform Association rejoiced in the ruling. "'Christianity is the law of the land,'" it proclaimed while quoting the Court. "The Christian church, therefore, has rights in this country. Among these is the right to one day in seven . . . that it may be devoted to worship of . . . God."[36]

Thus the "Christian nation" ruling became ammunition in the battle for a national Sunday law in the spring and summer of 1892, during the debate on the closing of the Chicago World's Fair on Sunday. "A flood of small petitions and memorials," reported the Boston *Daily Globe,* "is rolling in upon Congress demanding that all appropriations of the government in aid of the Chicago World's Fair shall be made with the proviso that the fair shall not be opened on Sundays. So bold and dictatorial are some of these memorials that Senator Vest was constrained to rise in his seat . . . and protest that they practically amounted to political black-mail. In many cases they are accompanied by the threat that any member of Congress who shall vote any aid . . . for the Columbian Exposition, except with the Sabbatarian proviso, will be systematically boycotted at the polls by the denominational constituencies cited in the memorials."[37]

Congress, Jones noted, caved in to the wishes of the churches "because it was demanded *with threats*." President Harrison, as previously mentioned, signed the first national Sunday legislation into law on August 5, 1892. The quill that the president had used was immediately placed in a silk-lined case and sent to the president of the American Sabbath Union. It was a high day for the Sunday forces. They had, they believed, accomplished a major step in bringing about the millennium.[38]

Jones saw the events in a radically different light from the National Reform Association. On May 14 and May 21, 1892, he preached two sermons in the Battle Creek Tabernacle entitled "The Late Decision of the Supreme Court, and the Image of the Beast." He electrified his audience by telling them that the image of the beast had been formed on February 29 in the Court's *Holy Trinity* ruling. "All that remains," he asserted, "is to give life to it by the enforcement of whatever religious observances any bigots may choose, who can control the civil power." Next he pointed out that Adventists had preached this event for 40 years. Now it was time to get ready. After all, he proclaimed, "it is nothing but the unbelief of our own people that keeps back the loud cry of the third angel's message to-day." Any Adventist who did not agree with him, Jones claimed, is not qualified to sound the alarm against the worship of the beast. That statement was undoubtedly a backhanded reference to Uriah Smith, who he believed was too cautious in his prophetic interpretations.[39]

His presentations did not impress everyone. Most of the people, however, were stirred, observed General Conference secretary W. A. Colcord, "though a few . . . went to sleep and some were criticizing it almost before they got out of the Tabernacle." Smith took exception on apparently excellent biblical grounds. He held that the miracles spoken of in Revelation 13:14 must take place before the image is made. S. N. Haskell, who at first tended to agree with Jones's interpretation, eventually came to see the logic in Smith's exegesis.[40]

It was only with a great deal of reluctance that Smith allowed Colcord to persuade him to publish Jones's sermons in the *Review*. Unfortunately, however, the editor could not resist taking a swat at Jones in public. In the issue that contained the last of Jones's sermons on the image, Smith published an article in which he flatly denied that the image had been formed, or that *Holy Trinity* had changed anything. He later explained his editorial policy in a private letter to one who questioned him for contradicting Jones in the *Review*: "When something turns up which is wrong, and the situation is such that it has to go in, I know of no other way than to publish in connection therewith an antidote to the same. . . . Having by long study, and years of observation in the work, become settled on certain principles, I am not prepared to flop over at the suggestion of every novice, an[d] I certainly should not think it proper to commit the *Review* to such a course."[41]

Smith's editorial policy depressed Ellen White. It made her "heart ache" to see conflicting viewpoints in the *Review*. To Haskell she deplored the fact that Smith had given "the trumpet a counter blast, to make of none effect the warnings given in the same issue. Even if he did see that Elder Jones was too fast," he should not have openly disagreed with him. The *Review* editor should have followed the counsel of Matthew 18 and talked the matter over with Jones. It was better to "let the articles of Elder Jones remain unpublished" than to show a split to the church's enemies.[42]

To Smith she wrote that Jones often used expressions that were too strong, but that he, as the older brother, should have cared enough to discuss the matter with the one he felt was erring. She counseled Jones to "avoid all impression[s] which savor of extremes," and to refrain from presenting articles to the *Review* that clashed with Smith's views, intimating that the Lord would remove Smith from the editorship if he refused to let light come to the people.[43] *Once again, we should note, Ellen White made no attempt to settle the theological issue. As* at Minneapolis, she functioned as a mediator between the two sides.

To General Conference president Olsen, it was Minneapolis all over again. Since 1888, he complained, "there has been a sort of watching one another's expressions, and taking advantage of certain utterances," which taken out of context would not stand the test.[44] Both sides were guilty of that problem. The spirit of Minneapolis was hard to kill.

In the meantime, the World's Fair national Sunday law had been signed on August 5. That action, Jones claimed, gave life to the image. His interpretation merely widened the distance between him and Smith. The denomination's periodicals settled down to a cold war in which the *Signs of the Times,* the *Sentinel,* and the *Home Missionary* supported Jones and his interpretation of the image, while the *Review* ignored both him and the topic. The one good thing about the deadlock, Colcord suggested, was "that our people will have to begin to think and study for themselves." The whole issue would raise its head again at the 1893 General Conference session when Jones would attack Smith's position publicly.[45]

The Smith-Jones struggle over the image of Revelation 13 is part of the background to the 1893 General Conference session. A more positive aspect, however, is that revival was in the air. Writings from Ellen White throughout 1892 indicated that she believed that the final events were rapidly moving toward culmination. The events leading up to the national Sunday law, and Jones's preaching on the formation of the image, had stimulated hope and expectancy. A great revival had begun in the fall of 1892 and was at its peak during the 1893 General Conference session. But before we examine that revival, we need to look at one more element that generated charismatic excitement in the early 1890s—the Adventist faith healing movement.

---

[1] OAO to J. S. Washburn, July 25, 1890.

[2] Reports of the Tennessee arrests appear periodically in the *RH* from 1890 through 1895. See also Everett Dick, "The Cost of Discipleship: Seventh-day Adventists and Tennessee Sunday Laws in the 1890's," *Ad Her* (Spring 1986), pp. 26-32.

[3] DTJ to ATJ, June 25, 1890; DTJ to C. Eldridge, Sept. 30, 1890; ATJ, *"Due Process of Law" and the Divine Right of Dissent* (New York, 1892), p. 5. (This volume is Jones's review of the King case.)

[4] *RH,* Nov. 17, 1891, p. 720; Feb. 16, 1892, p. 107; WAC to DTJ, Nov. 13, 22, 1891; 1893 *GCB,* pp. 324, 125, 126.

[5] The official transcript of the Blair Sunday bill hearing appears in 50th Cong., 2nd. Sess., *Senate Misc. Doc. No. 43.* Jones published an edited version in *The National Sunday Law* (Chicago, 1889). Blair made his remarks on Apr. 14, 1909, at the twenty-first anniversary celebration of the introduction of his Sunday bill. See "Important Facts and Issues," a handbill, c. 1910.

[6] E.g., Chicago *Daily Inter Ocean,* Apr. 1, 2, 3, 5, 7, 8, 1889; Battle Creek *Daily Journal,* Nov. [25], 28, Dec. 5, 11, 1889; Topeka *Daily Capital,* May 1889, passim.

[7] ATJ's testimony appears in *Religion and the Public Schools* (Oakland, 1889).

[8] ATJ, *Civil Government* (1890 ed.), pp. 80, 81.

[9] *RH,* Jan. 21, 1890, p. 40; OAO to E. G. Olsen, Feb. 6, 1890.

[10] *RH,* Feb. 25, 1890, pp. 124, 125; OAO to G. C. Tenney, Mar. 20, 1890; ATJs testimony is found in *Arguments on the Breckinridge Sunday Bill* (Oakland, 1890).

[11] WAS to F. J. Hutchins. Aug. 3, 1892.

[12] For a report of this hearing, see ATJ, *The Captivity of the Republic* (New York, 1893). For a helpful treatment of the world's fair, see Ben McArthur, "The 1893 Chicago World's Fair: An Early Test for Adventist Religious Liberty," *Ad Her* (Winter 1975), pp. 11-21.

[13] 1895 *GCB,* pp. 146, 334; *RH,* Apr. 9, 1889, p. 240.

[14] 1889 *GCB,* pp. 75-79.

[15] *Ibid.,* pp. 7, 77.

[16] *Ibid.,* pp. 7, 24; WAC to ATJ Sept. 27, 1891. See also the 7th edition (1894) of Crafts' *Sabbath For Man,* p. 435.

[17] *RH,* Mar. 19, Jan. 8, 1889, pp. 184, 32.

[18] *RH,* Feb. 11, 1890, p. 90.

[19] WAS to H. P. Hosler, Dec. 15, 1892; WAS to EJW, Dec. 15, 1892; WAC to R. M. Kilgore, Dec. 19, 1892; WAC to ATJ, Dec. 16, 1892.

[20] *AS,* July 3, 10, 17, 1889, pp. 178, 179, 192, 193; ATJ, *Appeal From the U.S. Supreme Court Decision Making This "A Christian Nation"* (New York, 1893), pp. 38, 39.

[21] *RH,* Feb. 18, 1890, p. 106; *AS,* June 26, 1889, p. 176.

[22] WAC to ATJ, Sept. 27, 1891; WCW to EJW, July 15, 1889; WCW to ATJ, July 15, 1889.

[23] Chicago *Daily Inter Ocean,* Apr. 15, 1889, p. 7. The correspondence between Jones and Crafts has been published in *Rev. W. F. Crafts Against the Editors of the American Sentinel: The Charges and the Defense, Together With the Report of the Committee of Investigation* (Oakland, 1889).

[24] E. H. Gates to EJW, June 30, 1889; Colorado Springs *Republic,* June 28, 1889.

[25] Colorado Springs *Republic,* June 28, 1889; W. F. Crafts to JHK, June 6, 1889.

[26] CHJ to GCC, Aug. 5, 1889. The findings of the Oakland investigation are in *Rev. W. F. Crafts,* pp. 72-75; those of the General Conference investigation are in H. W. McKee, J. O. Corliss, and DTJ to W. F. Crafts, July 25, 1889.

[27] *AS,* Mar. 1, Oct. 4, 1894, pp. 65, 312; CHJ to EGW, Feb. 6, 1894; WCW to ATJ, Feb. 14, 1890; DTJ to R. M. Kilgore, Mar. 16, 1890; DTJ to J. H. Morrison, Mar. 17, 1890; JHK to OAO, June 30, 1892.

[28] EGW to [ATJ], Oct. 13, 1895 (this letter was penned in May 1894, see MS 22a, Nov. 20, 1895); EGW to [SNH], Jan. 30, 1895.

[29] *AS,* Nov. 22, 1894, p. 368. EGW to [ATJ], Oct. 13, 1895, (see note 28); EGW to ATJ. May 1, 1899.

[30] Executive Committee of the National Religious Liberty Association to the Editors and Publishers of the *American Sentinel,* Jan. 25, 1891; ALW, "The Story of the Salamanca Vision," unpub. MS, May 5, 1954.

[31] 1893 *GCB,* pp. 125, 126; cf. 1895 *GCB,* pp. 434, 435, 504, 507, 508. (Ital. sup.)

[32] *AS,* Oct. 10, Nov. 7, 1895, pp. 313, 314, 345, 346.

[33] EGW, MS 22a, Nov. 20, 1895; EGW to ATJ, Nov. 21, 1895.

[34] CPB to OAO, Dec. 9, 1896; 1899 *GCB,* p. 95; ATJ, *The Ten Commandments for Sunday Observance* (Battle Creek, Mich., 1909).

[35] Anson Phelps Stokes, *Church and State in the United States* (New York, 1950), vol. 3, pp. 570, 572; *Holy Trinity v. United States.* (Ital. sup.)

[36] *Christian Statesman,* May 21, 1892, quoted in ATJ, *Appeal From the U.S. Supreme Court Decision,* p. 40.

[37] Quoted in Stokes, *Church and State,* pp. 159, 160.

[38] ATJ. *Appeal From the U. S. Supreme Court Decision,* p. 50: *RH,* Aug. 9, 1892, p. 512.

[39] Jones's sermons were published in *RH,* May 31, June 7, 14, 21, 1892, pp. 337-339, 353, 354, 369, 370, 385-387.

[40] WAC to OAO, May 17, 23, 1892; WAC to EGW, July 12, 1892; SNH to OAO, Sept. 12, 1892.

[41] WAC to EGW, July 12, 1892; WAC to OAO, May 23, 1892: *RH,* June 21, 1892, p. 392; US to ATR, Sept. 21, 1892.

[42] EGW to SNH, Aug. 22, 1892.

[43] EGW to US, Aug. 30, 1892; EGW to ATJ, Sept. 2, 1892.

[44] OAO to SNH, July 25, 1892.

[45] SNH to OAO, Sept. 12. 1892; WAS to M. C. Israel, Aug. 11, 1892; WAC to ATJ, June 6, 7, 1892; WAC to OAO, June 29, 1892; *AS,* Oct. 20, 1892, pp. 321-323; *RH,* Oct. 25, 1892, p. 664; WAC to SNH, June 21, 1892; 1893 *GCB,* pp. 6, 9, 181, 361, 498, 507.

CHAPTER VII

CHARISMA IN ACTION: ADVENTIST FAITH HEALING IN THE EARLY 1890S

F riday night [June 6, 1890] a meeting was held at Bro. W. H. Hall's house, which lasted till 3 o'clock in the morning, and they report eleven cases of healing during that meeting." Thus announced Dan T. Jones, secretary of the General Conference of Seventh-day Adventists, to O. A. Olsen, the denomination's chief executive.[1]

FAITH HEALING FANATICISM

The June 6 meeting was only one of several in a "healing-wave that had come over Battle Creek." Likewise, the 11 were merely a portion of a "large number of cases of healing" that had been reported. On the Sabbath afternoon of June 7 the Battle Creek Adventists witnessed a meeting in which many testified "to the goodness of God in hearing their prayers." In addition, "there were also quite a number of those who had been healed there to bear testimony to the fact of their healing." The leaders in this faith-healing revival were a Sister Marks, who claimed to have "the power to impart the Holy Ghost by the laying on of hands, and to cast out devils," and a Sister Parmele.[2]

Dan Jones concluded that if this were the healing power of God, he would be the last to discourage it. He was also careful to point out that he found no evidence of fanaticism. Five days later, however, he was not nearly as positive in his evaluation. "From what I have learned of it since I wrote you last," he reported to Olsen, "I am quite well convinced that the movement is not from the right source, and that it will be wisdom and duty to check it, by using mild means of course, if mild means will do."[3]

98

Whatever "means"—mild or otherwise—Dan Jones and his administrative colleagues used to quell the healing wave, they must have been effective since the issue did not surface as a problem again until the late summer of 1891. On the other hand, Dr. John Harvey Kellogg, director of the Battle Creek Sanitarium, claimed that the interest in healing continued throughout the interim, but was not particularly annoying since it did not receive much publicity.[4]

The presence of D. T. Bourdeau's article on "Praying for the Sick" in the *Review and Herald* of December 1890 tends to support Kellogg's assessment. Bourdeau left no doubt in the minds of his readers that they could expect a true gift of healing as a part of the latter rain when many "shall be made perfectly healthy." But he quickly pointed out that there were also many spurious gifts of healing: "A wily foe understands how powerful for good is the true gift of healing; therefore he has multiplied counterfeit gifts of healing, by which to reach hearts and turn honest souls away from the truths for these times." As a result, Bourdeau suggested, the gift must be tested. The crucial test seemed to be whether the healer endorsed the whole Bible—that is, the Adventist interpretation of it.[5]

Adventist faith healing became prominent once again during the summer of 1891. This time, however, instead of little-known church members, some of the denomination's foremost preachers now propounded it. For example, at the influential Harbor Springs educational convention on August 4, A. T. Jones and W. W. Prescott (president of Battle Creek College and secretary of the Seventh-day Adventist Education Society) reported the healing of a Dr. Douse in answer to prayer. Then on August 21 Jones wrote from the Mount Vernon, Ohio, camp meeting that "the power of the Lord is present to forgive, to cleanse, and to *heal.*" The meetings, he noted, were the most "powerfully impressive" he had ever seen. "The large tent was nearly full, and the whole congregation was weeping, many of them aloud, and praising God, and praying for mercy and grace. Oh, it was wonderful. . . . And it is going to continue and grow more powerful and more precious."[6]

The exact extent of the power and the magnitude of the charismatic blessing was yet to be seen. More accounts were soon on their way. On August 25 John N. Loughborough—respected Adventist pioneer minis - ter—reported to Olsen: "After meeting last night Bro. [A. T.] Jones and myself prayed with two sisters that were healed. This morning twelve presented themselves, at the close of the morning meeting, who had faith to be healed. All were healed in answer to prayer. Since then some three or four of the ministers have been kept busy much of the day praying for the sick." At least 25 had received healing since the previous evening. The Ohio experience repeated itself at the Illinois camp meeting.[7]

As we might expect, not everyone was happy with the new gift. Foremost among the movement's detractors was Kellogg. As early as August 23 he complained that Jones, in his eschatological excitement, was telling the students studying to become medical missionaries that it was useless to spend time in preparation since mission work would not continue for more than a couple years.[8]

The real crisis in the faith healing movement took place on September 30 when John Hobbs died on the campus of soon to open Union College in Nebraska. Hobbs, reported the secretary of the General Conference, had been healed that summer at the Michigan camp meeting.[9]

The circumstances of Hobbs' death infuriated Kellogg. He flatly condemned "the fanatical zeal of some of our leading brethren in what they are pleased to call the exercise of faith." To him it was presumption rather than faith. Kellogg claimed that he had kept quiet about the faith healings as long as they involved only persons of little influence. But now that prominent individuals had taken a lead in the healing ministry he saw nothing but disaster on the horizon.

Hobbs, Kellogg reported, had come to him several weeks before for an examination. He found him to be suffering from a "grave" form of diabetes. The doctor put Hobbs on a careful and thorough treatment and the patient had made some improvement. Then, just before the Michigan camp meeting, Hobbs wrote Kellogg for advice concerning marriage and going into teaching. Kellogg advised him to do neither, but to devote himself to taking care of his health for a few months.

Kellogg's recommended treatments came to an abrupt halt when Hobbs attended the Michigan camp meeting. While there he "was prayed for and pronounced healed." As a result, Kellogg reported, Hobbs "denounced the dietetic rules, . . . declared that I had been starving him—that he was cured and able to eat anything,—went to Lincoln, was married, and day-before-yesterday, just one week after his marriage, died."[10]

Kellogg went on to expose the case of a Miss Hammond, who had been stricken with typhoid fever. On the Sabbath of September 20, Loughborough had prayed for her, then had announced from the Battle Creek Tabernacle pulpit that she had been healed, noting that it was one of the most remarkable instances of healing that he had seen since 1844. To demonstrate the validity of her healing and the strength of her faith in it, Miss Hammond was encouraged to leave her sick bed, even though her temperature was 104°, and made to walk. "She fainted away once or twice," Kellogg recalled, "but they still insisted that she must show her faith, and even insisted on taking her out to ride." She returned with a temperature of 105° and rapidly sank into a comatose state. Mrs. W. H. Hall—the faith-healing extremist in this case—and others insisted that to allow the young patient to have medical treatment would demonstrate a lack of faith and that those who did so would be responsible if she died. "I presume," Kellogg remonstrated, "now that she is dead, [that] those who have been chiefly instrumental in her death will say that death was caused by lack of faith."[11]

The doctor wrote to W. C. White that somebody had "to speak out against this foolish exercise of faith." He then indicated that neither White's father nor mother had ever showed any sympathy with such irresponsible practices. "They always continued the employment of proper means in connection with prayer and the exercise of faith, asking God to bless the means used." That, he claimed, was in stark contrast with those who were teaching that to use any medical means in the cure demonstrated a lack of faith.[12]

The General Conference president was also perplexed with "this wholesale manner of healing." While not completely siding with Kellogg, Olsen made it plain that in praying for the sick he always asked God's will to be done rather than demanding that God heal them. Some of the Adventists in Battle Creek, he suggested, seemed to be taking the latter course.[13]

The October 21 *Review,* meanwhile, published an article on "Frauds in Faith-Healing." After exposing a non-Adventist faith-cure physician, it went on to note that the very prevalence and prominence of such men was "strong evidence that God is preparing to pour out his Spirit in healing power during the latter rain, and hence Satan is seeking to deceive as many as possible, and blind them to the genuine work of divine power."[14]

The Battle Creek Adventists were undoubtedly caught in the tension between their fear of false charismatic gifts and the pneumaticological expectations of their eschatology. They did not want to accept the false, but they feared rejecting true gifts. Thus Adventists were especially vulnerable in the early 1890s as the national Sunday law crisis daily thundered the signs of the times. It is in the context of such exciting events that we must understand the Adventist faith healing movement. The Adventist community was inflamed with eschatological anticipation.

Despite the excitement, Kellogg's October 2, 1891, letter reporting the deaths of Hobbs and Hammond was merely one salvo in a barrage of epistles against what he deemed to be a fanatical faith-healing movement. During the next year he would repeatedly request W. C. and Ellen White, who were in Australia and New Zealand, to take a public stand on the issue.

On October 21 Kellogg outlined what he understood to be the theory of A. T. Jones and W. W. Prescott. First, before being prayed for, individuals should be convinced in their own minds that it is God's will for them to be healed. Second, if they believe they have evidence that this is the case, then they should call the church elders, be anointed and prayed for, and then it is their *duty* to believe that they are healed. Third, there can be no doubt that they have been healed, since the Bible rule has been carried out and the promise is certain when the rule is followed. Fourth, however, after the prayer "healed" individuals must not expect all the manifestations of their disease to be gone, because the devil will tempt them to disbelief through the appearance of the old symptoms. As a result, "it is his duty to cling to his faith and not yield to the suggestion that he is not healed." Fifth, persons prayed for in this manner must be publicly announced as healed, despite the devil's evidence to the contrary. They are to "walk out on faith" as a testimony to the Lord's power.[15]

Kellogg concluded that such a course was neither biblical nor sensible since a person could be in error regarding his impressions concerning the Lord's will. Furthermore, the doctor pointed out, there is a test that can be applied to healing cases—let a competent physician critically examine the "healed" individual. Next Kellogg lashed out at "the glaring inconsistency of maintaining that the person is healed when he is not healed." He illustrated his point by the case of Brother Brigham who had been "healed" by prayer and "orificial surgery" innumerable times, and who continued to demonstrate "the curative power of faith" by painfully "hitching" his way up the Battle Creek Tabernacle aisle on two canes, but who was still as paralyzed as ever. The doctor then went on to bemoan the fact that Hobbs had even been declared healed during his funeral sermon.[16]

In January 1892 Kellogg wondered out loud if it were "possible that the Lord undertakes to do a miracle in these cases of healing and make[s] such a botch job of it?" Back in October 21 he had carefully pointed out that he was not sure how much Prescott, Jones, and Loughborough were behind the fanatical events in Battle Creek, since he had not personally interviewed them. That task he would undertake early in 1892.

While it has not been possible to discover the exact beliefs of those Adventist leaders in regard to faith healing in 1891, enough evidence exists to implicate them in the main outlines of the problem. On the other hand, as will become evident during our discussion of developments in 1891-1892, Jones, Prescott, and Loughborough's less-prominent followers seemed to have carried their beliefs to further extremes than they did.[17]

THE BROADER FAITH HEALING MOVEMENT

At this point it is important to note that the Adventist faith healers were not operating in a vacuum. Not only was this period of American history the time of the development of "mind cure" and "mental therapeutics" by such religionists as Mary Baker Eddy, but, much more importantly for the Adventists, it was the era in which the faith-healing wing of the holiness movement was reaching maturity in conservative Protestantism. We find many parallels between the holiness revival of the post Civil War decades and the development of Adventism's "holiness" emphasis in the period following the 1888 righteousness by faith renewal. A. T. Jones was at the center of many of those parallels.[18] It is undoubtedly more than coincidental that the Adventist faith healers had beliefs similar to those of the holiness advocates. A rapid survey of the latter's literature should be sufficient to highlight the similarities.

We find one of the clearest expositions of the holiness doctrine of faith healing in R. Kelso Carter's *The Atonement for Sin and Sickness; or, A Full Salva-tion for Soul and Body,* published in 1884. Carter observed that the church "has been limiting the atonement of Jesus Christ." While sin and sickness are from the devil, holiness and health are from God. Building upon Psalm

103:3 ("who healeth ALL thy diseases"), Carter developed the thesis that "God now heals bodily sickness, precisely as He now heals soul sickness, by His power alone, unaided by any [medical] means whatever; and that He does it through and by virtue of the perfect Atonement of Jesus Christ." Building upon a theory of the dual nature of humanity, Carter developed a dual theory regarding the effects of the atonement. The atonement, he argued, saves believers from afflictions of both body and soul. He pronounced any attempt to explain faith healing by natural law as "radically wrong, and as very dangerous to the spirit of childlike faith. . . . A 'son of God,' must be content to take his Father's word, without any endorsement."[19]

Carrie Judd took a similar position to that of Carter. In 1881 she penned: "Our part is simply to reckon our prayer as answered, and God's part is to *make faith's reckonings real.* This is by no means a question of *feeling* faith, but of *acting* faith. . . . Christ bore our sickness as well as our sins, and if we may reckon ourselves free from the one, why not from the other?" Like Carter, she also taught in her *Prayer of Faith* (1880) that the use of medicine or relying on human help demonstrated a lack of faith and sinful unbelief. Christ is the Great Physician of both soul and body.[20]

Another influential treatment of the topic was A. B. Simpson's *Gospel of Healing* (1888). Coming very close to the Adventist's post-1888 interest in the centrality of the redemptive power of Christ and faith in Him, Simpson bases his argument upon Matthew's interpretation of Isaiah 53:4: "Himself took our infirmities, and bare our sicknesses" (Matt. 8:17) on the cross. Thus the cross accomplished both redemption and divine healing. An individual must accept the accomplished provision by faith since it is always God's will to heal. While the symptoms of disease may not immediately disappear, one should view them as "trials of faith." "Simply ignore them and press forward, claiming the reality, at the back of and below all symptoms. Remember the health you have claimed is not your own natural strength, but the life of Jesus manifested in your mortal flesh."[21]

Finally, we should note A. J. Gordon's *Ministry of Healing* (1882). Reflecting on Matthew 8:17, Gordon writes that "the yoke of his cross by which he lifted our iniquities took hold also of our diseases; so that it is in some sense true that as God 'made him to be sin for us who knew no sin,' so he made him to be sick for us who knew no sickness. . . . In other

words the passage seems to teach that Christ endured vicariously our diseases as well as our iniquities."[22]

This short overview of holiness teachings on faith healing demonstrates
that the Adventists were in tune with the ideas of contemporary faith healers, even though they did not agree with all of their theology. Because of
those theological differences, the Adventists consistently found the holiness
faith healers falling short of the test of Isaiah 8:20 ("to the law and to the testimony: if they speak not according to this word, it is because there is no light
in them"). According to the February 23, 1892, *Review*, they were therefore
an expression of the type of false healers whose very presence foreshadowed
the pouring out of the true gift in the latter rain.[23] On the other hand, however, the Adventist faith healers in the early 1890s were apparently quite
willing to adopt many of the faith healing "truths" that the devil had carefully
wrapped in the deceptive package of an erring theology.

SEEKING BALANCE BETWEEN FAITH HEALING
AND HEALTH REFORM

December 1891 saw the Battle Creek situation take a new turn. For one
thing, Kellogg experienced a serious illness. While his recuperation period
gave him time to think and deepen his Christian experience, it also meant
that he was away from the sanitarium for an extended period. During his
absence, Kellogg claimed, two of his most trusted physicians—Drs. Neall
and Beilhart—"became such thorough converts of the doctrines taught by
Eld. Jones and Prof. Prescott that they undertook to carry out exactly what
they were taught." Thus Dr. Neall began advising patients that they did
not need treatment, but should have "faith" that the Lord would heal
them. As a result of the "general disturbance" they caused in the hospital,
both physicians had been released from employment.[24]

As Kellogg saw it, the faith healing "thing is becoming epidemic." He reacted in two ways. The first was to institute prayer sessions for the sick in
the sanitarium. The second was to meet with Jones on January 9, 1892,
"to carefully avoid a war and to have a friendly talk" in case Jones's position had been misrepresented to him and, as was probable, Kellogg's had
been misrepresented to Jones.[25]

Complicating the faith healing difficulty between Jones, Prescott, and
Kellogg, was the fact that the doctor was upset because they were not solidly

behind health reform, a problem that had aggravated more people than Kellogg. The doctor was particularly out to stop the use of pickles and vinegar, in addition to flesh foods, in the college cafeteria. In his eyes, the college did not adequately cater to vegetarians. Beyond that, he and Prescott were locked in battle over the weighty issue of "fried carrots" being served at the college. He just could not fathom why 200-300 students had to suffer because of "one man's obstinate refusal to see the light."[26]

The health reform issue was both intimately and intricately linked to the faith healing controversy. And, as we shall see, when one problem was solved, the other was also.

Kellogg's meeting with Jones and Prescott on January 9 was but the beginning of a drawn-out process of reconciliation. From Kellogg's perspective the first meeting was a dismal failure. Jones and Prescott left his office still holding that if persons had faith they would be healed. Kellogg had hoped to convince them that in nearly every instance in which prayer had been offered for the sick there had been a failure, but he was unsuccessful. His antagonists merely replied that failure resulted because "they did not have faith."[27]

On the other hand, the meeting between the leaders of the disputing factions did set the stage for a clearing of the air. In the ensuing weeks Prescott spent several evenings through the midnight hours studying the Bible and the positions of Jones and Waggoner with Kellogg. Both the doctor and the General Conference president looked back to those studies as being pivotal in Kellogg's experience. As we might expect, it appears that the doctor was giving Prescott a few lessons at the same time. Soon after the January 9 meeting Jones preached on faith healing in the Tabernacle, and, according to W. A. Colcord (secretary of the General Conference), "righted the thing up from all sides." On one side, Jones spoke out against those who had abused the gift, noting that those who had made God a mere servant in the matter had acted wickedly. On the other side, he condemned those connected with the sanitarium who claimed that the health work had superseded faith healing.[28]

The date of Jones's sermon is extremely significant, since it was given before Ellen White's counsel on faith healing arrived from Australia. It therefore indicates that Prescott, Jones, and their colleagues were not as extreme as their "followers." The January 9 consultation had indeed had a clarifying effect, but still a great gulf loomed between Kellogg and Jones and Prescott.

Ellen White penned her first reply to Kellogg's request for a public statement regarding faith healing on January 21, 1892, and it had arrived in Battle Creek by March 10. Her approach to the topic was balanced. Noting that "the path of presumption lies right along side of the path of faith," she wrote that she was in favor of both prayer for the sick and the establishment of sanitariums where they could have proper medical treatment. "Let no one yield to the suggestions of the enemy of all righteousness and think that because we are near the end of all things, we can have faith, and have all our infirmities removed, and that there is no need for institutions for the recovery of health. Faith and works are not dissevered." In praying for the sick she wanted to follow God's will. Physical healing, as she saw it, was not an unconditional aspect of the atonement. There was only one way that she could pray for the sick: "Jesus, you understand all about this case. If it is for the good of this soul, and for the glory of thy name, raise this brother or sister to health."[29]

On March 11 Ellen White wrote to Kellogg, indicating that the issue of praying for the sick is a "very delicate question" that would probably not be satisfactorily settled for many minds. Her position was, after having prayed for the sick, to "work all the more earnestly, with much prayer that the Lord may bless the means which his own hand has provided."[30]

On April 15 Ellen White wrote the doctor again, pointing out that not all was well with his own soul. She implied that he and his fellow physicians in Battle Creek had tended to exalt science above God and that there was great danger in departing from the simplicity of Bible faith in the power of God. (They were charges that the doctor would subsequently deny.) She had hoped that his sickness and his "gracious recovery through the mercy of God" would have cleared up much of the "fog" that had obscured his spiritual vision. He needed, she indicated, to reach a higher standard in spiritual things. She concluded the letter by entreating Kellogg "to come close to Jesus."[31]

During the summer of 1892 Ellen White sent two more documents on the topic of praying for the sick to Battle Creek. In them she highlighted the fact that Christians must always pray that God's will be done in heal-

ing, since "it is not always safe to ask for unconditional healing," and that
health reform and faith healing go hand in hand. In other words, there is
no use asking for healing if one continues on in poor health habits.
Interestingly enough, Ellen White herself had been seriously ill during
most of the faith-healing controversy. Following her own advice for others, she concluded in November 1892 that her illness had been "a part of
God's plan, and He always knows what is best. I have had a rich experience during this long illness. I have become better acquainted with the
Saviour. . . . The Lord Jesus was never more precious to me than now."
Counting her sickness a "privilege," she was undoubtedly pondering the
ways of God as she sought to advise the church in the "delicate" spiritual
issues of human existence.[32]

Her counsel did much to close the breach caused by the faith-healing
dissension. Writing on March 10, 1892, General Conference President
O. A. Olsen expressed his opinion that her January 21 communication
would do much to relieve the tension. He felt bad that Prescott, Jones, and
Waggoner had used "extreme expressions" and had at times taken "extreme positions" on the topic. He feared that their incautious stance would
neutralize the amount of good they might otherwise have accomplished.[33]

Kellogg also wrote to Ellen White of his appreciation of her counsel on
praying for the sick, inferring that her position was the one he held. In addition, the doctor reported on another meeting that he had had with Jones
and Prescott in April. He stated that they had scoffed at what Kellogg
claimed was her position on faith healing, suggesting that they had Bible
grounds for knowing beyond doubt when a person had been healed.
Kellogg pressed Jones to the wall until Jones finally admitted that he really
could not be absolutely certain regarding the success of a healing because
"he could not tell whether the individual had faith or not to accept the
blessing offered him." The doctor then forcefully argued that Jones would
be responsible for the death of anyone who gave up medical treatment because of faith in a bogus healing. At that point, according to Kellogg, Jones
capitulated, saying: "How can I read the sick man's mind?"[34]

Then Kellogg took on Prescott who had been claiming that he knew
with certainty when a healing had taken place because he had had instances in which "the Lord spoke to him in what seemed to be an audible
voice." The doctor quickly dispatched that argument to his satisfaction,

but apparently not to that of Jones and Prescott, since they would later use the "hearing-the-voice" argument disastrously in their support of Anna Rice's so-called prophetic gift in 1894.[35]

While the April meeting between Kellogg, Jones, and Prescott might not have been a complete success, it was a turning point in the faith healing controversy. It is probable that Prescott resumed his evening studies with Kellogg after that encounter.[36]

The developing reconciliation did not stop Kellogg from thundering to Ellen White on May 27 that Jones and Waggoner's teachings on faith healing were still causing problems. He did have to admit, however, that there seemed to be a lull in the fanatical spirit that had dominated the issue for some months past. About this same time he wrote that he was seeking to make the spiritual aspect of healing more prominent in the sanitarium.[37]

The fruits of Kellogg's mutual indoctrination with Prescott were also becoming apparent. On June 20 the doctor joyfully reported that Prescott was becoming more favorable to health reform. He also expressed the hope that "the time may not be far distant when the chief apostles of the doctrine of Righteousness by Faith—Brethren Jones and Waggoner—will begin to take a more consistent position in relation to health and temperance principles."[38]

By early September 1892 Kellogg happily declared that "the brethren seem to be taking a more sensible course in relation to praying for the sick." The devil, he held, had undoubtedly urged them into an extreme position to compromise their influence. Since the long talk he had had with Jones and Prescott in April, he had heard no more of methods that they had previously employed. "I have good reason to believe that they have reformed."[39]

At the same time, the experience apparently had changed the doctor. O. A. Olsen noted that Kellogg spoke at the Michigan camp meeting in the autumn of 1892 with more spirit-filled earnestness than ever before. He told the congregation that his sickness of the previous year had taught him his dependence upon God. As Kellogg talked, Olsen reported, "he became so affected at times that he could not speak, just broke down." In fact the whole congregation joined in with him. Jones and Prescott, who were on the platform, "just wept for joy, and praised God aloud for what the Lord was doing for the Dr., and through him for the people."[40]

While the problem between Kellogg and Jones and Prescott had been solved on the faith-healing front, it had not been completely resolved with Prescott in the area of health reform. In November and December Kellogg was fuming at the slow progress the educator was making in employing health principles in Adventist schools. He was much happier with Jones, whom he wanted to employ at the sanitarium for a few months as a teacher.[41]

MOVING FROM ONE EXTREME TO THE OTHER

If Kellogg was pleased with Jones in December 1892, he must have been euphoric in early 1893 when the latter preached at the General Conference session that "God intends health reform . . . to prepare his people for translation." Thus Jones had turned the position some had held in 1890—that faith healing was to prepare people for translation—on its head. Later in the 1893 session he would tell the delegates that if they practiced health reform they would not need ever to take a vacation because they would not need to rest. Noting that he worked day and night, he proclaimed that if "you get the health reform . . . it is all nonsense about having a vacation." Jones, in his usual manner, could be just as extreme on any idea once he saw its truthfulness. Meanwhile, both he and Prescott were busy calling for the fullness of the loud cry of the Holy Spirit at the 1893 General Conference session. While Prescott listed the gift of faith healing among those they soon expected the Holy Spirit to pour out, his and Jones's minds had rapidly moved onto a new charismatic excitement. After all, Jones had recently received a "testimony" from Anna Rice who he believed was a second Adventist prophet. Unfortunately, Olsen would not let him read the Rice testimony to the delegates. That bit of charismatic excitement would have to wait until January 1894 (see chapter 9).[42]

By the autumn of 1893 Kellogg was able to report that "Jones is preaching stirring health and temperance sermons at the camp-meetings," and that Prescott was waking up to the health work also. In November Kellogg indicated that both men had not only corrected their course on faith healing, but they "are straightening up as fast as they can on the health question." He also rejoiced that they were "taking hold of the work in good earnest," and that Jones was giving a series of 12 lectures at the college on health subjects. "He gets things badly twisted up sometimes when he undertakes to teach anatomy and physiology; but he means well." More important from the doctor's perspective was the fact that many Adventists would be influenced toward health reform by the influential Jones, who was then at the height of his power.[43]

The final stroke in the healing of the rift between Jones, Prescott, and Kellogg came at the 1894 educational convention, during which Prescott finally sided with Jones and took "a strong stand for the right" on health reform. As a result, "it was voted that all the schools should adopt a vegetarian diet."[44] Not only had these leading preachers swung around on the issue of health reform, but the doctor was more than willing to admit the occurrence of a bonafide healing. On February 9, 1894, for example, the Battle Creek *Daily Moon* reported that Mrs. T. A. Kilgore had been "deprived of a tumor which the best physicians in the country pronounced incurable, and the surgeons at the sanitarium refused to operate upon . . . , knowing the operation would result in certain death."

The sanitarium physicians had performed exploratory surgery, but had closed the incision once they saw the extent of the problem. Kellogg wrote to Kilgore to come quickly because his wife had but a short time to live. Mrs. Kilgore, in the meantime, "prayed long and earnestly to God to remove all trace of tumor and disease." While praying she "felt a peculiar prickling sensation as if a mild current of electricity" passed through her. Three weeks after the healing the *Daily Moon* could report that she was "the picture of health." Kellogg, the newspaper noted, was fully convinced that she had been healed by God since her case had been beyond human help. "No one could have been more surprised than I," the doctor claimed, "when she came to my office and told me that she was well." Here was a case that lent itself to verification by physical examination. Thus Kellogg was quite happy to acknowledge the miracle, especially since it lacked any "fanatical" or illogical elements. F. M. Wilcox took the healing to be an evidence of the arrival of the loud cry power of the Holy Spirit.[45]

Between 1894 and the turn of the century Adventist healing was less prominent, but it did surface with A. F. Ballenger in the late 1890s with some of the same claims in the "Receive Ye the Holy Ghost" movement.[46] While Jones was behind Ballenger's emphasis, by 1901 Jones himself was on a new path. For example, at the 1901 General Conference session he stood firm against those "vicious short cuts" that expected healing without following health reform and medical treatment. "In nine tenths of the cases we [ministers] are to teach them that there is something needed more than prayer; and in the other tenth case that *with* the prayer something is also needed." That something, he had written in his 1899 *Review* editorials, was "God's 'saving health' [which] is, and always has been, an essential part of the everlasting gospel." While he was not against faith healing, he was certain that God did not perform miracles for people who refused to correct the physical causes of their illness. He was fond of telling people that they did not need prayer. Rather, they needed to correct their health habits. Jones had learned important lessons from his faith-healing experience of the early 1890s. Perhaps he had "overlearned" his lesson, since by November 1898 he was teaching that health reform is the avenue to perfect holiness. After all, he wrote, "perfect holiness embraces the flesh as well as the spirit."[47]

E. J. Waggoner seemed to agree with Jones. At the 1899 General Conference session he was preaching that the gospel of health is to fit Adventists for translation. He did not ever expect to be sick since Jesus "actually, literally" took our diseases upon Himself. "Just as you can not conceive of Jesus' losing a day's work from sickness, so it ought not to be conceivable of Seventh-day Adventists' losing a day's work from sickness. . . . The life of Jesus in mortal flesh will do in us what it did in him." Waggoner, in fact, expected to "live forever" because of the benefits of the gospel of health.[48]

While Jones and his colleagues had shifted from a stress on faith healing to placing the emphasis on healthful living by the late 1890s, some of their readers undoubtedly interpreted their ideas concerning perfect holy flesh fit for translation in terms of their earlier emphasis on faith healing. By 1899 the excitement that would evolve into the holy flesh movement the next year was alive and well. As we saw in chapter 4, Stephen N. Haskell, who had spent most of the 1890s overseas, expressed shock at many of the wild ideas he found upon returning to the United States. Not only did he discover the holy flesh fanaticism, but he found it rooted in a faith healing context in which believers would be healed from all physical deformity and then "could not die." After listening to an hour or two of fanatical testimonies, the next morning, Haskell reported to Ellen White, "I arose early . . . and [publicly] read a testimony you sent me several years ago at the time Brethren Jones and Wagoner [sic] was [sic] carrying the praying for the sick to an extreme and it fully described the meeting of the sick we had the night before."[49]

Ellen White's counsel once again helped quell the immediate fanaticism, but it did not kill it, as the eruption of the holy flesh excitement of 1900 verifies. By that year, health reform, the outpouring of the Holy Spirit, "perfect" living, and translation faith had become inextricably linked in sectors of the Adventist psyche. The true and the false continued to remain in tension.

---

[1] DTJ to OAO, June 8, 1890.

[2] DTJ to OAO, June 13, 8, 1890.

[3] DTJ to OAO, June 13, 1890.

[4] JHK to WCW, Oct. 2, 1891.

[5] RH, Dec. 9, 23, 1890, pp. 754, 786, 787.

[6] WCW to Mary C. Mortensen, Aug. 4, 1891; ATJ to WAC, Aug. 21, 1891.

[7] JNL to OAO, Aug. 25, 1891; OAO to Eld. E. H. Gates et al., Sept. 21, 1891.

[8] JHK to EGW, Aug. 23, 1891.

[9] WAC to OAO, Oct. 1, 1891.

[10] JHK to WCW, Oct 2, 1891.

[11] JHK to WCW, Oct. 2, 21, 1891.

[12] JHK to WCW, Oct. 2, 1891.

[13] OAO to WCW, Oct. 9, 1891.

[14] RH, Oct. 21, 1891, p. 642.

[15] JHK to WCW, Oct. 21, 1891.

[16] Ibid.

[17] JHK to OAO, Jan 10, 1892; JHK to WCW, Oct. 21, 1891.

[18] See, e.g., chapters 12 and 13.

[19] R. Kelso Carter, The Atonement for Sin and Sickness; or, A Full Salvation for Soul and Body (Boston, 1884), pp. 2, 6, 17-19, 214, 24, 25.

[20] Carrie F. Judd, "Faith Reckonings," Triumphs of Faith, January 1881, pp. 2, 3, in Donald W. Dayton, Theological Roots of Pentecostalism (Grand Rapids, 1987), p. 126; Carrie F. Judd, The Prayer of Faith (Chicago, 1880), pp. 83, 82.

[21] A. B. Simpson, The Gospel of Healing, (New York, 1888), pp. 12-16, 27, 28, 36, 37.

[22] A. J. Gordon, The Ministry of Healing: Miracles of Cure in All Ages (Brooklyn, 1882), pp. 16, 17.

[23] RH, Feb. 23, 1892, p. 116.

[24] JHK to EGW, Dec. 28, 1891; WAC to WCW, Dec. 23, 1891; JHK to WCW, Jan. 27, 1892; cf. JHK to WCW, Mar. 27, 1892.

[25] JHK to WCW, Jan. 27, 1892; JHK to EGW, Dec. 28, 1891; JHK to OAO, Jan. 8, 1892.

[26] JHK to OAO, Jan. 8, 1892; OAO to F. D. Starr, Aug. 14, 1891; see also, Gilbert M. Valentine, "William Warren Prescott: Seventh-day Adventist Educator," (Ph.D. dissertation, Andrews University, 1982), pp. 94-96.

[27] JHK to OAO, Jan. 10, 1892; JHK to WCW, Jan. 27, 1892; cf. WAC to OAO, Feb. 12, 1892.

[28] JHK to EGW, May 25, Sept, 9, 1892; JHK to WCW, Sept. 9, 1892; OAO to EGW, Sept. 28, 1892; WAC to DTJ, Feb. 7, 1892.

[29] EGW to the Brethren and Sisters in Battle Creek, and to all who need these words, Jan. 21, 1892.

[30] EGW to JHK, Mar. 11, 1892.

[31] EGW to JHK, Apr. 15, 1892; JHK to EGW, May 27, 1892.

[32] EGW, MS 26A, Aug. 5, 1892; EGW to JHK, Aug. 5, 1892; EGW to ATR, Nov. 7, 1892.

[33] OAO to EGW, Mar. 10, 1892.

[34] JHK to EGW, Apr. 21, 1892.

[35] *Ibid.;* see chapter 9; cf. JHK to OAO, Jan. 10, 1892.

[36] JHK to EGW, May 25, 1892.

[37] JHK to EGW, May 27, 25, 1892.

[38] JHK to WCW, June 20, 1892.

[39] JHK to WCW, Sept, 9, 1892; JHK to EGW, Sept. 9, 1892.

[40] OAO to EGW, Sept. 28, 1892.

[41] JHK to OAO, Nov. 9, Dec. 26, 1892; cf. JHK to EGW, Jan. 24, 1893.

[42] 1893 *GCB*, pp. 88, 89, 515, 461.

[43] JHK to OAO, Sept. 19, Nov. 19, 1893; cf. WCW to JHK, Sept. 20, 1893; JHK to WCW, Nov. 2, July 17, 1893. See also, *Ad Her*, (Spring 1986), p. 53.

[44] JHK to EGW, Aug. 10, 1894.

[45] "Cured by Prayer," Battle Creek *Daily Moon,* Feb. 9, 1894; FMW to JHK, Feb. 8, 1894.

[46] Albion F. Ballenger, *Power for Witnessing* (Oakland, 1900), p. 147; Edwards and Land, *Seeker After Light*, p. 51.

[47] 1901 *GCB*, p. 452; *RH*, Nov. 7, 14, 1899, pp. 720, 736; Nov. 22, 1898, p. 752.

[48] 1899 *GCB*, p. 53; cf. WMH to EGW, [Sept. 1901].

[49] SNH to EGW, Oct. 3, 1899.

CHAPTER VIII

CHARISMATIC EXPLOSION: THE GREAT REVIVAL OF 1893

W e are living in a very interesting time," O. A. Olsen wrote in August 1892, 10 days after the signing of America's first national Sunday law. "Everything seems to be hurrying so fast toward the final consummation. The rapidity with which one event follows another in the fulfillment of prophecy is truly remarkable."[1]

Expectancy of the end of all things permeated the air for Adventists. On February 18, 1892, Ellen White wrote that "Protestantism is now reaching hands across the gulf to clasp hands with [the] papacy, and a confederacy is being formed to trample out of sight the Sabbath of the fourth commandment."[2] Eleven days later the Supreme Court ruled on its "Christian nation" decision, and on August 5 the United States got its first national Sunday legislation. Jones stood at the forefront of prophetic interpretation in Adventist circles. His messages on the forming of the image and the giving of life to the image of the beast had sensitized Adventists to their place in prophetic history.

Some in the church had been expecting the outpouring of the latter rain and the loud cry ever since the 1888 General Conference session. The Sunday law agitation had put the Adventist Church in the spotlight as nothing else had ever done. Referring to that publicity, Olsen, in 1890, pointed out that Adventists had "long talked about the loud cry of the third angel's message. If it is not just upon us, I don't understand it." His connection of the loud cry with Sunday legislation was no accident. Ellen White had plainly linked them in the 1888 edition of *The Great Controversy.* Coupled with that anticipation was the fact that the early

1890s had seen unparalleled expansion in Adventist missions around the globe. The Adventist world in the summer and fall of 1892 was heavy with anticipation.[3]

PRELUDES TO REVIVAL

The first stirrings of revival came during the autumn 1892 camp meetings. Jones, the featured speaker, reported that "the Michigan meeting was the greatest we ever saw. . . . The brethren who were in the 1844 movement and were present at Lansing, said that it was equal to 1844 and some thought it even surpassed 1844." Olsen agreed with him, writing that "we had some droppings of the latter rain. . . . In the afternoon there were not less than fifty on their feet to speak, and between twenty and thirty were speaking at once. . . . It may seem as though there would be a great deal of confusion, but that was not the case. While many were speaking, yet it sounded as one voice of praise and glory to God for his wonderful love and salvation in Christ Jesus."[4]

Michigan was not the only state that experienced revival. The same phenomena spread across the land. It is "by far the best campmeeting season that we have had," Olsen reported. "As a result, it is very evident . . . that the Message is rising, and that we shall soon see the truth go with mighty power." He believed that the church was on the verge of the "loud cry."[5]

By the end of October 1892 W. A. Colcord, secretary of the General Conference, was convinced that the loud cry had begun, with Jones as its foremost proponent. The clincher, however, came in the November 22 *Review and Herald*. In that issue Ellen White claimed that "the time of test is just upon us, for *the loud cry of the third angel has already begun in the revelation of the righteousness of Christ,* the sin-pardoning Redeemer. *This is the beginning of the light of the angel whose glory shall fill the whole earth.*" Jones lost no time in preaching this confirmation of the loud cry to the Adventist Church. The next Sabbath he presented "a stirring sermon on the 'latter rain' and the loud cry of the third angel's message" in the Battle Creek Tabernacle.[6]

Revival broke out in Battle Creek the following week. It began in the college when chapel exercises extended several hours to accommodate student testimonies, and in which between 50 and 100 were reportedly converted. Even the school "infidel" responded after reading *Steps to Christ* alone in his room. From the college the revival spread to the local church, the Review and Herald office, and the sanitarium. It was, stated W. A. Spicer, "no revival of the ordinary kind, but has seemed to be more directly by the agency of the Spirit of the Lord." He believed it to be an outpouring of the latter rain. Olsen was of the same mind. The revival had not been planned, but was the work of God. The General Conference president had not seen anything like it before. Even Uriah Smith attended all of the meetings and listened with deep interest.[7]

The results of Michigan's "latter rain" revival were immediate in many cases. I. H. Evans, president of the Michigan Conference, reported in early December that 500 Adventist farms had been put up for sale in the state. "The brethren [are] wanting to dispose of their possessions and get things in shape" for the final events. "When this spirit becomes general," Spicer asserted, "and believers throughout the world are praying to the Lord for a special manifestation of his power, truly his work will be cut short in righteousness."[8]

One result of the revival was that it stimulated Battle Creek College to offer short courses to prepare quickly a large number of older individuals for missionary work. Those courses would give a larger place to the Bible than the regular college program. College president W. W. Prescott, meanwhile, had felt inspired to hold a major series of evangelistic meetings in the Congregational church so that the non-Adventist community could share in the blessings of the revival. The meetings later shifted to the Battle Creek opera house, where Jones assisted Prescott.[9]

Jones was the spearhead of the latter rain movement, and he would play that role at the soon-coming General Conference session, at which he would present 24 sermons on the third angel's message. A. F. Ballenger worked hard to get Olsen and Colcord to agree to having Jones's messages (as published in the *General Conference Bulletin*) read in each Adventist church daily during the session so that prayer for the latter rain would spread throughout Adventism. Thus "the Bulletin [sic] would serve as arteries through which the life-blood could be pulsated from the General Conference to all our people throughout the country." Surely, "God would not turn a deaf ear to the pleadings of his people" for the latter rain. As we might expect, Jones was excited about the plan, but Olsen was cool to it since "such occasions as the week of prayer would lose their force."

Ballenger retorted that if the latter rain came, the church would not have need of weeks of prayer. The president's will, however, prevailed.[10]

Expectations for the coming General Conference session ran high. W. F. Caldwell, an Adventist of fluctuating experience who would soon be involved in his own "loud cry" movement, wrote to Olsen on January 16, 1893, proclaiming: "As sure as the Lord liveth, my Brother, this is the last conference that will ever sit on this earth." He requested permission to preach his "loud cry" message to the delegates. Olsen flatly refused, and soon after the session Caldwell left for Australia to preach, on the basis of a compilation of Ellen White's writings, that the Adventist Church was in a terribly fallen condition and must therefore be Babylon. He arrived in Australia only to find that she was dead set against his particular "loud cry" message. She wrote to him that "the Lord has not given you a message to call the Seventh-day Adventists Babylon." His "loud cry" died with a whimper, and Caldwell publicly confessed and rejoined the Adventists in their mission.[11]

It was not, however, only the excitable and the critical who felt impressed with the signs of the times and the importance of the 1893 General Conference session. Cooler heads also pulsated with anticipation. Olsen repeatedly wrote that the conference would "be the most important meeting of the kind ever held," because the world was rapidly "being brought to the final crisis."[12]

THE 1893 GENERAL CONFERENCE SESSION

In many ways the 1893 General Conference session was an "upper room" experience of prayer, confession (especially of unbelief in righteousness by faith as it related to 1888[13]), and exhortation. The object of the spiritual experiences was a greater outpouring of the Holy Spirit.

Two of the major speakers were Jones and Prescott—men who were beginning to work closer and closer as a team. Prescott had 10 sermons on the promise of the Holy Spirit, while Jones had 24 discourses on the third angel's message.[14] Their messages dovetailed as both emphasized that the denomination had been in the time of the loud cry since 1888, and that God was ready to pour out His Spirit upon a repentant church. Jones's studies ran through both the ministerial presession and the regular conference. He had more than twice the number of presentations as any other speaker, and his ideas set the tone for the entire session.

Prescott had no doubt that a "work that will be greater than pentecost has begun." The 1893 General Conference session, he proclaimed, would fit the leaders of the church for the closing work. The church had failed at Minneapolis. Using Christ's illustration of the unfruitful tree, he pointed out that Christ did not cut it down at the end of three years. In mercy He gave it a fourth year. It had been, Prescott told his attentive audience, four years since Minneapolis. Now was the deciding time—the time of shaking for the Adventist Church. Adventists needed to be just as earnest in praying for the Holy Spirit as did the apostolic church at Pentecost. Prescott was not certain there would ever be another General Conference session. Time was short indeed.[15]

Ellen White's messages from Australia tended to support the Jones-Prescott theses. Of particular importance was one written on January 9 and read to the conference on February 27. "The time of peril is upon us," she exclaimed. "The Lord is soon to come." The influence that grew out of resistance to the light in 1888, she intimated, had slowed down the work. "If every soldier of Christ had done his duty, if every watchman on the walls of Zion had given the trumpet a certain sound, the world might ere this have heard the message of warning. But the work is years behind."[16]

The conference delegates did not hear all of that letter, however. The unread part, while suggesting that Jones may have been premature in his statement concerning the formation of the image, definitely faulted Smith's course of action and commended Jones as having a timely message for the "starving flock of God."[17] Knowledge of her testimony undoubtedly emboldened Jones in his attitude and remarks toward Smith and his allies during the conference.

Olsen was also firmly in the Jones camp. He wrote on February 22 that Jones's lectures must have a thorough circulation throughout the world. Impressed by the meetings, the General Conference president noted that the place was "becoming more and more solemn on account of the presence of God." These meetings, he suggested, would mark a new era in the work of the denomination.[18]

Like Jones and Prescott, Olsen also believed that the church was unprepared for the loud cry because its ministers had still not imbibed the message of 1888 as anything but a theory. They could preach the doctrines, but they could not lead sinners to Christ, because they did not have a "living connection" with Him themselves. Justification, Olsen told the delegates, was "not a theory, but an experience."[19]

S. N. Haskell backed up Olsen on the significance of the 1888 message. It was not theology, as he saw it, but the experience of righteousness by faith. Haskell also believed that if the church had received it more fully, the denomination would be far in advance of where it was in 1893.[20]

Jones was at his self-confident best during the 1893 General Conference session. He set the tone for his sermons in his first message. "I do not care if it is the oldest minister in our ranks [a shrouded reference to Smith]; he must come and say, 'I do not know anything yet as I ought to know it; teach thou me.'"[21] Of course, Jones was the teacher with "the truth," and since it was truth there could "be no objection against it." Truth does not have two sides, so "we do not want to hear the other side." If God is leading someone, Jones suggested in a veiled reference to himself, that person can objectively interpret and teach the truth of the Bible without bias. During the conference he plainly told those who were resisting him that he had the facts. He also informed the delegates that there was no need to "hunt up anything in the Bible to see whether that tells the other side of it."[22] A man who saw things in terms of black and white, Jones was not bashful about reminding others that he was right and that they were wrong. That approach, of course, was not the most diplomatic way to win over his enemies.

In his messages Jones captured and illustrated the unity of righteousness by faith and religious liberty inherent in the three angels' messages of Revelation 14. After preaching several sermons on the forming of the image to the beast and its significance, he pointed out that the next thing to look for was the wrath of God. After all, they were already in the time of the loud cry. Thus they soon could expect the seven last plagues and the Second Coming. "The time is exceedingly short." The church, therefore, must totally separate from the world. Health reform would prepare the members for translation. The death penalty loomed over them, and they were to force the hand of the persecutors by continuing to work on Sunday. Not to do so was to worship the beast through its command to keep the first day of the week.[23]

Jones was certain that the latter rain had not yet fallen on the church to any great extent. That was because so many had resisted the Minneapolis experience and had not received Christ as both their justification and sanctification. They still had, he claimed, the Roman Catholic formula of faith plus works. In the time of trouble they would need to be like Christ—perfect. "If you and I," he told the delegates, "have not 'perfect obedience to the law of God' from the first breath we ever drew until the last one we ever draw, then eternal life does not belong to us." Christians, however, can be perfect when they are "in Christ" because "he is perfect." *He is both the Christians' justification and their sanctification. "His holiness is imputed" to them.*[24]

Accepting the centrality of Christ as preached at Minneapolis, Jones suggested, is crucial because only the pure can receive the latter rain. When the church spurned experiential faith in Christ in 1888, it in essence rejected the loud cry and the latter rain. Some, he noted, still had the spirit of Minneapolis. The denomination could find the solution to its problem in the counsel to the church of Laodicea. It needed to put on the white robe of Christ's righteousness. Righteousness, he pointed out, is rightdoing—not our rightdoing, but Christ's, which we accept by faith as already accomplished on the cross. Thus, according to Jones, both a person's justification and sanctification were completed on the cross. On the other hand, the justified, proleptically sanctified Christian also received the power of the Holy Spirit into his or her life at conversion. As the representative of Christ, the Spirit works within each individual. And "if Christ is dwelling in our hearts, *he will work in us* 'both *to will* and *to do* of his good pleasure.'" The focus of Christians will be not on their works but on Christ, who does the work in them. Their part is to surrender their wills to Him.[25]

According to Jones, therefore, sanctification proleptically takes place when people accept Christ who lived their life, but it is also the process of a lifetime. The Christian must live as Christ did on earth—in perfect submission to God the Father, who dwelt in Him and "did the works." He lived the perfect life through submission to God. Adventist Christians, Jones suggested, could do the same thing. Their task was continual surrender so that Christ through the Spirit could work in them.[26]

It was total reliance on Christ, Jones claimed, that many had resisted at Minneapolis. "What," he asked his hearers, "holds back the outpouring of the Holy Ghost? [Voice (from audience): "Unbelief."] Our lack of the righteousness of God, which is by faith,—that is what holds it back." *"This meeting,"* he asserted, must be the time for decision for each delegate. When they accepted righteousness by faith they would also receive the latter rain. Jones's appeals brought confessions from many who still harbored bitterness from Minneapolis.[27]

As Jones moved toward his final sermons he noted that the church was already in the sealing time for the 144,000. The sealing also was accomplished through faith. The topic of the sealing naturally raised the issue of the Sabbath, which was the opposite of the seal or mark of the beast—the Sunday Sabbath.[28]

Having reached this point, Jones had brought the two great themes of the third angel's message (the faith of Jesus and the Sabbath test) together. He was also in a position to demonstrate their connected relevance in the face of the nation's Sunday legislation and the proclamation of America as a Christian nation. In his mind, the topics were neither isolated nor irrelevant. They were, in their unity and timeliness, of utmost importance to the Adventist Church in 1893.

To Jones, the Sabbath was not merely an outward sign of allegiance to God, but a work of total surrender to Him. He described three classes of people who observed a day: Saturdaykeepers, Sundaykeepers, and Sabbathkeepers. A person could keep Saturday without knowing Jesus, but individuals could not observe the Sabbath without Christ living in them. Thus Sabbathkeeping, as opposed to Saturdaykeeping, is a sign of a person's sanctification, because Christ is in that individual. Sanctification, therefore, is Christ in us. "He is our sanctification." And sanctification, Jones taught, is progressive. "Sanctification and its ultimate . . . accomplished purpose, is the complete work of Christ finished in the individual. The image of Christ completely formed in the believer; so that when Christ looks upon the believer he sees himself. . . . That is sanctification." True Sabbath observance was the witness of completed sanctification, the sign that Christ was in the individual's heart and mind. The seal of God, therefore, was living a life, rather than merely worshiping on a day.[29]

God wanted to gather out a people, Jones proclaimed, to fill the new earth. Adventists, therefore, must cut loose from all in this earth, because the image to the beast had already been formed and nothing could ever reverse the flow of events, even if Congress repealed its Sunday legislation. The tide for ruin, insisted Jones, had been set. The Lord "is going to do something now." "There is no place now in the Seventh-day Adventist Church for hypocrites. . . . Those who are not going along with this work had better get out quick," because persecution would soon break upon the church in greater force. No one, he asserted, needed to leave the General Conference session without receiving the Holy Spirit.[30]

"Get ready to meet him [Jesus]," Jones urged in his final appeal, "for he is coming. Get ready to be like him; for that glory of which he has given us a part now will make us like him altogether in that day."[31]

Jones, like Prescott, was convinced that the conference would not close without a mighty outpouring of the Spirit. Thus he could not "risk" being absent from any of the meetings, he told the delegates, because he could not tell "at what meeting the Spirit may be poured upon us." He had preached mightily and convincingly, and many had made confessions regarding their resistance at Minneapolis, but still the outpouring had not come.[32]

One can only wonder what would have happened if Jones would have been allowed to use all of the powerful "spiritual gifts" that were at his fingertips at the 1893 General Conference session. A few weeks earlier he had given his approval to Anna Rice as a prophet of God. In the midst of the conference he had received a testimony from her that he desperately wanted to present to the assembled delegates. O. A. Olsen, however, had forbidden him to read it publicly. Jones, therefore, could only hint that great things were coming. "Thank the Lord," he told the delegates about a week into the meetings, "*he is not going to be content much longer with one prophet! He will have more.* He has done a wonderful work with one. And having done such a great work with one, what in the world will he do when he gets a lot of them?"[33]

It must have grated upon his impulsive nature to be restricted from using his most powerful tool to bring about the latter rain. What he could not do in the General Conference president's presence, however, he would do in his absence.[34] In December 1893, with Olsen safely 12,000 miles away in Australia, Jones would employ the Anna Rice testimony that he had received during the 1893 General Conference session to start a *real revival* that would make the one at the General Conference session of 1893 appear mild in comparison. That revival will be the topic of the next chapter.

AN EVALUATION OF THE SIGNIFICANCE OF THE 1893
GENERAL CONFERENCE SESSION

In the eyes of many of its participants the 1893 meetings were a re-sounding success. Olsen could write of the session as "the best Conference that has ever . . . been held by our people." The Lord's presence had been realized in a special measure, largely breaking the spirit of Minneapolis. Many others shared his evaluation.[35]

While those reports may be good and true, they do not tell the whole story. For example, the meetings certainly never fulfilled the hopes of Jones and Prescott. After all, nearly 120 years have passed since the 1893 General Conference session, yet Jesus has not returned. Some students of Adventism have pointed back to the 1893 meetings as an identifiable point at which the denomination failed in a special manner, since it did not receive the loud cry and latter rain in a greater way. They suggest that the secret for success today is to go back to the 1893 messages of Jones and Prescott so that the church can once again get on the track to divine power.

Though the 1893 sermons of Jones and Prescott offer a great deal of value, it seems wrongheaded to overemphasize the messages of that ses-sion as either an analysis of, or a solution to, the failure of the denomina-tion. Such a procedure is fraught with both historical and theological difficulties.

For one thing, even though Ellen White believed that the end was near in 1893 and that the loud cry had begun with the preaching of righ-teousness by faith in 1888, she also made similar statements at other times just as forcibly. For example, in 1883 she had written that "the angels of God in their messages to men represent time as very short. . . . It should be remembered that the promises and threatenings of God are alike con-ditional. . . . Had Adventists, after the great disappointment in 1844, held fast their faith and followed on unitedly in the opening providence of God, . . . the work would have been completed, and Christ would have come ere this to receive His people to their reward. . . . It was not the will of God that the coming of Christ should be thus delayed. . . . For forty years did unbelief, murmuring, and rebellion shut out ancient Israel from the land of Canaan. The same sins have delayed the entrance of modern Israel into the heavenly Canaan. In neither case were the promises of God at fault. It is the unbelief, the worldliness, unconsecration, and strife among the Lord's professed people that have kept us in this world of sin and sorrow so many years."[36]

Her statement is important not only because it sheds light in a general way on reasons for the delay of Christ's second coming, but also because it plainly indicates that Ellen White believed that Christ could have come soon after 1844. That idea has astounding consequences for those who would make too much of Jones, Waggoner, and Prescott's theology in 1888, 1893, or 1895. The implication is clear that Christ could have come before 1888—that is, before Jones and Waggoner ever preached their interpretation of the gospel. For that reason it is not helpful to build too much on the basis of their distinctive theology. It is not their message or the particular interpretation that they placed upon the gospel that is important, but the gospel message itself.

With the above fact in mind, it should be obvious that we should not place too much stress on the failure of 1893. Unfortunately, that has been the focus of certain Adventist ministers and laypeople who have sincerely sought for an answer as to why Christ has not yet come. Ellen White was not especially concerned with what some have viewed as the problem of 1893. In subsequent years she never fixated her thought on the failure of the denomination in either 1893 or 1888. However, she did emphasize continually the Christian's need of Christ and His saving grace. Also she continued to impress upon the church the nearness of Christ's return. In 1908, for example, she wrote to Jones that "we have now come to the last days of the work of the third angel's message. . . . This is the time of the latter rain."[37] It is strange that Ellen White's 1892 statement on the loud cry, as presented at the 1893 General Conference session, receives so much attention while her 1908 statement, which contains many of the same elements, gets almost totally ignored.

The explanation for the focus on 1893 rather than 1908 or some other date appears in the teachings of Jones, not in those of Ellen White. It was Jones and Prescott, rather than her, who built the 1893 excitement into grand proportions by exegeting her November 1892 statement in the light of their interpretation of the formation of the image to the beast in the summer of 1892. At this point, it is important to note that Ellen White never indicated any positive support for Jones's understanding of the formation of the image, nor did she ever have much to say about her 1892 loud cry statement. As far as we can tell, to her it was merely one of several similar declarations that she made during her prophetic career. We have no reason to single out the 1892 loud cry statement above the others, unless a person believes that Jones, having Ellen White's approval as the messenger of 1888, was, at that early date, incapable of major theological errors or of becoming unbalanced in his emphases.

If that is the case, however, a person faces the brutal fact that the ever-excitable Jones was not altogether a safe leader in 1893. Even though he had a timely Christ-centered message, he had also accepted the visions of Anna Rice (see next chapter) and would have presented her testimonies as a spur to revival in his loud cry message at the 1893 General Conference session if Olsen had not prohibited him from doing so. In the following year, in his advocacy of the Rice testimonies, it would be Jones himself who would do the most to squelch the great revival that had begun in 1893 and had continued into 1894. We should never forget that he had the perennial problem of extremism. Ellen White, in fact, would write to him soon after the 1893 General Conference session to warn him on that very point.[38]

In the wake of the Rice debacle, Ellen White would call Adventism away from a concentration on excitement and back to the gospel of salvation as found in the Bible. That had been her advice during the 1888 controversy, and it would be her recommendation throughout the 1890s. It is still the best counsel today as Adventism seeks to preach the everlasting gospel in the context of the distinctive message of the three angels of Revelation 14.

THE "SELLING TIME"

One direct result of the 1893 General Conference session was the movement for Adventists to sell their property and to move out of Battle Creek. Its inspiration came from Ellen White. Haskell had read a letter from her to the session delegates in which she said that the church had a world to warn, yet large numbers of Adventists were content to "huddle together" and "colonize." Given the needs of the work and the imminence of the end of time, she counseled "those who truly love God [to] step out from where there are large churches of Sabbath-keepers." She undoubtedly aimed her plea primarily at those congregated in Battle Creek.[39]

She had been urging Adventists to leave the city for missionary purposes since 1868. In particular, she had made a special appeal to that effect at the 1891 General Conference session, but had not received any significant response. In 1893, however, given the explosive Sunday law situation and the emphasis on the loud cry, her call found fertile soil.[40]

Jones soon began to preach that the "selling time" had arrived. Families should put their property on the market, move out of Battle Creek, and get ready for the coming of the Lord. After all, was not the church in the time of the loud cry?[41]

In October he became much more active in pushing an exodus, declaring in the Tabernacle on October 14 that those who had no special work for the Lord in Battle Creek should obey the testimonies and relocate to other places. Prescott joined him. About that same time, Ellen White penned a message to Prescott, indicating that if the people did not leave Battle Creek the Lord would send a "scourge" to "drive them out."[42]

That letter stirred up Prescott and Jones to even greater effort. "Our purpose," Prescott wrote, "is to keep up this agitation and try to persuade all to go who will do so." He claimed that between 100 and 200 people had already committed themselves to moving. Dr. Kellogg, sensing that many of the people were not prepared for what they were being stampeded into by the obvious sincerity of Jones and Prescott, organized "exodus classes" for the "exodusters," so that they would be able to cope more successfully and make a larger contribution to their new communities.[43]

Ellen White, meanwhile, had become deeply concerned with the excitement that Jones and Prescott were stirring up in Battle Creek. She still believed that people needed to go elsewhere, but she advised caution on the part of Jones and Prescott. Hasty moves, she wrote, could bring regret and disillusionment rather than victory. "I am troubled," she penned, "when I consider that there may be even some of our teachers [i.e., Jones and Prescott] who need to be more evenly balanced with sound judgment." Her last point was particularly troublesome in the case of those two leaders, because the people had almost unbounded confidence in their judgment. Her letter also contained warnings to the Battle Creek congregation to proceed with greater caution. They were not to heed the rash counsel of their advisers, who did not understand all the implications of their admonitions.[44]

Her counsel was not an abdication of her earlier position, but a mandate for Jones and Prescott to avoid the extremes and rashness that was their special weakness. The testimony was read to the leaders of the Battle Creek church in late January 1894. It had its intended effect. The exodus movement did not stop, but it avoided unhealthy extremes. Jones, meanwhile, had sold his property by early 1894.[45]

The treasurer of the General Conference hoped that Ellen White's statements would stop the "pressure" that Jones and Prescott were placing on the people, and that it would provide individuals with the incentive to prepare better for any move. The General Conference leadership followed this more conservative position. Yet the matter of leaving Battle Creek was not dropped. By November 1894 the Battle Creek church had been divided into districts, and instruction in Bible, health, and missionary work was being given to the members so that they would be more able to "let their light shine in other places" "when the Spirit of the Lord urges them to move out." Unfortunately, by November 1894 Jones and Prescott's advocacy of Anna Rice as a prophet earlier in the year had destroyed much of its momentum.[46]

---

[1] OAO to I. J. Hankin and wife, Aug. 15, 1892.

[2] EGW, MS 27, Feb. 18, 1892.

[3] *RH,* Jan. 29, Mar. 5, 1889, pp. 73, 160; DTJ to C. T. Swartz, Feb. 14, 1890; OAO to Mrs. N. H. Druillard, Apr. 1, 1890; EGW, *The Great Controversy* (Oakland, 1888), p. 443; WAC to J. W. Scoles, Oct. 23, 1892.

[4] ATJ to EGW, Oct. 8, 1892; OAO to SNH, Sept. 26, 1892.

[5] OAO to ATR, Oct. 17, 1892; cf. ATJ to EGW, Oct. 8, 1892; A. J. Breed to OAO, Oct. 16, 1892.

[6] WAC to W. H. Saxby, Oct. 31, 1892; WAC to R. C. Porter, Oct. 27, 1892; *RH,* Nov. 22, 1892, p. 722; WAS to EJW, Nov. 28, 1892. (Ital. sup.)

[7] LTN to E. G. Olsen, Dec. 1, 1892; WAS to D. A. Robinson, Dec. 8, 1892; WAS to J. T. Boettcher, Dec. 12, 1892; WAS to WCW, Dec. 2, 1892; OAO to EJW, Dec. 16, 1892; OAO to EGW, Dec. 28, 1892.

[8] WAS to J. S. Washburn, Dec. 13, 1892.

[9] OAO to EGW, Dec. 28, 1892; WAS to WCW, Feb. 24, 1893.

[10] AFB to OAO, Dec. 18, 1892; AFB to WAC, Dec. 18, 21, 1892.

[11] W. F. Caldwell to OAO, Jan. 16, 1893; OAO to W. F. Caldwell, Jan. 18, 1893; *RH,* Sept. 19, 1893, p. 606.

[12] E.g., OAO to A. [F]r[o]st, Jan. 17, 1893; OAO to C. A. Washburn, Jan. 5, 1893; OAO to WCW, Jan. 25, 1893.

[13] See "Report of Conference for the Consideration of the Subjects of Righteousness by Faith and the Relation of Faith and Works, Held in Dr. Kellogg's Parlor on the Evening

After the Sabbath," Feb. 18, 1893, unpub. MS.

[14] *RH*, Feb. 7, 1893, p. 88; 1893 *GCB*, p. 1.

[15] 1893 *GCB*, pp. 39, 65, 105, 384, 504.

[16] *Ibid.*, pp. 419-421.

[17] EGW to W. Ings, Jan. 9, 1893.

[18] OAO to J. J. Nichols, Feb. 22, 1893; 1893 *GCB*, p. 188; *RH*, Feb. 7, 1893, p. 92.

[19] 1893 *GCB*, p. 189.

[20] *Ibid.*, pp. 217, 218.

[21] *Ibid.*, p. 6.

[22] *Ibid.*, pp. 9, 11, 108, 361.

[23] *Ibid.*, pp. 87, 88, 115, 123, 89, 125, 126.

[24] *Ibid.*, pp. 377, 183, 243, 494, 167, 344, 178, 179.

[25] *Ibid.*, pp. 183, 184, 242, 245, 178, 179, 298, 299.

[26] *Ibid.*, pp. 301, 344, 345.

[27] *Ibid.*, pp. 383, 377.

[28] *Ibid.*, pp. 416, 438.

[29] *Ibid.*, pp. 439, 451, 455, 454.

[30] *Ibid.*, pp. 464, 472, 517, 499, 498.

[31] *Ibid.*, p. 523.

[32] *Ibid.*, p. 400; OAO to EGW, Mar. 21, 1893.

[33] SNH to EGW, Jan. 4, 189[3]; ACR to ATJ, Feb. 21, 1893; C. McReynolds to LTN, Mar. 22, 1894; 1893 *GCB*, p. 153.

[34] C. McReynolds to LTN, Mar. 22, 1894.

[35] OAO to P. Potter, Mar. 7, 1893; OAO to EGW, Mar. 21, 1893; CHJ to WCW, Mar. 30, 1893.

[36] EGW, MS 4, 1883, n.d.

[37] EGW to ATJ, July 25, 1908.

[38] EGW to ATJ, Apr. 9, 1893.

[39] 1893 *GCB*, pp. 131-133.

[40] *Ibid.*; 1891 *GCB*, pp. 181-183.

[41] OAO to H. Clausen, Mar. 14, 1893; A. J. Breed to OAO, Aug. 21, 1893.

[42] *RH*, Oct. 17, 1893, p. 660; EGW to WWP, Oct. 2, 1893; W. H. Edwards to OAO, Oct. 31, 1893; LTN to SNH, Oct. 31, 1893.

[43] WWP to OAO, Nov. 1, 1893; WWP to EGW, Nov. 8, 1893; JHK to WCW, Oct. 29, Nov. 2, 1893.

[44] EGW to WWP and wife, Dec. 22, 1893; cf. LTN to IDVH, Jan. 31, 1894.

[45] FMW to EGW, Jan. 31, 1894; LTN to OAO, Jan. 5, 189[4], (this letter is incorrectly dated as 1893).

[46] W. H. Edwards to OAO, Mar. 2, 1894; OAO to EGW, Nov. 29, 1894; OAO to ATR, Dec. 9, 1894.

CHAPTER IV

PROPHETIC CHARISMA: A SECOND ADVENTIST PROPHET AND THE REVIVAL OF 1894

B y the winter of 1893-1894, A. T. Jones was the most influential—the most listened-to—voice in Adventism, with the possible exception of Ellen White. In relative obscurity five years before, he had become the denomination's unrivaled champion in the legislative battles stimulated by the Sunday issue. Beyond that, by 1893, with Waggoner in England and Ellen White in Australia, he was Adventism's foremost proponent of righteousness by faith in the United States.

His enemies of 1888 had been largely silenced. Butler was just coming out of a health-related retirement in Florida, and Smith was teetering on the brink of dismissal from the *Review* editorship, with Jones as the heir apparent. The best his enemies could do was heckle him from the sidelines. It was Jones who dominated the center of action—especially since his proclamation of the formation of the image to the beast in 1892 and his spearheading of the latter rain movement at the 1893 General Conference session. Ellen White, F. M. Wilcox, and others noted that many Adventists treated his voice as if it were that of God.[1] Thus his actions on the last Sabbath of 1893 were fraught with important consequences for the denomination. They were all the more influential because they took place in the atmosphere of revival and expectancy that had permeated Battle Creek's Adventist sector for more than 18 months. The revival of 1894, in fact, was a continuation of the remarkable one of 1893.

THE GREAT JEWELRY OFFERING

The Sabbath afternoon of December 30, 1893, climaxed what had up to that time been a most successful Week of Prayer. After that afternoon one could in many ways view it as the greatest revival in the history of the Battle Creek church.

The turning point came when Jones stood before the people, claiming to have two testimonies for them. One, he noted, was from Sister White, while the second was from an unnamed author. He had received the latter during the 1893 General Conference session 10 months previously, and he would "hold it back no longer." After reading Ellen White's testimony, he presented the second one. Then, Jones reported in the *Review*, "the meeting took a peculiar, though most blessed turn." The unidentified testimony had insisted on entire separation from the world, from pride, and from outward adorning. It emphasized "plainness of dress, and especially a 'tearing off' of gold, etc., instead of wearing it on the body, 'as the heathen do.'" After Jones finished reading, Prescott arose, saying "My sheep hear my voice, and they follow me."[2]

At that point Jones turned the service into a revival meeting. The people were obviously moved—they had heard "the voice." Nearly 300 responded "in penitence and tears" to his altar call for "the unsaved," 66 of them for the first time.[3]

During the altar call one woman handed Jones a very "magnificent" gold watch, along with a note. It read: "For fear that my dead husband's watch may stand between me and the blessing of God, I give it for the work in Wellington, New Zealand, or wherever else it can be used in the wide 'harvest field.'"[4]

At the testimony meeting that followed, someone turned another watch over to Jones. At that time he made an appeal "to know who would obey the call of the Lord and 'tear off' the gold, and strip themselves of such ornaments. . . . From that moment there was a steady move, one after another, for more than an hour, bringing up gold watches, gold chains, gold rings, gold bracelets, gold sleeve-buttons, diamond studs and pins; costly furs and plumes; money in cash and drafts; and gifts of houses and lots; amounting in all, at a fair estimate, to over six thousand dollars."[5]

The spirit of dedication continued at the Sunday evening meeting when an additional $14,397 came in for the Lord's work—$8,972 in cash and $5,425 in real estate. The grand total was $21,347—a stupendous amount, considering that the nation was in the midst of a stringent depression and that Adventist ministers and editors received from between $15 to $18 per week. It was probably the largest donation ever given by the Battle Creek church. In today's purchasing power it would be equivalent to a figure of perhaps $800,000. Prescott and Jones had also heard "the voice" in its call for sacrifice. In all sincerity, Prescott gave an offering of $5,000, which, claimed a General Conference officer, was all that he had in the world. Jones was equally sacrificial. By January 5 he had "sold out" his Battle Creek property and committed himself to join the "Exodusters," who were planning to leave in the spring.[6]

The financial dividends were not the only fruits of the revival. The next Friday 46 were baptized, followed by 142 the next day in the Tabernacle, making a total of 188 baptisms stemming from the Week of Prayer and the revival at its close. Some people believed that the fruits of the meetings were the result of the effort of the entire week, but most of them gave credit to the anonymous testimony that Jones had read just before the revival began. Thus many who spoke during the Sabbath afternoon meeting credited the new prophet with the meeting's success. "I thank God," said one woman a few weeks later, "that a new gift of prophecy has come among us."[7]

The unidentified testimony had come from a young woman by the name of Anna Rice, also called Anna Phillips (although Phillips had never been her legal name). On the evening of January 4 another meeting convened. Jones, to his credit, cautioned the congregation regarding what they had experienced Sabbath afternoon. He had previously warned L. T. Nicola, secretary of the General Conference, in his use of the Rice testimonies, since they had not been fully proven yet. Unfortunately, Nicola noted, Jones had been much more careful in private than he had been in public with her writings.[8]

Some of Anna Rice's followers showed even less prudence than Jones. Elder D. T. Bourdeau, for example, arose at the January 4 meeting "and cautioned the brethren and sisters against sinning against the Holy Ghost by saying that the Rice testimony was from the devil." He would, he said, "sooner have his 'neck cut off'" than to speak against them.[9]

"HEARING THE VOICE"

Prescott was also less reticent than Jones. His favorite saying during this period was "know the voice." On the Sabbaths of January 27 and February

3 he preached at the Tabernacle on the gift of prophecy in the last-day church. His interpretation was that all God's remnant would have the gift of prophecy, not so much in prophesying as in being able to "know the voice" of a true prophet. Prescott claimed that he could tell while listening to an epistle whether it was from God or not. He cited the experience of one man, who, after hearing only six lines of a Rice testimony, had heard the voice and decided that it was from the Lord.[10]

The hearing the voice test, however, was not original with Prescott. He had gotten it from Jones, who had preached that message at the Lansing, Michigan, camp meeting the previous September. Jones had noted in his sermon that there would be more prophets before the end of time, and that a person could test them by recognizing God's voice in them. That was a safe test, he asserted, because *the devil cannot imitate the voice of Jesus Christ. No, sir. . . . He may speak in the very words that are in the Bible, but it is not the voice of Jesus. No, sir.* " Jones, therefore, exhorted his hearers to learn to recognize the voice of God, since His sheep will know His voice and follow Him.[11]

Jones and Prescott were sure they were hearing the voice of God in the Anna Rice testimonies. They would publicly read a selection from Ellen White and then one from Anna Rice, asking their congregation after each whether they heard the voice. The answer was invariably positive. The president of the Kansas Conference reported that Jones had read a Rice testimony at his camp meeting in September 1893, and not one in 100 could tell that it was not from Ellen White.[12]

The very nature of the test, however, was designed for disaster since it allowed no room for counsel with others. For that reason, neither Jones nor Prescott asked for Ellen White's evaluation of Rice's alleged gift. Nor did they seek the advice of those with more experience than they had. They heard the voice, and that was enough for them. Unfortunately, they trapped themselves in a cul-de-sac of their own making. After all, if people had not heard the voice, how could they possibly give valid counsel?[13]

Jones had been Anna's confidant from the very beginning. Her first testimony alluded to him as an authority in the church, and in the latter half of December 1892 she sought to validate her prophetic claim through his approval. After all, she reasoned, had not Ellen White said that he had advanced light? If he approved her gift, then she believed that she was truly a prophet.[14]

For his part, Jones had encouraged her right along, repeatedly (up through early February 1894) urging her to write out her testimonies. He told her that their fruit in the December 30 revival at Battle Creek had proved the validity of her work. But he was not yet aware of the testimony that Ellen White had written in Australia on December 23, 1893, rebuking him for his course in supporting Anna Rice's work. On the other hand, he knew of a letter dated November 1, 1893, to J. D. Rice, Anna's father by adoption, in which Ellen White censured Rice for presenting Anna's visions "in a light which leaves the impression . . . that I have sanctioned or endorsed this work." She flatly pointed out that she had "not had the least confidence" in Anna's claims, "or the claims anyone has made in her behalf." Jones, however, had explained that testimony away as applying to Rice for his part in making the visions public. Wholeheartedly behind the visions, he totally ignored Ellen White's rejection of Anna's prophetic role. Others, such as S. N. Haskell and L. T. Nicola, were more cautious, even though some believers branded them as being unchristian for their lack of enthusiasm for the Rice testimonies. They had a "wait-and-see" policy.[15]

The Rice testimonies spread across the nation with astounding rapidity, being printed in Ohio, South Lancaster, Massachusetts, and Battle Creek, Michigan, and being otherwise duplicated in every possible form. Some paid up to a day's wages for a copy of a Rice testimony, while one man sat up the entire night reading and meditating upon them. In addition, church leaders began presenting them to their constituencies at camp meetings and other gatherings. The Anna Rice movement threatened to take Adventism by storm.[16]

The excitement was sufficient to bring what Nicola called the prophecy "cranks" out of the woodwork. Those who thought they had special spiritual gifts began to demonstrate their charisma openly. One man, according to Nicola, claimed to have the "gift of 'roaring.'" That gentleman went to Jones to see if he could hear the voice. Jones heard one, but said it was not the voice of God. A few days later the "roaring man" left town in the night, "leaving many bills unpaid." Several other prophets also arose and began distributing testimonies, including the wife of the president of the New England Conference.[17]

The General Conference president, getting wind of all the prophetic excitement while he was in Australia, felt "considerable anxiety" about what he would find when he reached the United States. He had been reading the chapter in *The Great Controversy* entitled "Progress of the Reformation," and the parallels in false charismatic revival that had followed Luther's preaching of justification by faith in the sixteenth century and what was happening in Adventism in the 1890s immediately struck him. He was particularly impressed with Luther's desire to be preserved "from a church in which there are none but saints."[18]

THE VOICE OF ELLEN WHITE

The Anna Rice movement came to an abrupt halt in mid-February when Jones received a testimony from Ellen White that told him in the "plainest manner" that he had been wrong in supporting Miss Rice. Ellen White told him that she was surprised that he had got caught up in "a matter so readily that does not bear the divine credentials." She counseled him to weed out of his public utterances everything that was extreme and extravagant, because he had all too many excitable followers who desired strange and wonderful new light and were "always ready to go off on some tangent." "One fanatical streak exhibited among us," she exhorted, "will close many doors against the soundest principles of truth."[19]

Prescott was at Walla Walla College in Washington when the testimony for Jones arrived in Battle Creek. He intended to read a Rice testimony to the faculty and students. Haskell sought to dissuade him on the eve of the meeting, but to no avail. The next day, just in time to avert a further crisis, a copy of the testimony arrived at Walla Walla and Prescott quickly revised his plans. Ellen White's word had settled the question for him. "Now," he told Haskell, "I will take some of the same medicine that I have given to other people."[20]

That, however, was not the only bitter medicine that Prescott and Jones had had to swallow that winter. Just three weeks before, Prescott had read to the leaders of the church the testimony that he had received regarding his and Jones's overly hasty actions in the Battle Creek exodus movement.[21]

Jones was just as repentant as Prescott for his part in the Rice affair. He "wept like a child" when he received the message from Ellen White. In addition, he worked hard to reverse the effects of his advocacy of the Rice testimonies by seeking to stop their continued circulation. Jones even sought to recall and burn those already sold, but that undoubtedly proved to be an impossible task.[22]

Olsen returned to the United States to find two most humble men. He described Prescott as a "whipped dog." Commiserating with them, he noted that since Satan could not defeat them in a frontal encounter, he seemed "to have taken the rear and crowded these men too far." In their enthusiasm for the things of God they had reached such a rate of speed that "they left the track."[23]

Jones's and Prescott's open admission of their fault helped them maintain the confidence of many of the leaders of the church. Olsen claimed that he felt touched with tenderness when he saw their repentance. To him it was "an indication that the Lord has not left us, and that his reproof comes for our good." On the other hand, he recognized that Jones's indiscretion had made it impossible for him to replace Smith as editor of the *Review,* a move that many had desired. F. M. Wilcox also still had full confidence in Jones, claiming that he might have followed the same course himself if he had been in Jones's position as one of the foremost leaders of the church. E. W. Farnsworth, president of what later became known as the Northern Union Conference, was also supportive, noting that he had "heard old Bro. White say that if we would show him a man who never made any mistakes, he would show us a man who never *made anything.*"[24]

Such support, however, did not mean that everyone was reconciled to Jones's and Prescott's reliability as leaders. Wilcox feared that some would use the men's mistake "as a pretext for showing further fight" against the principles that Jones had been preaching in regard to righteousness by faith and religious liberty. Many, Olsen claimed, were already reasoning that way. Olsen was also deeply concerned that the "other side" would make the most of their error. Smith, on the other hand, exulted over the Ellen White testimony that Jones received in regard to Rice. He "was glad to see that Jones element getting a whack on the snout." The debacle also gave the anti-Jones forces more leverage on the General Conference Book Committee as they successfully blocked the publication of some of his manuscripts.[25]

In the aftermath of the Rice affair, Jones demonstrated that he could be a truly responsible and caring person to the major victim of the whole episode—Anna Rice. Anna was a sincere young woman with a simple faith in God. The whole business, Ellen White claimed, was not her fault, but that of those who had encouraged her in her visions. Haskell pointed out that her simplicity was evident in the fact that she allowed herself to be legally adopted by J. D. Rice when she was more than 25 years old. Elder Rice said he had adopted her because she had given him a testimony indicating that he should discontinue normal sexual relations with his wife or he "could not enter heaven," and that Anna was to be the Rices' "'baby from the Lord,' a 'child of promise.'"[26]

Anna, for her part, claimed that she needed protection if she was to be the Lord's prophet. The adoption was finalized in December 1892. After that she always called the Rices Mama and Papa. Never having had a home of her own while growing up, she was happy to be their obedient child. With these facts in mind, it is no wonder that Ellen White was shocked that Anna's claims had taken Jones in. The woman was truly a simple, dependent person unprepared for the hard knocks of life.[27]

The greatest shock in Anna's life occurred when the testimonies began to arrive from Ellen White. They left her almost hopeless. One of the first results was that her Adventist "friends" "branded" and deserted her. "My friends that were so numerous," she wrote, "all seemed to sink at once. The brethren that had written so freely to encourage me on, I heard no more from, excepting Bro. Jones, he saw my danger and stood by me . . . until he thought I had gained a foothold again." It is no wonder that she urged Ellen White to help the Adventist people to become loving.[28]

In Jones's relationship to the young woman he showed himself at his best, not only as a caring person but also as a courageous Christian. Anna had written to him that he probably should avoid her when he came to the California camp meeting to escape hurting his influence with the people. He corresponded back that she was not to hide herself or "shun to be seen speaking" to him. To the contrary, he told her, one of the first things he wanted to do upon arrival was to speak to her and her mother so that they could have all the care he could provide. This episode is a rare glimpse of A. T. Jones at one of the tenderest points in his ministry. His concern undoubtedly helped Anna get back on her feet. In subsequent years she worked as a Bible instructor in California and Indiana.[29]

One of the discouraging things that took place in the wake of Ellen White's testimonies regarding Anna Rice was that several who had given watches and other items during the Week of Prayer wanted them back after the repudiation of her visions. That worried some of the church leaders, who felt that the Holy Spirit had been leading toward revival during the whole week and that the gifts were the fruit of the entire Week of Prayer, and not merely the result of Jones's presentation of the Rice testimony. More disturbing was their fear that some who had been genuinely converted would lose confidence in their experience.[30]

The Anna Rice affair was not the brightest point in the history of Adventism during the 1890s, but even mistakes are not disastrous if people profit from them.

GOOD LESSONS FROM A BAD EXPERIENCE

Of the many lessons that came out of the episode, perhaps the most important centered on the role of Jones in the Adventist Church. Soon after the 1893 General Conference session, Ellen White had written to him that his enemies were watching him, expecting that he would "over-reach the mark, and stumble, and fall." She pleaded with him at that time to be humble and not to make extreme statements, but, as the Anna Rice crisis demonstrated, he had failed to assimilate her counsel.[31] The lesson he failed to learn in prosperity he would now have to gain in adversity.

His vulnerability stemmed from the fact that the people accepted anything he uttered as "truth." In March 1894 Ellen White chided the Battle Creek church for placing him where God should be. They should not regard all he said "as if inspired of God" just because God had given him precious light. It concerned her because they "eagerly seized" his words and took them to their "extreme meaning." He himself did not help that practice. She consistently had to rebuke him for using extreme and sensational language that excited the people.[32]

F. M. Wilcox summed up the problem nicely: "Elder Jones will make a statement, and make it as strong as it will bear, and then some of his disciples . . . will take his statement, and make it ten times as strong as he did." Olsen also mentioned Jones's power, claiming that a word from Jones ends all dispute in Battle Creek. Because of his influence among the members, Ellen White wrote to Jones in March 1894, he was the special target of Satan.[33]

Some Adventist leaders believed that his error in the Anna Rice affair was providential. "I sometimes almost feel," wrote Wilcox, "that the Lord may have permitted this mistake to be made, in order to balance our people up, and set them to looking at matters in a common-sense way. There was a time when many of the principles that Brother Jones has brought out were opposed, but lately the great mass of our people have hung on his words almost as though they were the words of God, and I do not know that there may be a providence in this thing, leading the people to see that they cannot give away their own judgment for the judgment of any one or two men."[34]

Thus the mistake was good for both Jones and the church. His temptation, Ellen White commented, had been to "glory . . . in self" and "success." His failure was a call back to the foot of the cross where he could lift up "the Man of Calvary" in a more single-minded manner. Therefore, his and Prescott's mistake could be "a great blessing to them." Their repentance, she wrote to Haskell, had "made it manifest that they do indeed hear the voice and accept it as from God."[35]

The incident was also good for the denomination, since the people, Ellen White noted, were "hanging upon" Jones's words. She utilized the problem as an opportunity to point both Jones and Prescott and the membership back to the Bible. "Satan," she penned, "would like nothing better than to call minds away from the word, to look for and expect something outside of the word. . . . They should not have their attention called to dreams and visions." In her several letters connected with the Rice affair, Ellen White constantly stressed the primacy of the Bible. That was the same message she had preached at Minneapolis.[36]

A second Minneapolis-related lesson coming out of the Rice mistake was that the various factions in the church needed to work together if they were to maintain spiritual balance. Haskell pointed out that Jones and Prescott had not been through the early development of Adventism and thus had not experienced the fanaticism evident at that time in regard to spiritual gifts. "Had they consulted with Uriah Smith and some of those who have been in the back-ground, and are looked upon as being 'out of date,' it would have saved them from making the mistake."[37]

Ellen White shared much the same opinion as Haskell regarding the need of the factions in Adventist leadership that had existed since Minneapolis to cooperate, but she placed the primary blame on Smith and the old guard. They, she declared, were to a large degree responsible for the crisis because they had held back from uniting in labor with "the faithful watchmen in these days of peril. . . . God . . . wants these men who think it is their duty to block the wheels, to put their shoulder to the chariot of truth, and roll it up the steep ascent. They should remember that Christ says of his disciples, 'All ye are brethren.'. . . The Lord's work needed every jot and tittle of experience that he had given Eld. Butler and Eld. Smith."

The Lord in His providence, she claimed, had allowed the crisis to show the older leaders their error in not uniting with the dynamic Jones and Prescott. "Truth is always aggressive."[38]

Not only did the conservative older leaders need the enthusiastic young leaders, but the opposite was also true. She wrote to Jones that he should not depreciate any of God's workers. Jones needed to respect "the old disciples who are the warriors of the faith," and who had experienced the difficulties in establishing the denomination in its early days. He needed their insight and experience.[39]

Thus, we might infer, the church is healthiest and most secure when its pluralistic factions learn to cooperate in aggressive action safeguarded by being anchored in a knowledge of how God has led His people in their past history.

Another lesson inherent in the Rice episode is that God does not cast off those who have made a serious error in carrying out His work if they are repentant. Haskell wrote to Ellen White in April 1894 concerning his fear about an unhealthy reaction against Jones and Prescott. Whereas, he pointed out, her support of them had formerly silenced nearly all criticism against them, he feared that a lack of support for them in their hour of trial might have a devastating effect on the church.[40]

Ellen White replied that she was quite anxious in regard to both Jones and Prescott, "but especially in regard to Bro. Jones who is so ardent in his faith, and does not manifest the caution he should in his statements by pen or voice." She went on to say that she had more confidence in them since they had made their mistake in the Rice affair than she had had before. "Bren. Jones and Prescott," she wrote, "are the Lord's chosen messengers, beloved of God. . . . While I cannot endorse their mistakes, I am in sympathy and union with them in their general work. . . . These brethren are God's ambassadors. They have been quick to catch the bright beams of the Sun of Righteousness, and have responded by imparting the heavenly light to others."[41]

A final lesson that the Adventist Church learned from the Rice episode was always to apply the biblical tests to spiritual gifts and to accept nothing on the basis of feeling, emotions, or novelty. The denomination has not had to repeat its lesson of 1894. On the other hand, the church needs to be aware of making the opposite mistake if spiritual gifts ever manifest themselves in its midst again. It is not impossible, for example, for God to reactivate the genuine gift of prophecy to challenge or correct tradition or administrative authority. In fact, on the basis of Joel 2:28-32, it appears that the church can even expect the prophetic gift in the future. At such a time an understanding of the experience of Jones and Prescott in 1894 will be of special value.

---

[1] EGW to Brethren and Sisters, Mar. 16, 1894; FMW to SNH, Mar. 5, 1894.

[2] LTN to OAO, Mar. 2, 1894; *RH,* Jan. 2, 1894, p. 11; ACR to ATJ, Feb. 21, 1893.

[3] *RH,* Jan. 2, 1894, p. 11.

[4] *Ibid.*

[5] *Ibid.*

[6] *Ibid.,* p. 16; W. C. Sisley to Dear Brother, c. Feb. 1, 1899; A. O. Tait to OAO, Jan. 1, 1894; W. H. Edwards to OAO, Jan. 4, 1894; LTN to OAO, Jan. 5, 1894.

[7] *RH,* Jan. 9, 1894, p. 32; LTN to OAO, Jan. 5, Mar. 2, 1894. (Ital. sup.)

[8] ACR to EGW, Mar. 18, 1894; LTN to DTJ, Jan. 11, 1894; LTN to OAO, Mar. 2, 1894.

[9] LTN to OAO, Mar. 2, 1894; LTN to DTJ, Jan. 11, 1894.

[10] *RH,* Jan. 30, Feb. 6, 1894, pp. 80, 96; LTN to IDVH, Jan. 31, 1894.

[11] *HM* Extra, November 1893, pp. 6, 7.

[12] LTN to OAO, Mar. 2, 1894; C. McReynolds to LTN, [1894].

[13] LTN to A. J. Breed, Feb. 26, 1894; LTN to E. G. Olsen, Feb. 28, 1894; LTN to OAO, Mar. 2, 1894.

[14] SNH to EGW, Jan. 4, 189[3]; ACR to EGW, Mar. 18, 1894.

[15] ACR to EGW, Mar. 18, 1894; ATJ to ACR, Jan. 3, 1894; EGW to Brethren and Sisters, Dec. 23, 1893; EGW to Brother and Sister Rice, Nov. 1, 1893; SNH to EGW, Nov. 30, 1893; LTN to OAO, Mar. 2, 1894.

[16] LTN to OAO, Mar. 2, 1894; LTN to JNL, Feb. 22, 1894; LTN to E. G. Olsen, Feb. 23, 1894.

[17] LTN to OAO, Mar. 2, 1894; LTN to SNH, Mar. 2, 1894.

[18] OAO to WCW, Mar. 5, 1894.

[19] LTN to E. G. Olsen, Feb. 23, 1894; EGW to ATJ, Jan. 14, 1894.

[20] SNH to EGW, Mar. 9, 1894; WWP to LTN, Feb. 26, 1894.

[21] FMW to EGW, Jan. 31, 1894.

[22] OAO to EGW, Mar. 29, 1894; LTN to A. J. Breed, Feb. 26, 1894.

[23] OAO to EGW, Mar. 29, 1894.

[24] *Ibid.*; FMW to WWP, Feb. 23, 1894; EWF to LTN, Mar. 13, 1894.

[25] FMW to ATJ, Mar. 1, 1894; OAO to WCW, May 31, 1894; A. O. Tait to OAO, Oct. 7, 1895; Book Committee Min, Sept. 8, 1895; J. Kolvoord to F. D. Starr, [September 1895].

[26] EGW to SNH, June 1, 1894; SNH to EGW, Mar. 9, 1894; ACR to EGW, Mar. 18, 1894; J. D. Rice to EGW, Aug. 21, 1894.

[27] ACR to EGW, Mar. 18, Oct. 14, 1894.

[28] ACR to EGW Mar. 18, Oct. 14, 1894; ACR to ATJ, July 29, 1894.

[29] ATJ to ACR, Apr. 26, May 24, 1894; J. D. Rice to EGW, Oct. 14, 1894; P. T. Magan to WCW, Sept. 19, 1901.

[30] FMW to WWP, Mar. 8, 1894; LTN to A. J. Breed, Mar. 9, 1894.

[31] EGW to ATJ, Apr. 9, 1893.

[32] EGW to ATJ, Mar. 15, 1894; EGW to Brethren and Sisters, Mar. 16, 1894.

[33] FMW to M. C. Wilcox, Apr. 16, 1894; EGW to ATJ, Mar. 15, 1894.

[34] FMW to SNH, Mar. 5, 1894.

[35] EGW to ATJ, June 7, 1894; EGW to SNH, June 1, 1894.

[36] EGW to ATJ, June 7, 1894; EGW to WWP and ATJ, Apr. 16, 1894. See Knight, *Angry Saints*, pp. 100-115, for an extensive treatment of EGW's uplifting the primacy of the Bible in the 1888 era.

[37] SNH to EGW, Apr. 20, 1994.

[38] EGW to SNH, June 1, 1894.

[39] EGW to ATJ, June 7, 1894.

[40] SNH to EGW, Apr. 22, 1894.

[41] EGW to SNH, June 1, 1894.

Truly Alonzo S. Jones

Ellet J. Waggoner and wife: Jones's "blood brother in the 'blood of the everlasing covenant'"

Uriah Smith: Jones's perpetual adversary in the
area of prophetic interpretation

W. W. Prescott: Jones's colleague in the 1890's and adversary in the early twentieth century

R. M. Kilgore: attempted to block discussion of the Galations issue at the 1888 General Conference session

Anna Rice (Phillips): The "Second Adventist Prophet"

Senator H. W. Blair: sponsor of the National Sunday Bills of 1888 and 1889 and the Constitutional Amendment to Christianize the nation's public schools in 1888

William H. Healey (and family): originator of the California conspiracy myth

Mrs. A. T. Jones

G. I. Butler: president of the General Conference, 1871-1874, 1880-1888

Wilbur Crafts, Ph.D.: champion of the Sunday-law forces

Above: The young Dr. J. H. Kellogg: Jones's associate in their war against the denomination early in the twentieth century

Right: A. G. Daniells: General Conference president. 1902-1922

Alonzo T. Jones claims he built the Farmington church in Washinton Territory with his own hands.

Left: W. C. White in the 1880s.

Bottom Left: I. D. Van Horn baptized Jones and later became his brother-in-law

Ellen G. White: the target of Jones's admiration and animosity

The elderly A. T. Jones

CHAPTER X

LOGICAL EXTREMISM AND THE TOTAL SEPARATION OF CHURCH AND STATE

A. T. Jones had battled valiantly against Sunday laws up through the summer of 1892. With the signing of the first national Sunday law in August of that year, however, he claimed that Congress had now given life to the image to the beast of Revelation 13. That act shifted the focus of his religious liberty activities. He would proclaim at the 1893 General Conference session that Adventists no longer had a responsibility to go to Washington to attend hearings or bring petitions against religious legislation. The mark of the beast had been established, and it could never be disestablished, even if Congress repealed its legislation. "The thing is done," Jones declared unequivocally. The United States government was "now confirmed in the hands of the professed Protestant churches." The task of the Adventists would subsequently be to warn the world against the worship of the beast and its image—a task that did not belong to the denomination before August 1892.[1]

The forming of the image did not mean that Jones's religious liberty work had ended, but that it would have a different emphasis. Part of it would be in calling the attention of Protestants to the fact that they were wrong in keeping Sunday because it was in reality a papal rather than a biblical institution. He found the four articles in the *Catholic Mirror* of September 1893 to be an excellent tool for that job. The *Catholic Mirror* articles demonstrated from a study of the Bible that Adventists were the only consistently biblical Protestants, since the Bible provided no justification for Sunday. The articles challenged Protestants either to admit their debt to the Roman Church or to keep the biblical Sabbath.

Such an argument proved to be excellent ammunition for Jones's guns, and he was soon off preaching the message of the *Mirror* and flinging its challenge in the face of American Protestantism. He was also instrumental in getting the articles published as *Rome's Challenge: Why Do Protestants Keep Sunday?* The booklet sold hundreds of thousands of copies.[2]

Beyond warning Protestants of their error and danger, Jones continued to battle for the total separation of church and state. That was not a new interest for him, since he had always operated on the assumption that the American ideal was 100 percent separation, but it did figure more prominently in his controversial positions as the nineties wore on.

In 1889 he had written for the annual Week of Prayer readings that America's "total separation of Church and State and the perfect religious liberty thereby assured, have been a beacon-light of progress to all other nations for a hundred years." Jones, of course, was unable to refrain from stretching total separation to its farthest logical conclusion. Thus at the 1895 General Conference session he would proclaim to the delegates that *"if we accept a point, or make a statement, which, if carried out to its utmost possible bearing, could lead to a union of Church and State, then that thing is teaching a union of Church and State."*[3]

With that logic in mind, it is not difficult to see why he would argue against such practices as military chaplains, national days of fasting and prayer, appropriations to churches, tax exemptions for churches, Bible reading in the schools, and the national Sunday law as examples of church-state union in the 1891 edition of his massive *Two Republics*.[4] His purpose in that book was to compare the United States with republican Rome, in order to show how America was making the same fatal mistake as the ancient nation in uniting church and state.

Seventh-day Adventists, he claimed in 1895, were not straight on the total separation of church and state. While they accepted it in theory, they often failed to live up to it in practice. Thus they were just as much in error as the National Reformers.[5]

In the separation of church and state, as in all other issues, Jones saw everything in terms of total black or total white. He had no place for those who desired to take moderating or contextual factors into consideration. A true fundamentalist of the purest sort, he had no room for compromise of any kind. His airtight logic led him into interesting positions on such topics as Christian citizenship, tax exemption for church property, religion in the public schools, and the church's receiving of gifts from governments. Closely related to such positions was his no-compromise attitude on the issue of Sunday labor, which we examined in chapter 6.

CHRISTIAN CITIZENSHIP

Jones's position on Christian citizenship was about as extreme as it could be. Reaching its zenith in 1894, it found its fullest expression in his presentations on the third angel's message at the 1895 General Conference session.

As usual, he built his argument from a *carefully selected* collection of Bible verses. He used them to establish a foundation for his reasoning, then employed syllogistic logic to milk out the most extreme position possible from them.

The basic biblical platform for his doctrine of Christian citizenship was Philippians 3:20, which reads that "our citizenship is in heaven" (Revised Version). Jones then extended the passage to mean that a citizen of heaven rightly has no business with any other government. After all, he queried, are we not God's ambassadors? "An ambassador is one sent, and accredited by one government as the representative of that government to another country. Now the principle of ambassadorship prohibits him from any interference whatever with the political concerns of the government to which he is accredited." Therefore, while governments are of this world, Christians have been born into the heavenly world, and have no business with earthly governments.[6]

He was not unaware of Jesus' saying that Christians should render to "Caesar the things which are Caesar's." His point was that if we worship God with all our mind "there is none of the man left for the service of Caesar." "Ye cannot serve God and Caesar" any more than you can worship God and mammon. "No man can serve two masters."[7]

The only logical thing, Jones asserted, was for every earthly government to "drop every man that professes to be a Christian from its roll of citizenship." Because the state did not do that, he pointed out, the Christian had conflicts in the present world.

It does not take much thought to see what Jones's position meant for Christian living. Obviously one would not vote, even though—as a resident alien—he would pay taxes. Likewise, a Christian would not "*start* any procedure in connection with civil government." The church, meanwhile, he read from one of his *Sentinel* articles, "can consistently and *rightly* disregard any and all legislative acts, judicial decrees, or executive powers, put forth upon religious questions (or that touch religious practices); because she ever denies the right of government to touch religion or any religious question in any way." This, he pontificated, "is *present* truth."[8]

Not all of Jones's Adventist contemporaries agreed with his radical position, even though many of them probably looked upon it as being light from God. Even O. A. Olsen, otherwise overly cautious in rebuking his coworkers, questioned "the propriety of making some of these statements in the pulpit." He was even more concerned with their going into print. To Ellen White he wrote that much of what went through the *Sentinel* was a burden on his mind, even though he had said but little. Ellen White, for her part, constantly cautioned Jones in regard to extremism. On one such occasion she wrote to him that "we should not work in such a manner as will mark us out as a people who seem to advocate treason. We should weed out every expression in our writings, our utterances, that . . . could be misrepresented so as to make it seem antagonistic to law and order."[9]

Jones's teachings on Christian citizenship also upset L. T. Nicola, secretary of the General Conference. He reported in the summer of 1894 that Prescott, as usual, was in full accord with Jones's interpretation of the implications of "My kingdom is not of this world," and that a Christian's civic responsibility ended with submission to the state. "Prof. Prescott," Nicola wrote, "acted precisely as on all former occasions when Eld. Jones was prescribing—he took the dose just as directed." Nicola also told Olsen that in Jones's recent presentation of the topic of citizenship "the extreme and unnecessary positions received more than their share of earnestness and syllogistic logic."[10]

Jones's perspective on Christian citizenship had obvious implications for his positions on tax exemption, government gifts, and religion in the public schools. Their most important significance, however, was probably related to his later attitude on church organization (see chapter 13), a position he would fully develop by the turn of the century. In the struggle over church structure, Prescott would eventually go over to the side of Arthur G. Daniells—president of the General Conference after 1901. After that change, Prescott, instead of being Jones's most devoted follower, would be one of his most formidable adversaries in a controversy that shook the denomination for nearly a decade.

COMBATING RELIGION IN THE PUBLIC SCHOOLS

One of the most important institutions in the mainline Protestant battle to Christianize America was the public school. The public school, however, like every other institution of postbellum America, found itself beset by enemies. A professor at Union Theological Seminary vividly described the plight of American Protestants in 1873. "Infidel bugles are sounding in front of us, Papal bugles are sounding behind us. And evangelical Protestants are not standing shoulder to shoulder."[11] Protection of Sunday sacredness, the temperance crusade, and the maintenance of Protestant Christianity in the public schools became three planks in the churches' program to keep America Protestant.

Catholics, who had their own view of America and the good life, did not always appreciate those ideals. If the public school could not meet their needs, they determined to create their own system of schools in which they could raise their children as Catholics. The Third Plenary Council, held at Baltimore in 1884, greatly furthered that goal. The Baltimore council decided to build a parochial school system that would include every parish in the nation. That decision set off a new wave of Protestant anxieties. At least part of that worry stemmed from the concern that Catholic education might get a share of the public school funding.

It was in this loaded context that the last quarter of the nineteenth century saw a large number of legislative bills aimed at (1) preserving the Protestant character of the public schools through the reading of the Bible (King James Version) and the teaching of nonsectarian (spelled "Protestant") religion; and (2) making sure that no public tax moneys went to support sectarian education. The Protestant strategy was to protect the educational status quo, since the schools were already generically Protestant in flavor. The Blaine amendment (1875), the Edmunds resolution (1875), and the Blair educational amendment (1888), along with several other pieces of federal legislation, sought to achieve that goal.

As we might expect, Jones was dead set against any religion being taught in the public schools. Likewise, he opposed Bible reading in them. He saw the slightest leniency on those points as a concession that would rapidly break down the wall of separation between church and state. In response, he preached against the Blair amendment at the 1888 General Conference session, he wrote about it in *Civil Government* in 1889, he testified against it before the United States Committee on Education and Labor on February 22, 1889, and he published *The Edmunds Resolution: Its Place in the Church and State Movement* in 1890. Furthermore, in 1891 in his *Two Republics* he set forth Protestant religion and Bible reading in the public schools as primary agents in the breaking down of the historic American position on the separation of church and state. The *Sentinel,* of course, did not remain silent on the topic. From Jones's perspective, the government had no business whatsoever in the teaching or the support of religion. To enter the field at all, the government had to establish some form of religion. That, however, the Constitution strictly forbade. Seeing those points in bold relief, Jones fought the battle with his usual zest.[12]

His exuberance on the topic tempered somewhat in early 1891 when Ellen White read a statement on the subject of the Bible and the public schools at the General Conference session. That statement, unfortunately not preserved, apparently went against his strictly separationist position. At any rate, he decided to say as little as possible on the topic, and he quieted the pages of the *Sentinel* in like manner. On the other hand, he was powerless to recall what he had already published.[13]

It is probable that Ellen White intended her 1891 comment to counter the attention given to Jones's objections to Bible reading in the public schools, since such publicity would further antagonize Protestants already upset with Adventists over the Sunday issue. Her statement, however, did not prevent an underground war between Smith and Jones and their colleagues in a less visible manner. In the ensuing struggle, Smith felt forced into expressing the sentiment that a "little religion in civil affairs" was all right. The pressure on him compelled him to admit that he believed that "if all the people wish it, they have a right to have the Bible and their views taught each day." That, Smith's opposers exuded, had nudged him toward the National Reform mentality.[14]

The topic surfaced again in 1893. Jones, apparently, had come out of the closet on the issue, since Ellen White wrote to him on April 9, 1893, regarding the problem. On the other hand, she may have received a manuscript copy of a pamphlet entitled *Shall Religion Be Taught in the*

Public Schools? that the Religious Liberty Association would release in May. While the pamphlet did not bear the name of an author, she may have suspected that Jones was somehow behind it. At any rate, he received her letter, and she had undoubtedly aimed it at his views.

She told him that while she did not feel it was right to bring the Bible into the public schools, she did not think that Adventists should make an issue over the question. To do so would "place us in a wrong light before the world." She was certain that if a law passed that legalized Bible reading in the schools, God would "overrule it for good." After all, the Bible does contain God's truth, including a knowledge of the true Sabbath. "My brother," she noted, "this objecting to the passing of a law to bring the Bible into the schools will work against us. . . . We should be exceedingly cautious in every particular lest we shut out a single ray of light from those who are in darkness. . . . It is very essential, as a people, [that] we take the greatest care that no provocation be given our enemies which they will make capital of against us, as a people, in a future crisis, in a matter of opposing so good a work as the introduction of the Bible into the public schools." Recalling her 1891 General Conference statement, which had been lost, she said, "I remember particularly this point, 'That anything that should give the knowledge of God, and Jesus Christ whom he hath sent, should not be obstructed at all.'"[15]

Thus Ellen White did not take a decided stand with Jones against the issue of reading the Bible in the public schools. She was pragmatic, while he was doctrinaire. As a result, she looked at the good that might come out of a bad practice through God's overruling providence, while Jones saw only the danger it had for the doctrine of total separation of church and state. This pragmatic versus doctrinaire dichotomy would run across all discussions between Ellen White and Jones on topics related to the separation of church and state. Her pragmatic attitude on the Bible reading issue, with its eye on the practical side, was quite in harmony with the stand she took against those with doctrinaire views at Minneapolis in 1888.

Jones replied to her letter in August, claiming that he was thankful for her counsel. He also noted that he well remembered her lost 1891 statement on the topic. The 1893 testimony, he told her, made the issue much plainer. Therefore he would stop printing material on the question, and do whatever he could "to turn all into the course pointed out by the Lord."[16]

FIGHTING TO PAY TAXES ON CHURCH PROPERTY

A major flaw in the Adventist practice of the separation of church and state, Jones pointed out in 1891, was their acceptance of tax exemption for church property. Such exemption, he rightly noted, was a major tool that the Emperor Constantine had used to weld church and state together in the fourth century. Tax exemption for church property, he correctly reasoned, is a form of state support for churches. It is in essence an indirect rather than a direct subsidy of religion by the state. Thus it is an "evil in itself." Beyond that, he said, it provided a basis for urging the claims of the National Reformers in their effort to Christianize Society.[17]

The denomination's religious liberty forces sought to publicize this issue, not only through Jones's *Two Republics*, but by two tracts on the topic written by non-Adventists. Adventist religious liberty advocates published and widely circulated both in 1891. Such efforts were part of an attempt to shape the thinking of the church and its leaders in what some saw as a crucial area of church-state relations.[18]

The major move to reverse the denomination's position on tax exemption took place at the 1893 General Conference session. On February 28 it was "*Resolved,* that we repudiate the doctrine that Church, or other ecclesiastical property should be exempt from taxation; and, therefore, further, . . . *Resolved,* that henceforth we decline to accept such exemption on our own behalf." Jones's 1891 criticism was beginning to bear fruit.[19]

The resolutions underwent considerable discussion before the delegates finally approved them in a somewhat altered form. Jones was active in those discussions. It was his view that the Adventists should not just decline exemption, but that they should "decidedly protest" against it. W. A. Colcord agreed with Jones, adding an amendment to Jones's amendment that emphasized that the church should not only decidedly speak against exemption, but that it should also work for "the repeal of such legislation as grants this exemption." The session adopted the amended resolution. The Seventh-day Adventist Church had now officially put itself on record on the tax issue.[20]

Complications and opportunities soon began to arise. On March 2 Jones and other Adventist religious liberty leaders traveled to Lansing, Michigan, to testify before the state legislature against a bill for the Sunday closing of barbershops. During the hearing one of the state legislators asked Jones where he stood on the bill currently before the House for the taxation of church property. He replied that he had not heard of it, but that he unreservedly supported such taxation. He was pleased to inform the legislator that the denomination had just taken official action on the question.

After the hearing on the barber bill concluded, the tax bill's sponsor approached Jones and asked him if he would be willing to testify before the House Judiciary Committee on behalf of his bill for the repeal of tax exemption. Jones was more than delighted to accept the invitation. His speech, in which he used the General Conference resolutions, had "excellent effect." The whole sequence from the General Conference resolutions through the tax bill hearings, Colcord claimed, was obviously providential.[21]

Not everyone, however, saw it that way. At that very time J. H. Kellogg and other Battle Creek leaders were in the midst of seeking to get tax-exempt status for medical missionary institutions, including an orphanage. They had enlisted the aid of the state representative for Battle Creek on their behalf. As a result, he had recently put forth a bill to that effect. Jones's March 3 speech regarding the denomination's position on tax exemption threw the friendly legislator into confusion on the question. He requested the General Conference, still in session, to clarify the matter for him. On March 5 the conference appointed a committee of five, including Jones, to come up with a solution. The committee reported the same afternoon that certain benevolent institutions, unlike purely religious institutions such as churches, "occupied confessedly disputed grounds." Taxing such institutions, it suggested, should be left up to the action of the legislature. The church would neither protest against nor request such exemption. The recommendation passed with two dissenting votes on March 6.[22]

Kellogg, to put it mildly, was upset with Jones and his associates. His bill failed to pass, and Kellogg had found himself "completely thwarted." Beyond that, he pointed out, "their action has brought all the venom and spleen of the Methodists and others, and has stirred up every bitter element against" the Adventists.[23]

Jones, on the other hand, saw the 1893 General Conference session actions as a great step forward in the cause of religious liberty. He would later use those actions as an argument against receiving free government land in Africa in the Solusi case (see below). In the meanwhile, the *Sentinel* continued to publish views against tax exemption from time to time.[24]

Ellen White remained silent on the issue until January 1895, when she wrote a letter to Haskell on the Solusi land-grant situation. Her remarks leave no doubt as to where she stood on tax exemption. "Our brethren," she wrote, "are not looking at everything in the right light. The movements they have made to pay taxes on the property of the Sanitarium and Tabernacle have manifested a zeal and conscientiousness that in all respects is not wise or correct. Their ideas of religious liberty are being interwoven with suggestions that do not come from the Holy Spirit, and the religious liberty cause is sickening, and its sickness can only be healed by the grace and gentleness of Christ. The hearts of those who advocate this cause must be filled by the Spirit of Jesus."[25]

Linking that counsel with that on the receiving of government land, she remarked that "it is very strange that some of our brethren should feel that it is their duty to bring about a condition of things that will bind up the means that God would have set free." Reading over her letter some time afterward, she penned the following additional comment between the lines: "Their business is not to close up the avenues. Let the Lord work in that line."[26]

REFUSING GOVERNMENT GRANTS

Closely related to tax exemption was the offer of 12,000 acres of free land to the church by the British South African Land Company for the establishment of a mission station in what is now Zimbabwe. The company was in effect the colonial government with full governmental powers.[27] Thus many viewed the land grant as a church-state problem. If tax credits were indirect aid, the land grant was direct governmental support to the church. The offer involved the denomination in a two-year internal struggle.

The issue of a government land grant in Africa first surfaced in February 1893 at the General Conference session. It immediately stimulated an official action by the General Conference against accepting such a gift, since "it is inconsistent for the Church to receive from the State pecuniary gifts, favors or exemptions." The issue seemed clear enough until one of the South African delegates pointed out that a company, not the government, would provide the land. That placed the matter in a somewhat fuzzy light for many church leaders, especially since one of the top company officials had become "governor" of the province where the land was located.[28]

The religious liberty leaders lost little time in seeing the problem. C. P. Bollman, Jones's coeditor on the *Sentinel,* wrote to F. M. Wilcox, secretary of the Foreign Mission Board, on August 30, 1894, that the denomination ought to keep clear of the offer. The next month the *Sentinel* came out with an article against the Catholic Church for receiving gifts from the government. It concluded the article by applying the principle to Adventists in Africa.[29]

Over in Africa, meanwhile, S. N. Haskell began a letter-writing campaign on behalf of accepting the land. He argued his point from the books of Ezra and Nehemiah, asking what the religious liberty officials would have done in that case. "Does not God's word plainly teach us that God runs the kingdoms of the earth in the interests of His own cause?" Operating on that basis, the Adventists in Africa accepted the land as a free grant.[30]

The missionaries' employing agency, however, began having second thoughts on the idea of a free grant. The General Conference president was also afraid that the missionaries might have gone too far. On December 2 Olsen recommended to the mission board that they should inform the company that they wanted to pay for the land.[31]

In the meantime, the *Sentinel* had aimed several digs at the African missionaries. The November 1 issue noted that the editors now had incontrovertible evidence that the company was "nothing less than a British Colonial government." Three weeks later the editors brutally aligned the Adventist missionaries with the "gospel of force" in a colonial land grab. "How the missionaries who have thus sold themselves for a mess of African pottage will succeed in serving two masters, remains to be seen," the *Sentinel* trumpeted, especially in view of "our Lord's declaration that it cannot be done."[32] That strongly worded gibe would have extensive repercussions.

Olsen rebuked Jones and Bollman on November 30 for their attack. They fired back a strongly worded epistle three days later in which they firmly defended their course, noting in effect that their appointed duty was to be the watchdog of the denomination on such issues. If the denomination was inconsistent, they pointed out, the fact would get spread around by its enemies, and would weaken the Adventist argument against those who would Christianize America through such things as Sunday laws.[33]

The most important protest against the *Sentinel* came from Africa. By January 1, 1895, Haskell had seen the November 22 *Sentinel.* On that day he fired off a battery of protesting epistles to Adventist leaders in America and Australia. One of them landed in the lap of Ellen White, still in Australia. She would reply with a most important letter.[34]

Before her letter could reach the United States, however, the 1895 General Conference session would be history. That session had much to say on the African land-grant issue. On February 20 a resolution sought to put the denomination on record as being against receiving all donations of land or other privileges from a government or "royal chartered company." It firmly stated that the denomination would pay "for all government land that may be secured in Africa or elsewhere."[35]

That resolution came up for discussion on February 24. Jones took the floor and "contended that our position on the entire separation of Church and State should be without a conditional 'but.'" He specifically addressed the problems raised by the books of Ezra and Nehemiah, claiming that they did not fit the present circumstances since the people had been in captivity and that the Persian authorities were just restoring what was rightfully theirs. Furthermore, he asserted, religious experience had progressed from the time of Nehemiah. Just as divorces and polygamy had been allowed in previous times, but now no longer, so it was with state aid. D. H. Lamson then rose up and suggested that one could not explain everything in Ezra and Nehemiah on the basis of entire separation from the state. Two full meetings of the conference dealt with the topic.[36]

The session finally adopted the resolution. The Sentinel announced that official action to the world as a witness to the fact that "Seventh-day Adventists are sincere in their belief in the complete separation of Church and State." The March 17 meeting of the Foreign Mission Board seconded the General Conference action. They voted, as Olsen had suggested in December, to purchase the land.[37]

It was not until four days after that action that Ellen White's letters on the topic arrived from Australia, even though she had written them on the last two days of January. She had addressed one of them to Haskell, but obviously she intended it for public circulation, while the second spoke to the leaders of the church.

She rebuked the editors of the Sentinel for their sharp thrusts in the November 22 issue, but she went way beyond that in her counsel to the church. Ellen White specifically mentioned the African land issue, indicating that God still owned the world. It "greatly distressed" her when the denomination's leading men (i.e., Jones and his colleagues) took extreme positions in matters that should have been left in the hands of God. "The Lord still moves," she penned, "upon the hearts of kings and rulers in behalf of His people, and it becomes those who are so deeply interested in the religious liberty question not to cut off any favors, or withdraw themselves from the help that God has moved men to give, for the advancement of His cause." She suggested that those men so concerned with repealing tax exemptions and rejecting the African land grant should read the book of Nehemiah. If they did so with humble hearts and the aid of the Holy Spirit, their "false ideas" would be "modified, and correct principles" would "be seen, and the present order of things" would be changed. "Nehemiah prayed to God for help, and God heard his prayer. The Lord moved upon heathen kings to come to his help." Also she protested against the zeal of such individuals as Jones, who manifested ardor ignorantly "when they ventilate their ideas about foreign fields of labor."[38]

Her letters found a positive hearing on the Foreign Mission Board. During its next meeting the board reversed the previous ruling about paying for the land. Olsen was also quite happy with the counsel. He confessed to W. C. White that he had been somewhat overwhelmed by "men of strong minds" and "great power of expression" who often took "extreme positions" on the religious liberty issue. Also he pointed out that the General Conference had decided the previous month to send Jones overseas. Hopefully, Olsen added, the exposure would enlarge his experience.[39]

Jones was not nearly so pleased with Ellen White's correspondence on the topic. He wrote his reply to her the same day he received her letter. Instead of admitting his error, as was his usual manner, he sought to shift the blame onto Haskell, who had, he claimed, miscommunicated with him. Rather than acknowledging any mistake on his part, Jones merely informed her that he had received the letter. Then he moved on to other business.[40]

The reason that Jones did not acknowledge his error was that he could not see where he was wrong. Bollman reported to Ellen White in May that both he and Jones were "*at sea*" on the land-grant issue. Her letters, he wrote, had undercut all their work on the separation of church and state. After all, the National Reformers also appealed to Ezra and Nehemiah, even for Sunday enforcement. Bollman entreated her to resolve the issue.

That, however, she declined to do, leaving it to the church to work out the implications in concrete sociopolitical contexts. By December 1896 Bollman had seen the wisdom in her position on the African land grant, but Jones continued to feel that they had been correct in their stand.[41]

In the land-grant question, as well as in the problems of religion in the public schools and tax exemption, we find Jones at odds with Ellen White. In chapter 6 we also saw the same difference in regard to ceasing labor in order to obey Sunday laws. She consistently chose the practical/pragmatic path that took contextual circumstances into consideration, while he consistently held to a doctrinaire polar extreme. His logical mind did not possess much ability for flexible interpretation, and he had a difficult time adjusting his views to differing contexts. As we have observed repeatedly, for Jones every issue was black or white, right or wrong. The use of reason in applying inspired counsel he did not view as a virtue. Ellen White, on the other hand, took the alternative position. Since neither of them changed over time, their basic difference in approach eventually set him up for a rejection of her writings (see chapter 16). Jones is a case in point of one who had swallowed the myth of the inflexible prophet.[42]

He took every position he touched to its logical extreme, irrespective of personal and contextual factors. Ellen White refused to follow him, and he could not completely go along with her. With their two different mentalities, it was inevitable that they would in time drift further and further apart. The church eventually would have to decide which of these two most prominent thought leaders it would listen to. The crisis, long in brewing, would come to a head in the first decade of the twentieth century.

[1] 1893 GCB, pp. 70, 71, 516, 517; cf. 1899 GCB, p. 162; AGD to WCW, May 27, 1901.

[2] WAS to AGD, Oct, 5, 1893; WAS to WCW, Oct. 5, 1893; FMW to A. La Rue, Jan. 24, 1894.

[3] 1893 GCB, p. 109; 1895 GCB, p. 66.

[4] ATJ, The Two Republics (Battle Creek, 1891), pp. 781-860. (Note: the 1895 edition of this book also carries an 1891 copyright, even though the content is quite different in the last 200 pages.)

[5] 1895 GCB, p. 503.

[6] Ibid., pp. 50, 51, 53.

[7] Ibid., pp. 66, 67.

[8] Ibid., pp. 85, 99, 101.

[9] OAO to ATJ, Feb. 7, 1895; OAO to EGW, Mar. 26, 1895; EGW to ATJ, Oct. 13, 1895.

[10] LTN to OAO, Aug. 23, 1894.

[11] Quoted in Handy, *Christian America*, p. 83.

[12] ATJ, *Civil Government*, (1890 ed.) pp. 43-67. *Religion in the Public Schools* (Oakland, 1889); ATJ, *The Edmunds Resolution* (Oakland, 1890); ATJ, *Two Republics*, pp. 820-829.

[13] ATJ to EGW, Aug. 14, 1893.

[14] WAC to F. W. Howe, Aug. 6, 1891.

[15] EGW to ATJ, Apr. 9, 1893.

[16] ATJ to EGW, Aug. 14, 1893.

[17] ATJ, *Two Republics,* pp. 295-297, 810, 811. For twentieth-century discussions on tax exemptions as indirect subsidies, see Richard E. Morgan, *The Supreme Court and Religion* (New York, 1972), pp. 103-107; Stokes, *Church and State*, vol. 3, p. 423; D. B. Robertson, *Should Churches Be Taxed?* (Philadelphia, 1968).

[18] A. P. M'Diarmid, *Should Church Property Be Taxed?* (Oakland, 1891); J. T. Ringgold, *Church and State* (Battle Creek, 1892), pp. 41-46.

[19] 1893 *GCB*, p. 437.

[20] *Ibid.*, pp. 484, 437, 444, 458, 475.

[21] *HM,* April 1893, p. 57.

[22] 1893 *GCB*, pp. 484, 486, 491.

[23] JHK to OAO, May 12, 1893; JHK to WCW, Aug. 7, 1895.

[24] Editors of the *American Sentinel* to OAO, Dec. 3, 1894; *AS*, Oct. 4, 1894, p. 307.

[25] EGW to [SNH], Jan. 30, 1895.

[26] *Ibid.*

[27] CPB to EGW, May 8, 1895.

[28] 1893 *GCB*, pp. 269, 437, 475, 486; *RH,* Aug. 21, 1894, p. 544; FMW to WCW, Aug. 17, 1894.

[29] CPB to FMW, Aug. 30, 1894; *AS*, Sept. 13, 1894, p. 287.

[30] SNH to FMW, Oct. 9, 1894; FMW to J. E. Graham, Oct. 10, 1894; FMW to WCW, Oct. 9, 1894.

[31] FMB Min, Nov. 13, Dec. 2, 1894; OAO to WCW, Nov. 8, 1894.

[32] *AS,* Nov. 1, 22, 1894, pp. 344, 368.

[33] The Editors of the *American Sentinel* to OAO, Dec. 3, 1894.

[34] SNH to OAO, Jan. 1, 1895; SNH to WCW, Jan. l, 1895; SNH to ATJ, Jan. 1, 1895; SNH to FMW, Jan. 3, 1895.

[35] 1895 *GCB*, p. 283.

[36] *Ibid.*, p. 340; OAO to WCW, Feb. 26, 1895.

[37] *AS,* Mar. 14, 1895, p. 82; FMB Min, Mar. 17, 1895.

[38] EGW to [SNH], Jan. 30, 1895; EGW, MS 41, Jan. 31, 1895.

[39] FMB Min, Mar. 29, 1895; OAO to WCW, Mar. 28, 1895.

[40] ATJ to EGW, Mar. 21, 1895.

[41] CPB to EGW, May 8, 1895; Dec. 9, 1896; EGW to CPB, June 18, 1895; WCW to OAO, June 7, 1895.

[42] For a discussion on the myth of the inflexible prophet, see G. R. Knight, *Myths in Adventism* (Washington D.C., 1985), pp. 17-25.

CHAPTER XI

THE NATURE OF CHRIST: SEEDS FOR A TWENTIETH-CENTURY REPLAY OF THE GALATIANS CONTROVERSY

The 1888 General Conference session at Minneapolis has been central to Adventism because it provided a desperately needed emphasis on Jesus Christ in Adventist theology and lifestyle. The great themes of Minneapolis, Ellen White pointed out to her son Edson in 1895, were "Christ crucified for our sins, Christ risen from the dead, Christ our intercessor before God, and . . . the office work of the Holy Spirit, the representative of Christ, sent forth with divine power and gifts for men."[1]

THE LAW IN GALATIANS, THE SPIRIT OF MINNEAPOLIS, AND THE NATURE OF CHRIST

As noted earlier, Jones, Waggoner, and, somewhat later, Prescott became the champions, along with Ellen White, of the righteousness by faith revival. Jesus and His saving grace was the center of their message. Christ received an emphasis in Adventist writing and preaching that He had never had before. Ellen White, for one, hoped that the cross would become the focal point and context for every Adventist teaching, both in terms of lifestyle and doctrine.

In the post-1888 decade that emphasis developed an interest in the nature of Christ and in His human experience as Adventism's reformers sought to plumb the depths of the meaning of His life and work for human existence. Their expositions brought forth many things that were both true and helpful, but not everything that Waggoner, Jones, and Prescott taught about Jesus was clearsighted, even in the Minneapolis and immediate post-Minneapolis periods. Waggoner, for example, taught a couple months after the General Conference session that it was impossible for Jesus to sin because God was in Him. Again, in *Christ and His Righteousness* (1890) he put forth semi-Arian views of Christ when he wrote that "there was a time when Christ proceeded forth and came from God." That semi-Arianism, which taught that Christ was not equal with God, had been prominent in Adventist theology from its inception in the 1840s. Just because Waggoner taught such views in the late 1880s and early 1890s, however, did not make them truth. Ellen White and others would reject both views—along with several of his other teachings—during the 1890s.[2]

Waggoner's semi-Arianism, however, was not controversial in the early 1890s. Nor, apparently, did anyone's salvation hang on a correct intellectual understanding of the topic.

Another Christological issue that encountered little disagreement in Adventist circles in the 1890s was the "sinfulness" of Christ's human nature. That position, like many other topics related to Jesus, had not been prominent in Adventist teaching before 1888. In fact, the two earliest mentions of the topic that I have been able to discover were written in February 1887 and January 1889.[3] Waggoner, Jones, and Prescott by the mid nineties, however, would develop the concept that Christ was just like every other child of Adam—including a tendency to sin—into a central feature of their understanding of righteousness by faith.

Their view of Christ's nature created no controversy in the Adventism of the 1890s. It was a generally accepted theological nonissue. But that would all change in the 1950s when it would become *the* theological subject for many Adventists on both sides of the question. M. L. Andreasen, who formed a student/mentor relationship with Jones in the late nineties and who had become one of the denomination's foremost theologians by the middle of the twentieth century, held that the doctrine of Christ's "sinful" nature is one of Adventism's "foundation pillars." To change that position, he suggested, was not only to give up historic Adventism, but to surrender belief in the testimonies of Ellen White.[4] Many have followed his lead. Others in the church believe that an adequate Christian belief in Christ must recognize that He was different from other humans in His tendencies toward sin. For more than 50 years Adventism has experienced a war of words over the topic.

Unfortunately, the struggle over the human nature of Christ is not the first theological sideline that has diverted Adventism's energies. The church had earlier derailed in the 1880s over the identity of the law in Galatians, a topic which some had magnified into landmark proportions. That controversy smoldered in the hearts of some Adventists for decades. Meanwhile, it kept them from the real task of the church and from letting God fully work in their lives. The same was true of the bitter battle over the "daily" of Daniel 8 in the first couple decades of the twentieth century. Each issue involved an interpretation of Ellen White's writings. In both cases the spirit of Minneapolis—with all of its inflamed passions over doctrinal differences, bitterness, criticism, sharpness, and evil surmising—was present. Ellen White said that the argument did not make much difference in either controversy. And in both cases she refused to settle the question, even though the battle had resulted from an interpretation of her writings that made the point under discussion a landmark in the eyes of the "old guard." To her they were nonissues. What the church needed to do, she urged, was to replace the spirit of Minneapolis with the spirit of Christ, get about its business, focus on the Bible as the "only rule of faith and doctrine,"[5] and express the love of God to a fallen world. It is reasonable to believe that if she were alive today she would take the same position in the battle over the nature of Christ.

The point of controversy in the Adventist struggle focuses on whether Christ was born with a moral nature exactly like ours—with all of its sinful tendencies—or whether He was incarnated with the moral nature of the prefallen Adam. The parallels between this issue and that of the law in Galatians in 1888 are enlightening. Both have been viewed as doctrinal "landmarks" or "pillars," and the denial of either position has been held to be a rejection of Ellen White. Furthermore, both have stimulated the spirit of Minneapolis. In many ways the nature of Christ controversy is a replay of the 1888 battle over the law in Galatians. Neither is an issue in salvation. At least we have no inspired evidence to the contrary. The law in Galatians controversy demonstrated that human landmarks and pillars are not necessarily God's.

According to Scripture, it is not theology that saves, but the Lord of that theology. Christian living, of course, needs to be informed by theological truth, but if that truth leads believers to partake of the spirit of Minneapolis, it is time for serious self-examination.

Because the major controversies over Jones's position on the nature of Christ did not arise until long after his death, this chapter—like chapter 5—departs from a strictly biographical format in order to treat a topic that became central in the latter half of the twentieth century to many people's understanding of Jones's historical significance in the development of Seventh-day Adventist theology. Building upon chapters 2 through 5, the present chapter interprets the controversy over the nature of Christ and the attitudes manifested in that battle as equivalent to the unfortunate experience at Minneapolis over the law in Galatians.

With the above background in mind, we will now examine A. T. Jones's view on the nature of Christ. We will then look at some possible relations that his teachings have to Ellen White's ideas on the same topic.

JONES ON THE NATURE OF CHRIST

Jones had a great deal to say on the Incarnation. This section will not attempt to survey that subject, but to state explicitly and briefly his theory on whether the incarnate Christ, in His moral nature, was like Adam before the Fall, or whether He came into the world just like all humans since the Fall—i.e., with an inborn tendency to sin. Even though at the 1893 General Conference session he alluded to the fact that Christ had flesh just like ours, and would often teach the subject after 1895, notably in his *Review* editorials[6] and in the *Consecrated Way to Christian Perfection* (1905), his fullest exposition of the topic took place at the 1895 General Conference session. He laced his 26 sermons on the third angel's message with his view on the subject, devoting six of them to it entirely. His later writings on the topic never differed significantly from his 1895 presentations. Those presentations, therefore, can serve as a base to set forth his position.

Without doubt, by 1895 Jones saw the total likeness of Christ's nature to that of other humans as central to his presentation of righteousness by faith, even though, outside of a few remarks in 1893, that emphasis had been absent from his writings before 1894. (Waggoner, on the other hand, had been teaching that Christ had sinful tendencies since February 1887.) In his 1895 presentations Jones pointed out that for three or four years the denomination had been studying the meaning of Christ's emptying Himself, but that he was quite convinced that his teachings were in advance of anything the church had previously heard on the topic.[7]

In his usual manner, Jones was quite explicit as he put his beliefs before the delegates. "Christ's nature," he claimed, "is precisely our nature." "In his human nature there is not a particle of difference between him and you." Christ did not come like the first Adam, "but as the first Adam had caused his descendants to be at the time at which he came."[8]

To get the full impact of this likeness, we need to realize that Jones had previously told the delegates that at the *"moment"* that Adam and Eve sinned there was "total depravity." For Jones the Fall did not merely mar the image of God in humanity—it obliterated it. Adam and Eve could not tell the truth to God in Eden, because their *minds* were in bondage to Satan.[9]

It was in this depraved human nature that Christ became like us with "not a particle of difference between him and you." There was, Jones claimed, "not a single tendency to sin in you and me that was not in Adam when he stepped out of the garden." Christ took our flesh in the Incarnation, with "just the same tendencies to sin that are in you and me. . . . All the tendencies to sin that are in human flesh were in his human flesh," yet "not one of them was ever allowed to appear; he conquered them all. And in him we all have victory over them all."[10]

Jones did not hold that Jesus was a sinner, even though at times he became careless in his language, even saying at one point that Christ "was sinful as we." That habit extended beyond his 1895 General Conference sermons. In 1896, for example, he would note four times in one article that Christ had "human flesh laden with sin." Again in 1894, in preaching at the Battle Creek Tabernacle on the nature of Christ's flesh, he defined sinful flesh as being "full of sin."[11]

His use of language is often confusing. Furthermore, Jones's extremes in expression and thought do not help the situation. In addition to those problems, it is often impossible to tell exactly what he had in mind. For example, we can interpret many of his discussions of Christ's nature to mean that Christ took our sinful nature vicariously, just as He bore our sins on the cross vicariously when He became sin for us.[12]

After accounting for all the careless language, exaggerations, and ambiguities in Jones's statements, however, it is still evident that he believed that Christ became incarnate in flesh just like ours, with all of its sinful tendencies. On the other hand, Jesus was without sin. He was, in fact, a demonstration to the universe that individuals can overcome sin in human flesh.

Jesus is an example in this matter for every Christian. Jones stated that "in Jesus Christ as he was in sinful flesh, God has demonstrated before the universe that he can so take possession of sinful flesh as to manifest his own presence, his power, and his glory, instead of sin manifesting itself. And all that the Son asks of any man, in order to accomplish this in him, is that the man will let the Lord have him as the Lord Jesus did."[13]

In other words, if a person surrenders to Jesus, God will do the same for him or her today. "God will so dwell yet in sinful flesh that in spite of all the sinfulness of sinful flesh, his influence, his glory, his righteousness, his character, shall be manifested wherever that person goes." Thus Jesus "is a Saviour from sins committed, and the Conqueror of the tendencies to commit sins." Christ offers "resurrection . . . power" to every believer. In short, Jones pointed out in 1905, by overcoming sin in sinful human flesh, Jesus had opened a "consecrated way" for each of His followers to do the same. Each can have "perfection of character . . . in human flesh in this world."[14] That, of course, he often noted, resulted not from human effort, but from the surrender of the will and from the indwelling of the Holy Spirit.

That type of living, he declared in 1897, would make God's people a demonstration to the universe. Their lives would proclaim: "Here are they that keep the commandments of God and the faith of Jesus."[15]

Not all the delegates at the 1895 General Conference session agreed with his position that Christ was like fallen humanity in every way. They challenged him with a statement from Ellen White that claims that Christ "is a brother in our infirmities, but not in possessing like passions." Jones tried to tersely pass off the quotation, but in his next sermon he had to deal with it extensively. His way around the problem was to differentiate between Christ's flesh and His mind. "Now as to Christ's not having 'like passions' with us: In the Scriptures all the way through he is like us, and with us according to the flesh. . . . Don't go too far. *He was made in the likeness of sinful flesh; not in the likeness of sinful mind.* Do not drag his mind into it. His flesh was our flesh; but the mind was 'the mind of Christ Jesus.' . . . If he had taken our mind, how, then, could we ever have been exhorted to 'let this mind be in you, which was also in Christ Jesus'? It would have been so already. But what kind of mind is ours? O, it is corrupted with sin also."[16]

Adam and Eve, Jones explained, "forsook the mind of Jesus" and accepted that of Satan. As a result, both they and we were "enslaved" to that mind.

Jesus came into the world with the flesh of Adam but the mind of God. He fought the battle at just the point where Adam lost—appetite. Thus he conquered Satan on his own ground, and "in Jesus Christ the mind of God is brought back once more to the sons of men; and Satan is conquered."[17]

Jesus never consented to sin with His mind, Jones claimed. His mind won over the flesh. Individuals can have that same mind by faith in Him through the indwelling of the Holy Spirit. They can therefore be "partakers of the divine nature." The solution is to be dependent upon God at all times. When individuals do this, "that mind which he gives to me will exercise in me the same faith it exercised in him."[18]

Jones's argument partly succeeded and partly failed in his attempt to explain how Christ's human nature did not differ "a particle" from ours, even though He did not possess our passions. A measure of success came from the fact that he managed to end his argument with Christ still possessing sinful flesh that had all the tendencies to sin experienced by every other human being. He also succeeded in that he demonstrated that the born-again Christian could have the mind of Christ through the indwelling of the Holy Spirit. The Christian, he argued, could have the same power through faith that Jesus had through faith. Jones's argument failed, however, in the sense that he had to admit that Jesus was not just like the non-Christian or the child who still had not accepted Christ by faith and, therefore, yet possessed the fallen mind of Adam. That failure, in the last count, meant that he had denied the premise that he had started with. He had been forced to admit that Jesus had "precisely our nature" only in terms of His flesh. He did not have our passions, because He did not have the fallen mind of Adam and Eve. In the end, therefore, Jones demonstrated that more than "a particle of difference" existed between Christ and other human beings.

While he may have lost his argument, he contributed many valuable insights, not the least of which is that a Christian can live the victorious life by being born from above by the Holy Spirit. In that is the secret of Christian living on the order of the 1888 message. At conversion a person can have the mind of Christ, something that Christ possessed, as Jones inferred in his argument, from His birth.

ELLEN WHITE CONFUSES THE ISSUE[19]

As noted earlier, the nature of Christ did not become a divisive issue in

Adventist circles until the 1950s. Between the mid-nineties up through that time the denomination's writers had been mostly in harmony with Jones, Waggoner, and Prescott that Christ had come in human flesh that had, like the fallen Adam's, all of humankind's tendencies to sin.

One major stimulus for a shift in the position of several denominational thought leaders in the 1950s was the "discovery" of the "Baker letter." Coupled with that was a sensitivity to the criticisms of certain evangelicals that Adventists "sinful tendencies" Christology was less than adequate.

Ellen White penned the controversial letter to W.L.H. Baker in early February 1896. Its recipient was an ordained minister in the Central Australian Conference who had worked with Jones and Waggoner at the Pacific Press in California in the 1880s. Since that letter has become so important in Adventist theological discussion, and since some scholars have seen it as an indirect rebuke to Jones, Waggoner, and Prescott, we will quote it at some length.

"*Be exceeding careful*," Ellen White wrote, "*how you dwell upon the human nature of Christ. Do not set Him before the people as a man with the propensities of sin.* He is the second Adam. The first Adam was created a pure, sinless being, without a taint of sin upon him; he was in the image of God. He could fall, and he did fall through transgressing. Because of sin, his posterity was born with inherent propensities of disobedience. *But* Jesus Christ was the only begotten Son of God. He took upon Himself human nature, and was tempted in all points as human nature is tempted. . . . But *not for one moment was there in Him an evil propensity.* . . .

"Bro. Baker, avoid every question in relation to the humanity of Christ which is liable to be misunderstood. . . . In treating upon the humanity of Christ, you need to guard strenuously every assertion, lest your words be taken to mean more than they imply, and thus you lose or dim the clear perceptions of His humanity as combined with divinity. His birth was a miracle of God; for, said the angel, 'Behold thou shalt conceive in thy womb, and bring forth a son, and shalt call His name Jesus. He shall be great and shall be called the son of the Highest'. . . .

"These words are not addressed to any human being, except to the Son of the infinite God. *Never, in any way, leave the slightest impression upon human minds that a taint of, or inclination to corruption rested upon Christ.* . . . The incarnation of Christ has ever been, and will ever remain a mystery. That which is revealed, is for us and for our children, but let every human being be warned from the ground of making Christ altogether human, such an one as ourselves; for it cannot be. . . .

"I perceive that there is danger in approaching subjects which dwell on the humanity of the Son of the infinite God. . . .

"*There are many questions treated upon that are not necessary for the perfection of the faith*. . . . Many things are above finite comprehension. . . .

"But every truth which is essential for us to bring into our practical life, which concerns the salvation of the soul, is made very clear and positive."[20]

Baker replied to Ellen White on March 6, 1896, thanking her for the letter, but without shedding any light on the exact nature of his "problem."[21]

Since the rediscovery of the Baker letter a great deal of controversy has arisen over its exact meaning. Many have been the explanations of the definition of "propensities." Some of them have been ingenious, while others have been contorted. Webster's dictionary, for whatever it is worth, says that propensity is "a natural inclination or tendency; bent." Ellen White appears at times to use the word in that way. In July 1889, for example, she wrote that "Satan is appealing to the lowest propensities of human nature. But these do not need cultivation. Like thistles and briars, selfishness, self-love, envying, jealousy, evil surmisings, self-esteem, will grow up luxuriantly if only left to themselves." A decade later she seemingly equated propensities with tendencies while discussing the unfallen Adam, who had "no corrupt propensities or tendencies to evil." In 1897 she made a related comment: "There should not be the faintest misgivings in regard to the perfect freedom from sinfulness in the human nature of Christ."[22]

In 1890 she made a similar statement in what appears to be a rebuke related to Waggoner's January 21, 1889, article in which he both asserted that Christ was born with "sinful tendencies" and repeatedly claimed that Christ could not sin, because he was the "manifestation of God." "As Christ," she wrote, "humbled Himself to the nature of man, He could be tempted. He had not taken on Him the nature of the angels, but humanity, perfectly identical with our own nature, except without the taint of sin. A human body, a human mind, with all the peculiar properties, He was bone, brain, and muscle. A man of our flesh, He was compassed with the weakness of humanity. . . .

"Our Lord was tempted as man is tempted. He was capable of yielding to temptation. . . .

"But here we must not become in our ideas common and earthly, and in our perverted ideas we *must not think* that the liability of Christ to yield to Satan's temptations degraded His humanity and *He possessed the same sinful, corrupt propensities as man*.

"The divine nature, combined with the human, made Him capable of yielding to Satan's temptations. Here the test of Christ was far greater than that of Adam and Eve, for *Christ took our nature, fallen but not corrupted.* . . . To suppose He was not capable of yielding to temptation places Him where He cannot be a perfect example for man, and the force and the power of this part of Christ's humiliation, which is the most eventful, is no instruction or help to human beings."[23]

Ellen White's statements on Christ not having fallen humanity's propensities to sin must be taken in the context of quotations that seem to imply the opposite. For example, in December 1896 (just a few months after the Baker letter), she published in the *Review* that Christ "took upon him our sinful nature." Then again, in 1900 she wrote that "he took upon himself fallen, suffering human nature, degraded and defiled by sin." Those were not isolated statements. In both May and September 1896, for instance, she claimed that Christ took our "fallen human nature."[24]

There is not the slightest doubt that Ellen White believed that Christ took upon Himself fallen, sinful human nature at the Incarnation. Whatever that nature consisted of, however, it is clear that it did not include any evil propensities to sin—those "thistles and briars" of selfishness, self-love, and so on.

That position harmonizes with other statements she made through the years on the topic. Children, she pointed out, do not have an "inborn inclination" to "do service for God." Christ, by way of contrast, had a natural inclination to do right. In 1898 she wrote that "*it is not correct to say, as many writers have said, that Christ was like all children. . . . His inclination to right was a constant gratification to his parents. . . .* He was an example of what all children may strive to be. . . . *No one,* looking upon the childlike countenance, shining with animation, *could say that Christ was just like other children.*"[25]

In *Education* she commented that humans (including children) have "a bent to evil." On the other hand, as we have already noted, Christ had a bent toward good. Human children can get their bent corrected only through surrendering their wills to God, being "born from above," and accepting the power of the Holy Spirit in their lives.[26] Then they partake of the divine nature.

Even then, however, they are still not exactly like Christ in His humanity, because they have brought into their new spiritual life their past sinful habits and their well-developed tendencies, whereas Christ never had that distorting baggage. On the other hand, after being "born from above," they have the same power that He had to eradicate those sinful habits. That is the work of sanctification or character development. All born-from-above human beings thus fight on the same ground as Christ did. They can be thankful that "Christ did nothing that human nature may not do if it partakes of the divine nature."[27]

Notwithstanding that encouragement, Ellen White pointed out a paradox in 1895: (1) Despite the fact that "divine power was not given to Him in a different way to what it will be given to us," yet (2) "we can never equal the pattern" even though "we may imitate and resemble it." That paradox may find its roots in the reality that Christ never had to be sanctified in the same way other people do because He was unlike other children in their inborn inclination to wrong.[28]

In the long run Ellen White's statements, as noted above, moved in the same direction that Jones's argument took once he had to deal with the quotation that claimed that Christ did not have our passions. Each of them ended up by inferring that the inclinations and/or mind of Christ in His humanity were different from those of other children. Both Jones and Ellen White believed that Christ had "sinful nature," but Jones tried to include more in the "sinful" than she did. In that he failed in 1895, but that did not convince him to change his position. He continued to teach that Christ had sinful tendencies in His flesh,[29] a position that Ellen White had never explicitly stated, even though people could interpret many of her statements on the subject that way if they left out or redefined other of her comments.

Perhaps the best avenue to understanding her meaning of "propensities" is by seeing how one of the authors she used to prepare some of her material on the Incarnation employed the word. Henry Melvill was one of Ellen White's favorite writers. Several of her works indicate their mutual agreement on various points. The Ellen G. White Estate has her marked copy of

Melvill's Sermons. Tim Poirier, of the White Estate, has analyzed her use of him. His sermon "The Humiliation of the Man Christ Jesus," Poirier points out, is especially helpful in enabling us to understand and reconcile the apparent conflict in Ellen White's statements on the humanity of Christ. According to Melvill, the fall had two basic consequences: (1) "innocent infirmities," and (2) "sinful propensities." "By 'innocent infirmities,'" Poirier writes, "Melvill understands such characteristics as hunger, pain, weakness, sorrow, and death. 'There are consequences on guilt which are perfectly guiltless. Sin introduces pain, but pain itself is not sin' (p. 47). By 'sinful propensities' Melvill refers to the proneness or tendency to sin. In his summary of the discussion, Melvill makes it clear that, in his view, Adam had neither 'innocent infirmities' nor 'sinful propensities'; we are born with both, and Christ took the first but not the second."[30]

In other words, Melvill held that the incarnate Christ was neither just like Adam before the Fall or just like fallen humanity since the Fall (see figure 1). That appears to be the position Ellen White held, and it was

The Results of Sin	Adam Before the Fall	Adam After the Fall (and all people since then)	Christ
1. Innocent Infirmities	No	Yes	Yes
2. Sinful Propensities	No	Yes	No

FIGURE 1
Summary of Melvill's Understanding
of the Human Nature of Christ

certainly the one that Jones had to take in 1895, even though he later wrote as if he had never argued himself into that position. It might be convincingly conjectured that he never fully saw the complete implications of his 1895 argument.

We should note that Melvill's explanation fits quite nicely Ellen White's statement that caused Jones so much trouble at the 1895 General Conference session: Christ "is *a brother in our infirmities* [Melvill's 'innocent infirmities'], *but not in possessing like passions* [Mellvill's 'sinful propensities']." Similar statements are that Christ "was a mighty petitioner, *not possessing the passions* of our human, fallen natures, *but compassed with like infirmities*," that "Christ took upon Him the *infirmities* of degenerate humanity" as part of a 4,000 year inheritance, and that "Christ, who *knew not the least moral taint or defilement* of sin, took our nature in its deteriorated condition. . . . By taking upon Himself man's nature in its fallen condition, . . . He was subject to the *infirmities* and weaknesses of the flesh with which humanity is encompassed."[31]

Melvill's typology definitely fits Ellen White's use of similar concepts. His model is the only one that explains *all* of her statements on the human nature of Christ.

POSSIBLE CONNECTIONS BETWEEN JONES AND THE BAKER LETTER

Some students have hypothesized a connection between Jones and the Baker letter. That is not an impossibility. After all, his sermons were the central feature of the 1895 *General Conference Bulletin* and Ellen White composed the Baker letter in early 1896. O. A. Olsen wrote to Jones in the first part of the conference to express his appreciation that his studies were "written out so fully, and printed in the Bulletin [sic], to be sent out to our people in all parts of the world." Adventists in Australia looked forward to the *Bulletin* with anticipation. A. G. Daniells noted that the 1891 *Bulletin* sent "mighty pulsations . . . around the globe." Church members were "fairly convulsed" with the power of the messages as they read them. Correspondence indicates that the *Bulletins* of 1893 and 1895 received equal enthusiasm. Their messages were definitely influential.[32]

From what we know, it is quite probable that Baker, as an American missionary, shared that enthusiasm for the *Bulletin*. If so, Jones's sermons would have been fresh in his mind in the latter half of 1895. It is not necessary to prove that point, however, because the teachings of Prescott, Waggoner, and Jones on the sinful tendencies of Christ's human nature permeated the Adventist air in the mid-nineties. Beyond that, Ellen White had several times in the previous few years written articles for the Australian *Bible Echo* that pointed out that Jesus "came in the likeness of human flesh" and in the "likeness of sinful flesh."[33] It is important to note that while her many statements in the *Echo*, *Review*, and other places *could be interpreted* to support the Jones-Waggoner-Prescott wording of "sinful tendencies," she did not use that terminology, and one definitely would have to understand her words in other ways in the light of the Baker letter and the other statements cited earlier in the chapter.

Prescott was probably an especially strong influence on Baker in 1895, since he had been in Australia for much of the year. On October 31 Prescott preached a rousing sermon at the Armadale camp meeting on righteousness by faith in which several times he alluded to the fact that Christ had the same flesh we have—"flesh of sin." Ellen White praised the sermon, observing that "Professor Prescott gave a most valuable lesson, precious as gold." She was overjoyed with his preaching of justification by faith, and that he had centered every aspect of the Adventist message on Christ. There was, she wrote, "hardly a discourse . . . given during the whole [camp] meeting that could be called a doctrinal sermon. In every sermon Christ was preached." The *Echo* later published Prescott's sermon in the January 6 and 13, 1896, issues.[34]

In light of the above discussion, it is plain that Baker had several lines of exposure to the Jones-Waggoner-Prescott "sinful tendencies" thesis by 1895. Jones was only one possible influence through his *Bulletin* sermons.

At this point, it is important to ask if Ellen White's approval of Prescott's sermon meant that she endorsed all that he may have said or implied in it. If we measure that question by her attitude toward Waggoner at the 1888 General Conference session, the answer is a resounding NO! On November 1, 1888, she flatly told the assembled delegates that "*some interpretations of Scripture, given by Dr. Waggoner, I do not regard as correct.*"[35] She did not specify where she believed he was wrong, but she certainly did not give him a blank check, even though she claimed that he was God's chosen servant, preaching God's message on justification by faith. Likewise, in 1895 she never explicitly stated that she was in full support of Prescott's Christology, but she did emphasize that he had the truth of salvation through Christ's grace and that he had put Christ at the center of his message. To say more than that is to read her endorsement with a great deal of interpretation. We should also remember, as seen in our previous discussion on the views of Ellen White, that "flesh of sin" (and related concepts) is open to more than one explanation.

Some students of the topic have suggested that Ellen White sought to rebuke Jones, Waggoner, and/or Prescott through Baker. But we have no evidence for that argument. It is true that she often did censure a collective teaching through personal letters written to a third party, but generally she had such letters quite widely circulated, as in the reprimand of the African land-grant problem through a letter to Haskell. The Baker letter, to the contrary, was a private one that never received circulation. If it had, we would find signs of it in the correspondence as individuals discussed it with each other. The truth is that the Baker letter was a reproof to Baker himself.

That conclusion leads to an obvious question. If Ellen White rebuked Baker—a little-known minister—for teaching things related to the Jones-Waggoner-Prescott thesis, why didn't she do the same to the giants in that viewpoint? The answer is probably twofold, if, in fact, Baker was espousing the same doctrines as they were. (This last point cannot be proved conclusively, even though it is highly probable.)

First, *Ellen White's role was not that of a theological policewoman,* even though many twenty-first century Adventists seem to have that view. She did not see herself as the theological arbiter, as noted earlier, in either the 1888 problem involving Galatians nor in the "daily" crisis that arose in the early twentieth century. Nor did she rebuke Waggoner and Kellogg's pantheism, which was evident in the 1897 *General Conference Bulletin.* The same goes for the whole issue of Adventist semi-Arianism and anti-Trinitarianism that had existed for decades without substantial reproof. She did not believe it was her role to refute every idea that she did not agree with. In 1890 she frankly observed that "there are errors in the church, and the Lord points them out by His own ordained agencies, *not always through the testimonies.*"[36]

Ellen White, contrary to our often mistaken impressions, was frequently silent on even serious issues. She often refrained from speaking until she had a definite word from the Lord on a subject. Thus she did not comment on the potentially destructive Anna Rice situation. She wrote to Elder Rice on November 1, 1893, that "letters have come to me presenting before me the case of Sr. Phillips [Rice], and inquiries have been made to me [concerning] what I thought of the matter. *I have not felt called out to encourage or condemn so long as I had no special light in reference to this case. . . . I decided to let the matter develop.*" To Jones she stated in January

1894 that she had left it up to the denominational leaders to correct the problem. Three months later she told Prescott and Jones that she had kept silent on the issue until "the Spirit of God . . . pressed me to speak."[37]

Her lack of comment on Jones and his colleagues' extremes in regard to deliberately breaking Sunday laws by publicly working is a similar situation. For years she held her peace, even though scores of Adventists went to prison. Her silence, however, did not mean agreement, although some may have interpreted it that way. In November 1895 she spoke to the topic in a way that eventually reversed the denomination's approach to the problem. She gave that counsel at a time when continuing the old policy would develop a crisis situation.[38]

From the above illustrations it should be obvious that it is not safe to rely on the silence of Ellen White to substantiate a position. J. H. Kellogg, however, used that very method with her in his pantheism. Because she did not make an issue of the topic in the late 1890s and early 1900s, he assumed that she agreed with him. That conclusion, as he eventually discovered, was far from the truth.[39]

A second possible reason why Ellen White reproved Baker rather than Jones and his associates is that the former may have gone to greater extremes in his teachings on the nature of Christ and, more important, he was doing actual harm in his particular context. After all, he was working among a people prejudiced against his American religion and who had some doubts as to whether Adventists were really Christians.[40] Her awareness of factors in Baker's specific situation may have stimulated her to write him a personal letter. By way of contrast, she may not have responded to the issue in general because she viewed other problems to be of greater importance.

Ellen White's letter to Baker hints of that possibility. "There are many questions treated upon," she wrote, "that are not necessary for the perfection of the faith. . . . But every truth which is essential for us to bring into our *practical life, which concerns the salvation of the soul,* is made very clear and positive."[41]

It appears that while Adventist theologians in the 1890s catered to dogmatism in their teachings, Ellen White was more interested in the practical application of Christianity to individual lives. To put it bluntly, she was not overly concerned with some of the doctrinal sidelines that stimulated ministers and laymen to aggressive and/or defensive heights. Her interest centered, as it had at Minneapolis, on whether people knew Jesus and had applied His grace to their lives so that they could reflect His loving character. While she staunchly defended the theological pillars of Adventism, she was not especially interested in debating the fine points of theology.

---

[1] EGW to J. E. White, Sept. 25, 1895.

[2] *ST*, Jan. 21, 1889, p. 39; EJW, *Christ and His Righteousness* (Oakland, 1890), pp. 21, 22.

[3] EJW, *The Gospel in the Book of Galatians*, p. 61; *ST*, Jan. 21, 1889, pp. 38, 39.

[4] M. L. Andreasen, partial autobiography, quoted in Virginia Steinweg, *Without Fear or Favor: The Life of M. L. Andreasen* (Washington, D.C., 1979), pp. 51, 52; M. L. Andreasen, *Letters to the Churches*, reprinted, (Payson, Ariz., 1980) pp. 10, 11, 18.

[5] *RH*, July 17, 1888, p. 449. On the larger issue of theological authority in the Minneapolis era, see Knight, *Angry Saints*, pp. 100-115.

[6] 1893 *GCB*, pp. 207, 301; *RH*, Feb. 18, 1896, pp. 104, 105; Nov. 16, 1897, p. 728; Apr. 11, 18, 1899, pp. 232, 248; Oct. 2, Dec. 11, 18, 25, 1900, pp. 633, 792, 808, 824; Jan. 1, 22, 1901, pp. 8, 56.

[7] EJW, *The Gospel in the Book of Galatians*, p. 61; 1895 *GCB*, p. 330; Jones's earliest extensive treatment on the topic seems to be recorded in the manuscript of his sermon presented at the Battle Creek Tabernacle on July 14, 1894.

[8] 1895 *GCB*, pp. 231, 233, 436.

[9] *Ibid.*, pp. 192, 191.

[10] *Ibid.*, pp. 233, 333, 266, 267.

[11] *Ibid.*, p. 302; *BE*, Nov. 30, 1896, pp. 370, 371; Sermon by ATJ at the Tabernacle, unpub. MS, July 14, 1894.

[12] *RH*, Nov. 16, 1897, p. 728; *BE*, Nov. 30, 1896, pp. 370, 371; ATJ, *The Consecrated Way to Christian Perfection* (Mountain View, Calif., 1905), p. 40.

[13] 1895 *GCB*, p. 303.

[14] *Ibid.*, pp. 377, 267, 433; ATJ, *Consecrated Way*, p. 84.

[15] 1897 *GCB*, p. 279.

[16] EGW, *Testimonies*, vol. 2, p. 202; 1895 *GCB*, pp. 312, 327. (Ital. sup.)

[17] 1895 *GCB*, p. 327.

[18] *Ibid.*, pp. 328-331.

[19] For a comprehensive study of all of EGW's published and unpublished statements on the human nature of Christ, see Woodrow W. Whidden II, *Ellen White on the Humanity of Christ: A Chronological Study* (Hagerstown, Md., 1997).

[20] EGW to Brother and Sister Baker, [Feb. 9, 1896; by mistake this letter was designated as B-8, 1895, but both internal and external evidence demonstrates an 1896 date]. (Ital. sup.)

[21] W.L.H. Baker to EGW, Mar. 6, 1896.

[22] EGW to Elds. Madison and H. Miller, July 23, 1889; EGW to GAI and SNH, Nov. 1899; EGW, MS 143, [December] 1897.

[23] *ST*, Jan. 21, 1889, pp. 38, 39; EGW, MS 57, 1890. (Ital. sup.)

[24] *RH*, Dec. 15, 1896, p. 789; *YI* Dec. 20, 1900, p. 394; *RH*, Sept. 29, 1896, p. 613;

EGW to OAO, May 31, 1896.

[25] EGW, *Counsels to Parents, Teachers, and Students* (Mountain View, Calif., 1913), p. 20; *YI*, Sept. 8, 1898, pp. 704, 705. (Ital. sup.)

[26] EGW, *Education* (Mountain View, Calif., 1952), pp. 29, 30; EGW, *Steps to Christ* (Mountain View, Calif., n.d.), pp. 18, 19.

[27] *ST*, June 17, 1897, p. 357.

[28] EGW, MS 21, November 1895; *RH*, Feb. 5, 1895, p. 81. Cf. EGW, *Testimonies*, vol. 2, p. 549. (Ital. sup.)

[29] E.g., ATJ, *Consecrated Way*, pp. 40, 41; see also note 6 above.

[30] Henry Melvill, *Melvill's Sermons* (New York, 1849), vol. 1, pp. 40-51; Tim Poirier, "A Comparison of the Christology of Ellen G. White and Henry Melvill," unpub. MS, Apr. 5, 1982 (published version in *Ministry*, Dec. 1989, pp. 7-9).

[31] EGW, *Testimonies*, vol. 2, p. 202; *RH*, May 19, 1885, p. 305; Aug. 17, 1886, p. 513; EGW, *The Desire of Ages*, (Mountain View, Calif., 1940), p. 117; EGW, MS 143, Dec. 12, 1897.

[32] OAO to ATJ, Feb. 7, 1895; 1901 *GCB*, p. 272; AGD to OAO, Feb. 17, May 14, 1893; EGW to SNH, May 12, 1893; OAO to WCW, Mar. 28, 1895; OAO to EGW, Feb. 27, 1895.

[33] E.g., *BE*, Sept. 15, Dec. 15, 1892, pp. 274, 370; Aug. 1, 1893, p. 242; Apr. 22, 1895, p. 123.

[34] *BE*, Jan. 6, 13, 1896, pp. 4, 5, 12, 13; *RH*, Jan. 7, 1896, p. 1.

[35] EGW, MS 15, Nov. 1, 1888.

[36] EGW to Brother and Sister Garmire, [Aug. 6], 1890. (Ital. sup.)

[37] EGW to Brother and Sister Rice, Nov. 1, 1893; EGW to ATJ, Jan. 14, 1894; EGW to WWP and ATJ, Apr. 16. 1894.

[38] EGW, MS 22a, Nov. 20, 1895; EGW to ATJ, Nov. 21, 1895.

[39] JHK to WCW, Dec. 6, 1903; JHK to EGW, Dec. 10, 1903.

[40] AGD to OAO, Nov. 22, 1895.

[41] EGW to W.L.H. Baker, [Feb. 9, 1896]. (Ital. sup.)

CHAPTER XII

CHARISMATIC EMPHASIS FROM THE CENTER: A. T. JONES AT THE PINNACLE OF POWER

By late 1897 A. T. Jones had reached the peak of his "official power" in his denominational career. The 1897 General Conference session had placed him for the first time on the powerful, 12-member General Conference Committee. Then, a few months later, he became editor of the *Review and Herald*, probably the most influential post in nineteenth-century Adventism.

From those authoritative positions Jones would seek to initiate and carry out reform of the denomination and its institutions. The very visibility and possibilities inherent in his positions, however, probably hastened his demise as an Adventist leader of the first rank. His impetuous nature, his caustic pen, his harsh treatment of people, and his bent toward logical extremism made it difficult for him to maintain credibility with both the church's leadership and its membership. Many of the same attributes that contributed to his success as a charismatic force in the church led to his failure when he sought to operate in the same way in the real world of formal power in which one had to make concrete decisions that would stand the test of everyday life.

Having tried and failed as an official (as opposed to charismatic) leader for four years, the year 1901 would find him on a downhill toboggan to disaster that was almost as rapid as his rise to prominence in the late 1880s. Absolutely certain that he was always right, Jones never could understand why the denomination could not follow him in his every reform right into the kingdom. Early in the new century he would become embittered, especially against A. G. Daniells and the new leadership—men

184

whose ideas differed from his. His bitterness would eventually lead him to conclude that the entire denomination, including Ellen White, had apostatized, and that he was the true Adventist. Such were the fruits of his extremist and arrogant tendencies—tendencies that his more courageous associates and Ellen White had sought to correct for nearly two decades.

The four years extending from 1897 to 1901, then, were his period of official power. One might plausibly argue that he had reached his peak of unofficial, charismatic strength in early 1894. At that time he was in line for official leadership, but his involvement in the Anna Rice crisis delayed that step for three years. Jones needed to be "laundered," and his credibility needed to be reestablished. Thus the period between 1895 and 1897 was one of transition. He went into that time as a charismatic leader, and would emerge from it in duly appointed leadership.

YEARS OF TRANSITION, 1895-1897

By early 1895 Jones sensed that he needed a change in his duties. Writing to Ellen White in late March, he noted that for some time he had felt that he had labored long enough in the English speaking work. Having been studying German, and thinking that he might evangelize and write for the Germans in the United States, he queried her to find out if she had any light on the topic. Jones also talked to O. A. Olsen about his plan, but the president soon put a stop to that. Olsen felt that Jones should labor in broader fields.[1]

That, however, did not mean that he believed that Jones could continue as before. Something had to change. The Battle Creek situation had become untenable. Jones and Prescott had been bickering with Uriah Smith for years, with both sides sharing fault. W. C. White, writing from Australia, sympathized with Olsen: "You stand just now in the position of a step-father to a big family of boys, who have been working rather independently, and who are now asked to work in union. Each one thinks he knows how matters ought to be, and quotes past experience to show that every move now being made is out of order."[2]

The solution was to break up the Battle Creek factions, perhaps by sending the three key men overseas for a time. None of them had international experience, even though the denomination was rapidly becoming a world church. Their lack of perspective had caused real difficulties, such as the

African land-grant problem, which might not have reached the crisis stage if more of the American leadership had had a broader outlook. A tour overseas would also get them out of each other's hair for a while. Smith was the first to begin his course in internationalism. He left in mid-1894 for a tour of Europe and the Near East. Olsen hoped that he could make some major changes in the editorial program of the *Review* in Smith's absence. His real desire was to change editors, but the only likely replacement—A. T. Jones—had recently discredited himself by supporting Anna Rice.[3] Since the church had no other viable alternatives, Smith resumed the editorship upon returning from Europe.

Jones and Prescott received their orders for experience enlarging field education in 1895. Prescott went to Australia, as the first leg of a trip around the world, while Jones toured 16 nations in Europe and the Near East. The General Conference president told him to stay in Europe "as long as he wished." He departed on May 8, 1895, and returned to Battle Creek 10 months later on March 8, 1896.[4]

As we might expect, Jones found high adventure in Europe. He and H. P. Hosler, president of the Adventist program in central Europe, traveled fourth class in the Mediterranean, which meant that they slept on the open deck. In addition, they got arrested and put under armed guard in Turkey, being suspected as Armenian partisans in a highly explosive political situation. That did not stop them, however. They continued to wander fearlessly without protection in Turkey, even though the Armenian Christians "said it was hardly safe to go out of the house," let alone "to be found out walking upon the hills." Through all of their adventures, Hosler wrote, "Brother Jones seems to be in his element." He could still play the part of a frontier soldier.[5]

The charismatic Jones not only did well in roughing it, but also made his impression on titled persons. He and Hosler, for example, spent three days with Count Papengouth on the isle of Capri. Jones gave the Count daily Bible studies. Papengouth, who had once traveled all the way to England just to hear D. L. Moody preach, stated that in 20 years he had "never been so blessed in Bible study as during our short stay." In gratitude, he offered to pay all of Jones's expenses for a trip to Palestine after the Adventist minister finished his work in England. We have no record of Jones's response to that generous offer.[6]

Did the tour accomplish its task in broadening him? It probably never hurt him, but S. N. Haskell was still fuming in 1900 that a trip clear around the world might wise him up on political issues.[7] The truth seems to be that Jones was an incurable American. He continued to write as if the United States form of government was the norm, and he persisted in interpreting world church and state issues in the light of the First Amendment to the United States Constitution. On the other hand, Prescott began to lose his provincialism. Their varying responses to broader experiences probably contributed to their eventual animosity toward each other in the early twentieth century in the realms of both spirituality and practicality.

One immediate result of Jones's overseas tour was that the General Conference Committee asked him to write several textbooks for use in Adventist colleges that would allow students to study history from the perspective of the Bible. His teaching along those lines in Europe had so impressed Hosler that he had recommended to the committee on March 17, 1896, that it allow Jones time to write his history books. The committee passed Hosler's recommendation the next day.[8]

Jones spent most of the remainder of 1896 in historical writing. His 410-page *Empires of the Bible* came off the press by the end of the year. In 1898 his 696-page *Great Empires of Prophecy* and in 1901 his 874-page *Ecclesiastical Empire* joined it. Those three volumes traced the history of the world, from the Bible perspective, from the Flood up through the 1890s.

The transition years of 1896 and 1897 saw a persistent call for Jones to go to Australia to direct the church's religious liberty program as the emerging nation developed its constitution, which most believed would contain a clause uniting church and state in some way. W. C. White opined that the constitutional discussions would provide an unprecedented opportunity to get Adventism before legislative bodies and the public.[9]

Olsen blocked the Australian proposition in 1896 on the grounds that Jones had just returned from Europe, he needed to finish his history books, and he had to attend the General Conference session in early 1897. George A. Irwin, elected as General Conference president in 1897, initially was agreeable to his going that year, but other needs for Jones's labors soon superseded the summons to Australia.[10]

Part of Irwin's eventual reluctance stemmed from the fact that Jones had recently been reappointed as editor of the *American Sentinel* because its subscription list was falling off and the magazine required livening up. His appointment had not been without controversy. A. F. Ballenger and C. P. Bollman, two of Jones's earlier editorial colleagues on the *Sentinel,* were both wrought up over his extremism on Christians not being citizens of the earthly nation in which they resided, a position, they believed, that not even Jones's circular logic could line up with either the testimonies of Ellen White or living in the day-to-day world.[11]

Bollman was particularly explicit in his warning, writing that "I esteem Brother Jones as highly as any man in the denomination, but I do think that past experiences ought to make us careful about being led by him into extreme positions. He was wrong on the Rice testimonies, and yet was just as sure he was right as he is now . . . on this question [of citizenship]. He, in company with myself, was wrong in regard to the landgrant in Africa, and he still sticks to it that we were right. He was wrong in the extreme position taken in regard to the taxation of church property. He was wrong in carrying his opposition to exemption clauses to the extent of protesting against their enactment where they were freely offered by the State of Tennessee. He was wrong in holding that our brethren could not work extra time to pay for . . . keeping the Sabbath in the chain-gang, and further, that as they could not work the extra time they could not work at all in the chain-gang; and that to work to pay for keeping the Sabbath was the same as to work on the Sabbath itself. When his words were read before Sister White she said, 'That is strange fire.'

"Now I have not a word to say against Brother Jones, but I do earnestly protest against his being allowed to stampede the whole denomination upon this question [of citizenship], and that in the wrong direction. Would it not be better for us to possess our citizenship 'in sanctification and honor' rather than to renounce it entirely?

"Do not misunderstand me, I do not ask that any man be muzzled, I only ask that the influence of the General Conference be not given to this extreme view which even Elder Jones does not and cannot follow out consistently in practice."

Ballenger, for his part, pointed out that truth in the *Sentinel* was more important than increasing the subscription list. But Jones became editor in spite of such protests.[12]

A weightier reason prohibiting his going to Australia in 1897 was that he accepted the editorship of the *Review and Herald* on September 24.

REVIEW AND HERALD EDITOR

Major dissatisfaction with Smith's conservative editorial policy had been in evidence since 1893. At that time some suggested that he was "too slow," "not original enough," and "did not get out of the ruts." Olsen and others definitely wanted him replaced in 1894. Much of the problem stemmed from the continual controversy between Jones and Smith over prophetic interpretation and other issues. Smith's reactionary stance on the image to the beast development in 1892 alienated large numbers of progressive Adventists. For years the *Review* carried little from Jones's pen, even though it listed him as a member of the editorial staff for part of that time. His general articles during those years appeared most often in the *Home Missionary*. As a result, to the dissatisfaction of many, an unhealthy rivalry broke out between the two papers. The *Review* ended up on the losing end in the battle between them for subscriptions.[13]

Their respective trips to Europe must have softened the feelings between Smith and Jones somewhat. Beginning in August 1896, the *Review* printed Jones's articles with regularity in an attempt to bolster its circulation. That move, however, did not stem the growing tide of criticism with Smith's editorial policy. The spring 1897 meeting of the General Conference Committee took up the editorial problem on several different days, finally summoning Smith to meet with them and to explain his position on certain controverted points. Jones told Smith before the committee that his editorials definitely needed improvement. Irwin and Hosler expressed concern that "the trumpet should be given a certain sound; [and] that the paper should be a true exponent of the progress of the third angel's message." At the conclusion of the March 28 meeting, the committee reluctantly reappointed Smith as editor.[14]

The problem surfaced again at its autumn meeting. Subscriptions had continued to decline. A. O. Tait pointed out that the readers wanted "live issues for this time." Irwin reiterated the need to give the trumpet a certain sound. And Jones incriminated Smith by declaring that "the editorial columns of the *Review* have failed to contain the third angel's message for the last six years." Until that changed, he proclaimed, the *Review* would not prosper. The next day, September 24, 1897, the committee appointed Jones to the editorship. Smith, who had served the *Review* for more than four decades, would be his associate.[15]

That appointment must have been the ultimate victory for Jones and the ultimate defeat for Smith in their long war with each other. Surprisingly enough, however, they seemed to work well together. The fact that Smith had been ill since his trip to the Near East, and that he was tired of struggling with the continuing subscription problem, all may have contributed to their harmony.[16]

Jones's task was clearly pointed out. He had a mandate to preach the message with a definite ring. "Now," the directors of the *Review* touted in announcing the change, "instead of speaking to comparatively few of our people in annual gatherings, he will address *all* of them *every week.*"[17]

As we might expect, Jones's new position delighted him. With characteristic "modesty," he claimed that he had been divinely appointed to the task. For years, he told the General Conference Committee afterward, he had been convicted that he was destined to be editor of the *Review*. He saw the position as a power base from which to reform the church. But not everyone was happy with the editorial change. It discouraged Ellen White, for example, and she would weep for joy when Smith once again assumed the office in 1901.[18]

The new editor did everything in his power to bring renewed life to the old *Review*. During his years as editor the paper featured illustrated articles on current events as signs of the times and it prolifically supported educational and health reform. Jones's editorials also sought to preach the message. For years he weekly editorialized on the denomination's need of the Holy Spirit for power in Christian living. He also ran shorter (up to one year in length) series on such topics as the gospel in Galatians, educational reform, Christian patriotism (including an exposure to his concept of Christian citizenship), the third angel's message, and current events in the light of prophecy. In short, he did his best to provide the readers with editorials and articles on topics that stood at the center of progressive Adventism.

Beyond contributing to the relevance of the content of the *Review*, Jones had an extremely active policy to bring in new subscribers. He not only sought to "hook" them with meaningful series of articles and editorials, but he also used more personal methods of bridging the gap between himself and his readers. Early in his editorship, for instance, he sent personal letters to each subscriber in an attempt to create a family feeling. That program, he claimed, had a very positive effect—one that a twenty-first-century reader, living in the age of massive junk mail, might not be able to appreciate.[19]

We should view his early editorship of the *Review* as a success. The contents of the paper greatly improved, and by February 1898 he had increased the subscription list by more than 20 percent. The General Conference president felt convinced that they had made the right choice in selecting him to be editor.[20]

Irwin's joyfulness, however, would not last. By 1900 he was berating Jones's "natural tendencies to *sharpness* and *combativeness,* because it not only does harm to people who are not acquainted with our truth, but it is also *causing him to lose his influence among even our own people.*"[21]

Irwin was not the only one concerned with the editor's sharp tongue. Ellen White pleaded with him to dip his pen "into the holy oil of grace and love." She particularly reacted to his antagonistic style, which, she lamented, was "natural" to him. Through his coarse, harsh words he often bruised souls. Worse yet, the "drops of gall" in some of his writings infected and "poisoned" many of his readers. Too often, she wrote to him, they talked and acted just like A. T. Jones. "Thus the evil is multiplied." "We may talk of the blessings of the Holy Spirit," she penned to Jones in obvious reference to his extensive editorials on the topic, "and pray in regard to receiving them; but unless the human agent is worked by the Spirit of God, he reveals that he has Him not. . . . Your entire being needs the divine touch." His harsh treatment of the Women's Christian Temperance Union especially upset her. That course of action, she wrote, had "nearly cut off all opportunity for us to work for this people."[22]

Ellen White never claimed that Jones was not proclaiming the truth, but she did indicate that his approach was not helpful. He was one who prided himself in telling the "straight truth." Other people's response, as he saw it, was their problem. Ellen White was more interested in results that won people to Christ than in the straight, often harsh, truth.[23] For her the central aspect of the gospel message was Christian love. From that perspective, Jones failed as both an editor and as a reformer.

Unfortunately, too many "reformers" entrap themselves in the same fate as Jones. The problem is doubly unfortunate, since whatever reforms they do achieve through harshness can hardly be called Christian. That truth, it seems, is at the very center of the 1888 message with its emphasis on the love of God and the spirit of Jesus.

THE ADVENTIST HOLINESS MOVEMENT

The theme that most often characterized Jones's *Review* editorials was the reception of the Holy Spirit to empower believers to live the Christian life. To him, the Lord had been leading His people step by step. The first step was the preaching of righteousness by faith at the 1888 General Conference session. The second step, Jones and other Adventists taught intensively from 1897 through the turn of the century, was the gift of the Holy Spirit. That truth, Jones stated in 1898, "is the message for to-day."[24]

He and his Adventist associates were not alone in their holiness emphasis. American Protestantism in general, and Methodism in particular, experienced a holiness revival in the post Civil War period. It reached its peak in the 1890s. "Within the last twenty years," C. I. Schofield commented with a great deal of plausibility in 1899, "more has been written and said upon the doctrine of the Holy Spirit than in the preceding eighteen hundred years."[25]

The holiness preachers emphasized perfect holiness (complete sanctification) and the Holy Spirit's work in the life of the believer. As it grew in strength during the late 1880s and early 1890s, the holiness movement spawned a large number of new denominations, including the Church of the Nazarene, the Christian and Missionary Alliance, and various Church of God groups. The years between 1894 and 1900 saw at least 10 separate religious bodies organize with sanctification as their major doctrine. The turn of the century would see even more radical groups arise, notably the Pentecostals and the Assemblies of God.[26]

Jones and his colleagues were quite aware of the trends in the larger religious world. Adventists, for example, were familiar with Hannah Whitall Smith's *Christian's Secret of a Happy Life*. Jones discussed it at the 1893 General Conference session, and the *Review* had a handsome advertisement for it in 1896. By that time both the Pacific Press and the Review and Herald Publishing Association were marketing the book, which was rapidly becoming a holiness classic. In 1898 Jones also indicated that he had been studying the Keswick movement (the leading holiness group in England) and Frederick B. Meyer's ideas for two or three years. Their teachings on Christian living, he suggested, were just good Adventist ideas with fancy names. He also included frequent excerpts from *The King's Messenger* (a holiness journal related to Methodism) in the *Review*. In fact, *The King's Messenger* was by far the most quoted non-Adventist journal during his editorship.[27] Of course, as we saw in chapter 7 and will see in chapter 12, Jones was also in tune with the faith healing and ecclesiological principles of the holiness movement.

Charismatic Jones, as we might expect, was quite susceptible to emotional expression in religion. During the 1892 revival at the Michigan camp meeting, for example, Jones and Prescott wept for joy on the platform and praised God "aloud for what God was doing." A year later at the General Conference session Jones told the delegates that perhaps it was time for Adventists to "praise the Lord, or say, 'Praise the Lord,' in meeting." One of the clearest illustrations of his holiness bent took place when he called for a "praise meeting" at the conclusion of one of his sermons at the 1895 General Conference session. The editor of the *Bulletin* summarized the audience response: "Here followed a praise-meeting, of which a Baptist minister who was present, seeing the large numbers praising God all at once, remarked: 'Some might be ready to say that such a number of voices makes confusion. But with all speaking together the praises of the Lord, surely, the Lord and the angels see only perfect harmony, and so do we.'"[28]

Ellen White from time to time warned Jones not to seek to create excessive feeling in his preaching, noting that he relied too much on emotion himself. To Prescott and Jones she wrote in 1894 that if they worked "to create an excitement of feeling," they would soon have more than they could "possibly know how to manage."[29]

Jones was not alone in the Adventist holiness movement. As noted earlier, "Receive Ye the Holy Ghost" was the theme of the 1897 camp meetings. At the forefront of the movement with him was A. F. Ballenger, who published *Power for Witnessing* in 1900, and Mrs. S.M.I. Henry, whose *Abiding Spirit* came off the press in 1898.[30] Ellen White also wrote a great deal on the Holy Spirit during the 1890s.

The same week that Jones became editor of the *Review*, Ballenger began a "Receive Ye the Holy Ghost" revival in the Battle Creek Tabernacle. Jones

ATJ-7

was his primary preaching assistant, speaking, for example, on October 2, 1897, on "the relation of righteousness by faith to the baptism of the Holy Spirit, which it is now time to receive." By January 11, 1898, Ballenger could report 240 baptisms and a genuine spiritual revival in Battle Creek. From Battle Creek he took his message to Union College and then to Boulder, Colorado. In both places he witnessed "sweeping" public confessions. "These are," Ballenger observed, "a few manifestations of God's earnest work in clearing the King's highway, in order that he may baptize his people with power from on high." He had previously preached his message with great success in Pennsylvania, Ohio, Illinois, and Indiana. Both Ballenger and Jones saw the new revival as a continuation of the aborted latter rain revival of 1893.[31]

It was in Indiana that Adventist holiness became Adventist Pentecostalism in what we now know as the holy flesh movement. The holy flesh concept had sprouted and grown in the soil of the "Receive Ye the Holy Ghost" message. Jones had undoubtedly stimulated some of the holy flesh excesses, even though he was not in harmony with the movement. It is significant that R. S. Donnell, the Indiana Conference president, had treated Jones as his mentor for his ideas regarding the latter rain in 1896. Also Jones had preached the key holy flesh doctrines of "translation faith" and "the power to overcome every tendency to sin" at least as early as 1889 and 1895, respectively. Most pertinent, perhaps, is the fact that he taught holy flesh through his *Review* editorials in 1898. On November 22, for example, he wrote that *"Perfect holiness embraces the flesh as well as the spirit;* it includes the body as well as the soul. . . . Do you not see by all this that in the principles of health for the body, and righteousness for the soul, both inwrought by the Holy Spirit of God, the Lord is preparing a people unto perfect holiness, so that they can meet the Lord in peace, and see him in holiness? Can you, then, despise or slight true health reform . . . ?" That teaching (which Ellen White would subsequently reject), along with other of Jones's ideas, provided an excellent base for a holy flesh theology.[32]

Despite the similarities between Jones's theology and that of the holy flesh advocates, he flatly repudiated their movement, claiming "it was darkness and would lead to fanaticism." They replied to him that it was new light that he had not received yet. Later they came to believe that both Jones and the General Conference had it in for them. The reason for his complete rejection of the holy flesh movement, despite its relationship to his own teachings, undoubtedly lies in the fact that its leading advocates differed from him in his strong stand on the sinfulness of Christ's human nature. He did not reject them primarily for their Pentecostal excitement. Along this line, it is significant that his final religious affiliation was with a group of tongues-speaking, Sabbathkeeping Pentecostals.[33]

Indiana was not the only place that "new light" was being preached. S. N. Haskell, returning to the United States after a long absence, encountered to his shock a number of fanatical movements across the country. He discovered that Adventist preachers were teaching that it was wrong to kill insects, that no one could receive the seal of God if they had even one gray hair, that deformed persons would be completely healed if they were to be part of the 144,000, and so on. Adventist holiness preachers, such as Luther Warren, were behind much of the new light. Haskell also found that such thought had leavened the thinking of a number of those in responsible leadership positions throughout the church and its institutions. The proponents of the new light claimed that Jones, Prescott, and Waggoner also believed it. Haskell doubted that they had reached such extreme conclusions, but he had to admit that it was in the line of their arguments if one took them to their natural conclusions.[34]

The denomination broke the backbone of the fanatical aspects of the new light movement during the first two years of the new century. Attention then shifted to stamping out its more sophisticated ally—pantheism, a teaching that Jones and Waggoner found quite compatible with their beliefs. Prescott had also imbibed pantheistic ideas in the late nineties, but he veered off from the course of Jones and Waggoner soon after the turn of the century.

To Haskell, the holy flesh movement (and its fanatical cousins) was "*a false application of righteousness by faith.*" Ellen White agreed, noting that "all may now obtain holy hearts, but it is not correct to claim in this life to have holy flesh. . . . If those who speak so freely of perfection in the flesh, could see things in the true light, they would recoil with horror from their presumptuous ideas. . . . While we can not claim perfection of the flesh, we may have Christian perfection of the soul. Through the sacrifice made in our behalf, sins may be perfectly forgiven."[35]

A major problem with the teaching of Jones, Waggoner, and Prescott on righteousness by faith is that they often overly literalized the Bible's teaching on the indwelling of the Holy Spirit. That problem made it difficult for them to resist pantheistic teachings, and it also set up many of their readers for the holy flesh perfectionism.

REFORMER AT LARGE

The period from 1897 to 1901 was the time that Jones had the greatest impact on Adventist institutional and organizational reform. He took up the reform cudgel with characteristic enthusiasm at the 1897 General Conference session. The records of the meetings picture him as the leading figure in a move to reshape the denomination in line with the testimonies of Ellen White. Throughout the conference, Jones, being the acknowledged authority on them, wielded recent communications from her in a powerful effort to bring about change.[36]

His keynote address on the first day of the meetings set the tone for what followed. "We are," he announced, "in trouble now. . . . We get into trouble by disregarding the Testimonies, and the Testimonies tell us just how to get out of that trouble." They indicated, he continued, that changes must come and that "many" of the leading individuals in the denomination's program must be replaced. "The temple needs cleansing." The testimonies had been rejected and the church needed to apply them. During the conference, Jones made explicit presentations calling for organizational and educational reformation. His plea was for Adventism to "come out of Egypt."[37]

The high point of his work and of the conference itself came on February 24 when he spent nearly the entire day reading and discussing messages of rebuke and reform from Ellen White. Olsen described the meeting nicely: "Last Wednesday was a remarkable day. All business was laid aside, and the time was given to Brother A. T. Jones, who took up the communications that had come to us for the last two or three years, and through these opened up the situation as it has been, and as it is now, and what the Lord would do for us under present circumstances. The power of God was in the meeting, and the word of the Lord took effect in a manner that I think I have never seen it before in a Conference. Many minds that had been troubled, found relief; many humble confessions were made by leading men. All acknowledged the testimony borne."[38]

Jones emerged from the 1897 session with what he believed was a mandate to reform the denomination. His newly acquired post on the General Conference Executive Committee put him in a position of power, and his subsequent appointment as editor of the *Review* strengthened his position. He was quite certain that he was God's chosen messenger to clean up Adventism, beginning with Battle Creek.[39]

The first task he undertook on his crusade was to deal with the hardcore problems in the management and operation of the Review and Herald Publishing Association. That was a task that Ellen White had pleaded with Olsen to do for years, but he had failed to take hold of the task adequately, even though he had made some feeble attempts. Few leaders were bold enough to take on the formidable leadership at the Review. The job fell to Jones, who, as noted earlier, was not one to shrink from a good battle. His first step was to lead a three-person task force, which included the General Conference president, to examine intensively every aspect of the Review's operation. The investigation lasted from July 25 through August 8, 1897. Jones's team came down hard on the tight-fisted policies of the institution's managers, and it reported a general lack of Christian principles.[40]

Ellen White wrote to him that he was doing the right thing, but that he had not gone far enough. "You have taken hold of the lesser evils," she penned. "Will the investigation now go to the higher responsibilities? Will every principle be considered?"[41] That gentle spur reinforced in him his sense of mission. As usual, however, he would go too far, eventually playing the part of the proverbial bull in the china shop.

Jones remained quiet for most of 1898, giving the Review and Herald management a chance to straighten up its own problems. But in late 1898, when their progress did not meet his satisfaction, he resumed his activity with full force, testimonies in hand. With complete confidence in his interpretation of Ellen White's counsel regarding the Review, he claimed that the management had robbed authors by not paying a sufficient royalty. He pushed the leaders hard to double the royalty schedule and to make restitution to those authors the publishing house had cheated in the past. That, he claimed, was the only way that the publishing association could again gain God's favor. His demand, reported the manager of the Review, would bankrupt the organization. A committee, including Jones, investigated the question of royalties, and requested that Jones make a compilation on the topic from Ellen White's testimonies.[42]

In the meantime the 1899 General Conference session had begun. Jones played essentially the same role as he did in 1897, insisting on the total reshaping of Adventism according to the testimonies.[43]

After shocking the delegates by reading an 1898 statement in which Ellen White claimed that it had been "some years" since she had "considered the General Conference as the voice of God," he called for corporate repentance for past sins. Three times during the meetings Jones helped to bring the conference to its knees in repentance and confession before God. Reform was what God was after, and Jones was convinced that he was God's man for the hour. He left the delegates with the impression that he had the complete approval of both God and Ellen White in his moves to "overturn" Adventism's institutions. His message was that those who did not cooperate with A. T. Jones were against the Lord. That was strong talk indeed, even for him.[44]

Not everyone was ecstatic over his performance at the 1899 General Conference session. Ellen White was particularly incensed, especially with his use of her writings. "*Do not*," she wrote to Jones soon after the meetings, "*when referring to the Testimonies, feel it your duty to drive them home. In reading the Testimonies, be sure not to mix in your filling of words;* for it is impossible for the hearers to tell what is the word of the Lord to them and what are your words. Be careful that you do not make the words of the Lord offensive. There are methods that are always right when worked by the Holy Spirit. There are wrong methods; quick, severe speech, words not the best adapted to win and to heal the wounded soul are of self." Her appeal to him, as usual, was to receive the Holy Spirit and His softening power.[45]

Ellen White interwove her counsel to Jones regarding the 1899 General Conference session with her critique of his exuberant and forceful tactics in reforming the Review office. She firmly rebuked him for both his extreme view on the royalties issue and for his pushy ways.[46]

But she was not the only one concerned over the situation. A. J. Breed, Adventist leader in the Midwestern states, appealed to denominational president G. A. Irwin, then in Australia, to ask her if Jones was indeed "divinely appointed to straighten up things at the Review and Herald." Irwin reported back in a manner that temporarily shattered Jones's self-confidence. Breed and I. D. Van Horn read Irwin's letter to him. Afterward, Jones prayed as Breed had "never heard a man pray. . . . He thanked the Lord for sending him the light, . . . and when we were through he wept on our necks, thanking us for coming to him as we did."[47]

Jones resumed his crusade for the reform of the Review administration in early 1900. He pushed for, and got, another investigation. Also he forced the manager of the Review off its board of directors, wrongly claiming that he had a testimony for that action. Irwin "mildly reproved" Jones for his high-handedness and called for an apology. That was too much for Jones, who, as a result, resigned from the General Conference Committee.[48]

Educational reform was also a major preoccupation for him in the period following the 1897 General Conference meetings. During the session he spoke several times on education, expounding upon themes that Ellen White was constantly writing about in her drive to establish the Avondale school in Australia as a truly Christian institution, in contrast to the denomination's tradition-bound colleges in the United States that had been heavily influenced by classical education. Jones preached on the science of salvation as being the basis of all true knowledge. In addition, he launched an all-out war on the Greek and Roman classics, the staple of nineteenth-century curricula, and he called for Adventist schools and other institutions to escape their captivity to Egyptian and Babylonian ways of thinking and acting.[49]

Soon after the General Conference session, Jones presented a series of evening meetings in the Tabernacle entitled "Principles of True Education." In those lectures he pounded home the themes that the Bible was the only basis for education and that any compromise with worldly education was a grand mistake. He plainly pointed out that G. W. Caviness, the current president of Battle Creek College and a "son-in-law" of Uriah Smith, was unfit to remain in his position. That was too much for the peace-loving Caviness, who promptly resigned.[50]

Caviness's resignation allowed the reform forces, led by Jones, Kellogg, and Prescott, to press E. A. Sutherland into the presidency. Sutherland, 32 years old, had been carrying out a successful program of educational reform at Walla Walla College in Washington. He had one advantage at Walla Walla, however, that he would not have in Battle Creek. In Washington he had been able to develop programs away from the pressures inherent in the seething atmosphere of Battle Creek. On the other hand, when Sutherland arrived at his new location, Jones and other exuberants swayed him into extremes that he might not have taken had he been able to plan carefully as he developed new approaches.

Late in March 1897 President Irwin, in a General Conference Committee meeting, assigned Jones the task of bringing Adventist schools "into line," since he had a burden "in this direction." Jones was not slow to snap up the opportunity. His *Review* editorials and articles for the next four years, and his presentations at the 1899 General Conference session, often featured the educational reform program. Close to his heart was the ideal of making the Bible the textbook in every subject. Other books were only "study-books" to help students understand the Bible. He aimed every aspect of his educational reform package at making Adventist institutions into "schools of the prophets." Eventually he published his basic educational theory as *The Place of the Bible in Education* (1903).[51]

By early 1898 Jones had been elected to the chairmanship of the Seventh-day Adventist Educational Society, the controlling board for Battle Creek College. To Ellen White he wrote that he accepted the position with reluctance, but that he would push reform based on her writings with enthusiasm. That he did with typical gusto. His goal was an "entire change of principles and methods." He believed that he was achieving his aims at Battle Creek College with the aid of Sutherland.[52]

Jones continued his reforms in Battle Creek until the spring of 1901. At that time the General Conference relieved him of the editorship of the *Review* so that he would again be "free to engage in evangelistic work in the field." His editorial successor was Uriah Smith.[53]

Jones's pinnacle of power, reforming years had been energetic and, in many ways, successful. But as suggested earlier, they may have provided for his downfall as a first-rank Adventist leader by overexposing his extremism and harsh manners to a larger audience. Irwin hinted at that possibility in 1903. While Jones "believes himself to be a reformer," Irwin commented, "I have always thought that he was more of a destructionist than a real reformer, because he goes at things in such a radical and ungentlemanly and unchristian way that he defeats the purpose that he evidently has in mind."[54]

After 1901 Jones would never again be a major force in Adventism. But that does not mean that his influence dried up overnight.

His later bitter course toward the church and its leaders seems to have its roots in the period from 1897 through 1901. It deeply hurt him that the denomination had failed to accept his reforming leadership. That rejection was most obvious in his attempted administrative restructuring of the General Conference itself. To that topic we will now turn.

[1] ATJ to EGW, Mar. 21, 1895; OAO to ATJ, Apr. 12, 1895.

[2] WCW to OAO, Sept. 1, 1895.

[3] OAO to WCW, Apr. 27, 1894; OAO to EGW, Mar. 29, 1894; LTN to A. J. Breed, Oct. 29, 1893; WWP to OAO, Nov. 1, 1893.

[4] OAO to SNH, Mar. 24, 1895; OAO to WCW, Mar. 28, Apr. 18, July 18, 1895; *RH*, May 21, 1895, p. 320; Mar. 10, 1896, p. 160.

[5] *RH*, Nov. 12, Dec. 3, 1895, pp. 731, 779; 1897 *GCB*, p. 337; H. P. Hosler to OAO, Oct. 23, 1895.

[6] H. P. Hosler to FMB, Dec. 4, 1895.

[7] SNH to WCW, Mar. 9, 1900.

[8] GCC Min, Mar. 17, 18, 1896.

[9] WCW to ATJ, GCC, FMB, May 13, 1897.

[10] OAO to WCW, Mar. 9, Apr. 25, May 21, 1896; GAI to WCW, May 18, 1897.

[11] CHJ et al. to GCC, Oct. 26, 1896; CPB to M. E. Olsen, Oct. 12, 1896; AFB to OAO, Nov. 2, 1896.

[12] CPB to OAO, Dec. 9, 1896; AFB to OAO, Nov. 2, 1896.

[13] LTN to A. J. Breed, Oct. 29, 1893; OAO to WCW, Apr. 27, 1894; OAO to EGW, Mar. 29, 1894; LTN to OAO, Dec. 7, 1893; WWP to OAO, Nov. 1, 1893.

[14] GCC Min, Sept. 23, Mar. 23, 25, 28, 1897.

[15] *Ibid.*, Sept. 23, 24, 1897; *RH*, Oct. 5, 1897, p. 640.

[16] GAI to EGW, Oct. 13, 1897; ATJ to EGW, Oct. 19, 1897; *RH*, Oct. 5, 1897, p. 640.

[17] *RH*, Oct. 5, 1897, p. 640.

[18] GAI to EGW, Oct. 13, 1897; ATJ to EGW, Oct. 19, 1897; EGW to Brother and Sister SNH, Feb. 5, 1902; see also *RH*, Nov. 30, 1897, pp. 753, 754.

[19] ATJ to EGW, Jan. 20, 1899.

[20] GAI to EGW, Jan. 30, 1898.

[21] GAI to EGW, Mar. 16, 1900. (Ital. sup.)

[22] EGW to ATJ, Apr. 28, May 1, 1899; Feb. 6, 1900; EGW to J. A. Burden, Sept, 2, 1907.

[23] [Confession of A. T. Jones], unpub. MS, June 13, 1901; EGW to ATJ, Apr. 18, 1900.

[24] *RH*, May 3, 1898, p. 292.

[25] Quoted in G. M. Marsden, *Fundamentalism in American Culture* (New York, 1980), p. 72.

[26] S. E. Ahlstrom, *A Religious History of the American People* (New Haven, Conn., 1972), pp. 816-822; J. L. Peters, *Christian Perfection and American Methodism* (Grand Rapids, Mich., 1985), pp. 148, 149; T. L. Smith, *Called Unto Holiness* (Kansas City, Mo., 1962), pp. 27-53; V. Synan, *The Holiness-Pentecostal Tradition* (Grand Rapids, Mich., 1997 pp. 22-44; G. Wacker, *Heaven Below: Early Pentecostals and American Culture* (Cambridge, Mass., 2001).

[27] 1893 *GCB*, pp. 358, 359; *RH*, June 23, 1896, p. 399; Mar. 15, 1898, p. 172.

[28] OAO to EGW, Sept. 28, 1892; 1893 *GCB,* p. 378; 1895 *GCB,* p. 368.

[29] EGW to ATJ, Apr. 14, 1894; EGW to WWP and ATJ, Apr. 16, 1894.

[30] GAI to EGW, Oct. 13, 1997; for Ballenger's role in this revival, see Edwards and Land, *Seeker After Light.*

[31] *RH,* Nov. 23, Oct. 5, Dec. 14, 1897, pp. 747, 640, 793; Jan. 11, 1898, p. 32; AFB to GAI, Apr. 18, 1898, Sept. 6, 1897; Edwards and Land, *Seeker After Light,* pp. 32-64.

[32] R. S. Donnell to OAO, June 2, 1896; Topeka *Daily Capital,* May 18, 1889, p. 5 (see chapter 4, note 20); 1895 *GCB,* p. 267; O. S. Hadley to EGW, June 1, 1900; *RH,* Nov. 22, 1898, p. 752. (Ital. sup.) See chapter 4 for a discussion on the relationship of holy flesh theology to righteousness by faith.

[33] I. V. Hadley to EGW, June 1, 1900; A. J. Breed to GAI, July 22, 1900; O. S. Hadley to EGW, June 1, 1900; *AS* (2), September 1922, pp. 7, 8.

[34] SNH to EGW, Oct. 3, Nov. 23, 1899; SNH to WCW, Oct. 25, Dec. 26, 1899; Feb. 5, 1900; R. S. Donnell, *What I Taught in Indiana,* (n.p., n.d.).

[35] SNH to EGW, July 27, 1900; 1901 *GCB,* p. 419. (Ital. sup.)

[36] 1897 *GCB,* pp. 311, 313.

[37] *Ibid.,* pp. 2, 4, 21, 22; 1897 *GCQB,* 1st Qtr., pp. 20-54; *RH,* Feb. 16, 23, 1897, pp, 112, 120.

[38] 1897 *GCB,* pp. 160, 314; *RH,* Mar. 9, 1897, p. 152; OAO to EGW, Feb. 26, 1897.

[39] ATJ to EGW, Oct. 19, 1897.

[40] EGW to OAO, June 19, 1895; EGW to Brethren, July 1, 1896; OAO to EGW, Nov. 6, 1896; ATJ, GAI, and JNL, "Informal Report of Committee on Investigation of Affairs in Review and Herald Office," unpub. MS, Aug. 8, 1897; GAI to EGW, Oct. 13, 1897; ATJ to EGW, Oct. 19, 1897.

[41] EGW to ATJ, Dec. 9, 1897.

[42] ATJ to EGW, Dec. 28, 1898; W. C. Sisley to EGW, Feb. 1, 1899; GCC Min, Mar. 19, 1899.

[43] See, e.g., 1899 *GCB,* pp. 62, 63, 74-76, 124.

[44] *RH,* Mar. 7, Apr. 4, 1899, pp. 160, 217, 218; 1899 *GCB,* pp. 68, 74, 179.

[45] EGW to ATJ, May 1, 1899. (Ital. sup.)

[46] EGW to ATJ, Apr. 28, May 1, Aug. 14, 1899; ATJ to EGW, July 6, 1899; W. C. Sisley to EGW, Apr. 13, 1899.

[47] A. J. Breed to GAI, June 1, Sept. 5, 1899.

[48] EGW to Brother and Sister SNH, Apr. 25, 1900; GCC, *A Statement Refuting Charges Made by A. T. Jones Against the Spirit of Prophecy and the Plan of Organization of the Seventh-day Adventist Denomination* (Washington, D.C., 1906), pp. 15, 16; GCC Min, Feb. 12, Mar. 25, 27, 28, 1900; ATJ to Secretary of the General Conference of SDA, Mar. 27, 1900.

[49] 1897 *GCB,* pp. 46, 47, 49-53, 59-66; 1897 *GCQB,* 1st Qtr., p. 48.

[50] J. H. Haughey to W. T. Bland, Apr. 7, 1897; C. S. Longacre to E. K. Vande Vere, Feb. 22, May 21, 1956. I have placed "son-in-law" in quotation marks because the Smiths had raised Caviness's wife from the age of 12 or 13, even though she was never formally adopted.

[51] GCC Min, Mar. 29, 1897; *RH,* July 5, Feb. 8, 1898, pp. 428, 92; Oct. 17, Nov. 14, 21, Apr. 25, 1899, pp. 663, 664, 731, 732, 751, 752, 264.

[52] ATJ to EGW, June 22, 1898; 1899 *GCB,* p. 68; *RH,* Dec. 12, 1899, p. 812; Nov. 6, 1900, p. 720.

[53] *RH,* May 14, 1901, pp. 312, 320.

[54] GAI to AGD, Nov. 3, 1903.

CHAPTER XIII

CHRISTIAN ANARCHY: CHARISMATIC CHURCH ORGANIZATION

The most important reform on A. T. Jones's agenda was that of the administrative structure of the Adventist Church. Adventism had established its organizational pattern in 1863 when the denomination had only a few thousand members. At that time it had no mission program nor any institutions, except its publishing plant. In the next quarter century, however, all that would change. By 1888 the church had a rapidly expanding mission program in several countries, its membership was growing in the United States, and it was acquiring an increasing number of schools, sanitariums, and publishing houses.

Because of the denomination's increasing complexity, the 1863 administrative structure was no longer sufficient. The problem, although evident in the late 1880s, developed into crisis proportions in the 1890s as the church underwent rapid expansion and growth in every aspect of its work. Even though its administrative machinery was hopelessly inadequate, Adventism limped along with its 1863 structure until in 1901 impending administrative breakdown and the urging of Ellen White virtually forced it to reorganize.

Adventism had been going through piecemeal organizational change from 1888 to 1901, but the 1901 transformation was thorough and based on a new principle. The old system had focused on the centralization of authority in a few men in Battle Creek. The new approach emphasized the diffusion of administrative power.[1]

A. T. Jones was at the center of the struggle for organizational reform. For him, however, the reforms never were anywhere near extensive enough. The repudiation of his program, along with the rejection of him as a first-rank leader of the church, set the stage for his apostasy in the early years of the twentieth century.

CHRISTIAN ANARCHY IN THE 1890S

By the time of his meteoric rise in 1888, Jones had already developed the seed thoughts for his philosophy of church organization. At the important Ottawa, Kansas, camp meeting of May 1889 he preached at least three series of sermons: one on righteousness by faith, a second on religious liberty, and the third on church organization. That trinity of topics was standard fare in the post-1888 period for him and his reforming colleagues. The General Conference session at Minneapolis had dealt with the first two subjects, but the third had largely gotten pushed aside by the other two during the conference, even though it had been slated for discussion.[2]

The heart of Jones's doctrine of the church in 1889 (and subsequently) was that "the church is the body of Christ" and Christ is its head. "*Christ is head,*" he proclaimed, "*not only of the body, but [of] every member of the body, every man. No man is the head of any other man, but Christ is head of every one and all.*"[3]

Undoubtedly he was basing his teaching on Paul's ecclesiology and Martin Luther's concept of the priesthood of every believer, but Jones would as usual take the notion to its logical extreme. In the process, he came to concentrate on people's responsibility to God, while underemphasizing their accountability to their fellow church members. Jones had part of Paul's analogy correct when he noted that Christ was the head of the body, but he fell short in understanding the various interrelated functions of Christ's body, which includes "administrators" or "governments." The New Testament view of the church incorporates officers who are to care for it and are to be obeyed for the health of the body. In neglecting that aspect of structure he ended up with a distortion of the biblical view of the church.[4]

A corollary of Jones's emphasis on the individual's direct relationship with Christ was his denigration of the role of clerical leadership. In 1889 he published a booklet for use in the important ministerial institutes established in the wake of the 1888 theological crisis. The booklet, in addition to other topics, contained "a large number of quotations from ancient and eminent writers in reference to the exaltation of the elders of the primitive Christian church which finally resulted in the establishment of the papacy."[5]

During much of his early ministry, Jones, as noted in chapter 1, had been exposed to W. L. Raymond, who had the problem of "complaining of all the leaders and finding fault with the General Conference." In addition, Raymond held that the general church body had no right to discipline individual clergy. While we do not fully know Raymond's exact teachings, and while it is impossible to determine the amount of influence he and Jones had on each other, it seems to be more than coincidental that the latter later espoused Raymond's theories and attitudes toward the church.[6] Jones's aberrant theories on church organization gained strength in his mind throughout the nineties.

He was not alone in his views on church organization. E. J. Waggoner also developed false views on the topic in the early 1890s. Writing to Jones in 1894, Ellen White claimed that "Elder Waggoner . . . has agitated strange theories. He has brought before some of the people, ideas in regard to organization that ought never to have had expression. I supposed that the question of organization was settled forever with those who believed the testimonies. . . . Oh how Satan would rejoice to get in among this people, and disorganize the work at a time when thorough organization is essential, and will be the greatest power to keep out spurious uprisings. . . . We want to hold the lines evenly, that there shall be no breaking down of the system of regulation and order. In this way license shall not be given to disorderly elements to control the work at this time. . . . Let not you nor Elder Waggoner be incautious now, and advance things that are not proper, and not in accordance with the very message God has given." Waggoner would eventually leave his denominational position in Britain because "the brethren . . . could no longer sanction" his "teaching that was tearing down all order and organization." For his part, he believed that the denomination was well on its way to papalism.[7]

It is a curious fact that all three leading ministers in the righteousness by faith movement in the 1890s—Jones, Waggoner, and Prescott—came to the same conclusions regarding organization. They stressed a person's individual relationship with and access to Christ to such an extent that they lost all balance in regard to the biblical role of the church as the corporate body of Christ. Their particular emphasis also left them vulnerable to other problems, such as pantheism with its perversion of the divine-human relationship. All three either came to accept pantheism or to use language that pushed biblical concepts of the indwelling Holy Spirit so far that many of their ideas and words had pantheistic aspects. Thus it was not a strange thing for Jones and Waggoner to join the Kellogg schism early in the new century.

Kellogg, meanwhile, had his own complaints with Adventist organization. His problems, however, were administrative rather than theological. He had no use for any church leaders who attempted to block the development of his programs. As early as 1895 we find him referring to conference presidents as "little popes."[8] By 1903 Kellogg and Jones would unite their forces over the issues of organization and administrative control.

It was at the 1897 General Conference session that Jones opened up his guns on behalf of organizational reform. Armed with a fistful of testimonies, during the conference's keynote address he called for administrative renovation, keeping up the pressure through the last of his presentations. "'Many of the men,'" he quoted from Ellen White in his first sermon, "'who have acted as councilors in board and council meetings need to be weeded out.' Notice," Jones exclaimed, "it says *many*."[9] The time had come for radical change, and he was determined to push it through.

One of his most explosive bits of ammunition came from an Ellen White testimony penned in August 1896. One sentence from that message particularly fascinated him: "It is not wise to choose *one man* as president of the General Conference."[10] He would continue to reiterate those words for the rest of his ministry. Taking them out of their context, he interpreted them to mean that the General Conference should have more than one president, or better yet, no president at all.

Jones and his allies successfully fought for both interpretations. One result was that the 1897 session decided to divide the world church into "three grand divisions," each with its own General Conference president. As it eventually worked out, however, the European and Australasian fields came to be thought of as "unions." That development left the president of the American field with the title of president of the General Conference in America and thus was somewhat short of Jones's plan for three coequal presidents.[11]

Soon after the 1897 session, he prevailed upon the leadership to drop the title of president altogether. As a result, the denomination had no

General Conference leader with that title for a few months. It was not long, however, before the title came into use again. Jones believed that the reversal was apostasy and that the church needed to repent of it.[12]

A second avenue of attack against the concept of a church president that he developed at the 1897 General Conference session focused on the idea of kingship. The whole notion of kingship, he pointed out, came from the apostasy of Nimrod. Human government itself was a sign of humanity's apostasy from God. When God established Israel it was to be a different kind of nation—God was to be its king. But Israel wanted to be like other countries. In choosing a king, they apostatized from God's leadership. Their rejection of Him led to Israel's downfall.[13]

Jones argued that Adventists were following Israel's path. If they had not, they already would have been in the kingdom. The problem, he claimed, was that Adventists were no happier with God's kingship than was Israel. God, he asserted, *wanted his church [Israel] to dwell alone, to have no ruler but himself,* no law but his law, no legislation of any kind but the Lord's word, no government but the Lord's. . . . So long as they needed any kind of legislation, of themselves, . . . that was evidence that they had forsaken God, that his law was not enough for them any more."[14]

The ideal, Jones never tired of repeating, was that Jesus Christ was the head of the church and would guide every individual member in it. The church needed no king (or president). "If God is not a sufficient ruler for Seventh-day Adventists, it is because they are not believing on him with all the heart. It is because they are so much like the heathen, that they must have a heathen government and heathen power to protect themselves from themselves, and to rule themselves." Adventism must come out of Egypt and Babylon and let God rule the church.[15]

Those were strong words, even for A. T. Jones, but his call would grow even more strident in the decade following 1897. The eradication of the conference presidency would become a consuming passion to him. His line of argument, of course, was much more evident by 1903, but it did not essentially differ from his earlier position.

The unfinished business of reorganization formed a central feature of the 1899 General Conference session. Once again Jones was at the center of action. On February 22 he claimed that the General Conference needed to be "revolutionized." He then read a statement (without its context) from Ellen White that brought the meeting to its knees. "*'It has been some years,'*" she had written in 1898, "*'since I have considered the General Conference as the voice of God.'*" "That," Jones pleaded, "calls for such repentance as has never been shown yet." From that point he led the delegates into an extended session of prayer.[16]

The next two days saw Waggoner, Prescott, and Jones, in the longest debate of the conference, seek to reorganize the church under the direct guidance of the Holy Spirit. The extended discussion revealed that all three men held the same position.[17]

Waggoner was first to speak. "*Perfect unity,*" he concluded, "*means absolute independence.* . . . This question of organization is a very simple thing. All there is to it is for each individual to give himself over to the Lord, and then the Lord will do with him just as he wants to. . . . 'Receive ye the Holy Ghost.' *The Holy Ghost is the organizer.*" Thus the "new light" on organization was seen as an integral part of the Adventist holiness movement and an extension of the principles of righteousness by faith.[18]

For Waggoner that doctrine was not anarchy. Rather, it was church government directly under God. Anarchy, he asserted, existed wherever you found any human organization. Thus, he pointed out, the Roman Catholic Church "is the very embodiment of anarchy." "Which do we want,—anarchy, or the Spirit of God?"[19]

The next day Prescott aired his view that all politics and parliamentary procedures came from the devil in his attempt to control humans. In an organization with a powerful General Conference president, all the devil had to do was to dominate one mind in order to have the whole organization. "If we get at it right," Prescott claimed, "there will be no officials here." "'All ye are brethren'" is the biblical ideal.[20]

Believing that the discussion was taking place under the direct inspiration of God, Jones told the conference to stop asking questions of Waggoner and Prescott. All the delegates needed to do was to seek the guidance of the Holy Spirit and the truth would naturally flow out.[21]

Not all agreed with him. L. D. Santee rose and read a long series of quotations from Ellen White on the principles of organization, and on how Satan would like to disorganize the denomination and create confusion.[22]

Jones then took the floor again, claiming that the suggestions of

Waggoner and Prescott were not disorganization. Rather, they were genuine gospel organization.[23]

All three of the reformers held the same position—that the Holy Spirit should be the only coordinator of individuals in the church. When all the church members were in tune with the Spirit, perfect unity would result. Human church government merely got in the way. The church needed to come out of Babylon. Their position, interestingly enough, was the opposite of the argument that James and Ellen White had used in the 1850s and 1860s in their hard-fought battle to establish the Seventh-day Adventist Church as an organized denomination.[24]

In his last formal presentation at the 1899 session, Jones once again pushed hard for total reform. He defined Christianity as "God's Christian republic,—a government of the people, by the people, and for the people,—God the Governor, and he governing *each one alone,* and that by the consent of the governed." Once more he called for repentance and confession, noting that God was raising up leadership to overturn the denomination. Without doubt he saw himself as that divinely appointed leader. Some, Jones claimed, would think that instituting the new principles would destroy organization, but what would really be eradicated would be "the wicked principles of Satan in the organization."[25]

The 1901 General Conference session would be the setting in which the denomination would find itself forced to choose its course in organizational reformation. Meanwhile, Jones urged his views between 1899 and 1901 in the *Review* and other publications.

The General Conference president, on the other hand, pressed for a different ideal. After discussing the extremes of too much and too little authority at the 1899 session, Irwin wrote that "the Lord wants organization and system in his work; but he does not want that organization to be arbitrary, and dictatorial."[26] He clearly took a sensible and moderate position, but moderation was not getting much of a hearing in the late 1890s. The Jones-Waggoner-Prescott forces outmaneuvered him at the 1899 General Conference session. Stronger moderate leadership would have to arise if things were to take a different course in 1901.

THE 1901 GENERAL CONFERENCE SESSION

The 1901 meetings did see such strong leadership, particularly in the persons of A. G. Daniells and Ellen G. White. Both had been in Australia for nearly 10 years. Their return signaled new directions in the power struggle over denominational reorganization. And their words meant all the more because they had recently been instrumental in organizing the Australian field in a manner that provided a pattern for the denomination at large. That plan was a radical break with the past, but it certainly was not as iconoclastic as the one urged by the Jones forces. Early in the 1901 General Conference session the delegates appointed Daniells to leadership in the move to reorganize the administration of the church.

Ellen White provided the spark for the reform initiative. She had been urging organizational changes for more than a decade, and by 1901 she had concluded that the denomination could not put it off any longer. On the day before the conference began she met with a group of leaders, including Daniells and Jones, in the library of Battle Creek College. In no uncertain terms she called for "new blood" and "an entire new organization." "There should be a renovation without any delay. To have this Conference pass on and close up as the Conferences have done, with the same manipulating, with the very same tone and the same order—God forbid! God forbid, brethren."[27]

Much that Ellen White said gave Jones the idea that she was behind his proposals. After all, she opposed the centralization of power in a few men, and she left no doubt that "kingly, ruling power" and any administrator who had a "little throne" would have to go. The Lord "wants the Holy Ghost to come in" to get the church out of its "rut." She noted that the whole principle of Adventist organization was wrong. President Irwin "should have a change," and any leaders that came in after him would have to be removed if they did not understand Christlike principles of organization.[28]

On the first day of the session, she again made her plea for reorganization, noting specifically that "God has not put any kingly power in our ranks to control this or that branch of the work." Her plea led Daniells to move that the conference set its regular business aside and that reorganization become the major agenda item. His motion carried.[29]

Jones interpreted Ellen White's statements as a validation of his position. In his sermon on the first evening of the session, he came out strongly for reorganization of the church and a change of leadership, and powerfully preached against any "kingly spirit."[30]

Most of the delegates, including Daniells, missed the central meaning of Jones's message, however. His real point was that reorganization begins with the individual. When individuals get right with God under the direction of the Holy Spirit, then, and only then, would the only Head of the church—Jesus Christ—guide the members. Whosoever, Jones claimed, shall be elected as president of the church will have no more authority after his election than he had before it, because Christ is the only head of the church.[31]

While much that Jones had to say regarding reorganization was true, it was, as noted above, based upon a distortion of the biblical view of the church as the body of Christ with its various gifts. In essence, he was again preaching his doctrine of Christian anarchy—that the only real organization of the church is that the Holy Spirit directly rules every individual member of the church. Partly because of the excitement of the occasion and partly because of Jones's circular reasoning, few saw his full meaning clearly. Daniells, in fact, was so impressed with Jones's "grand sermon" that he had him print it as a booklet entitled Church Organization. Then he personally distributed 500 copies. Only later did he come to see that he and Jones held diametrically opposite positions on the issue of organization.[32]

Jones's later messages in the 1901 meetings continued to hammer away at kingly power and each individual's direct relationship to God. At times he seemed to approve of a congregational form of church government, but even then he would veer off into radical self-governing individualism. That was the bottom line of his argument, and he would later write entire books on radical individualism as complete "religious liberty." By that expression he came to mean that each individual was responsible to God alone and not to any other human being.[33]

The 1901 General Conference session did restructure the denomination. Among the changes, four stand out as having particular importance: (1) the creation of union conferences that had supervision of local conferences dispersed the administrative authority from the General Conference officers; thus, (2) no small group could rule the church like kings; (3) most of the independent organizations related to the denomination (such as the Foreign Mission Board and the International Tract Society) became departments of the General Conference, the union conferences, the local conferences, and the individual churches; and (4) the

General Conference was to have no president. Instead, it was to have an executive committee that chose its own "chairman" and other officers. Point 4 was of special importance in Jones's mind.

Great changes had resulted from the 1901 General Conference session. Ellen White, who had been apprehensive as to how the meetings would go, testified near the end of the session that she "was never more astonished in all my life than at the turn things have taken at this meeting. This is not our work. God has brought it about." Jones would never forget her assessment of the meetings. He would subsequently hold that any reversions to the pre-1901 system were nothing short of blatant apostasy. That was particularly true in regard to the presidency.[34]

The 1901 session, unfortunately, did not manage to bring all parts of the Adventist institutional program under the umbrella of its new departmental system. The largest exception was the medical branch. In 1901 the Medical Missionary and Benevolent Association was an extremely powerful organization. It employed some 2,000 individuals. The General Conference, on the other hand, had only 1,500 under its direction. The relationship between the medical organization and the General Conference was a problem in 1901, and it would become even more troublesome by the 1903 General Conference session. The leader of the medical organization was J. H. Kellogg, a fiercely independent physician who did not look kindly on "semi-ignorant" preachers interfering with his plans and programs. As a compromise position, the 1901 church constitution allowed six of the 25 members of the General Conference Executive Committee to come from the Medical Missionary and Benevolent Association. That gave the medical wing a disproportionate amount of power. Kellogg, of course, had no objections to that.

On April 18, 1901, immediately following the General Conference session, the Executive Committee chose A. G. Daniells to be its chairman. In one of the ironies of Adventist history, Kellogg made the motion to appoint Daniells, and Jones seconded it. The two men would soon become deadly enemies of the denomination's new leader.[35]

YEARS OF CRISIS, 1901-1903

The years between the 1901 and the 1903 General Conference sessions were fraught with crises and conflict. They were also ones in which Jones would align himself with Kellogg in a power struggle against Daniells and Prescott (who had changed sides in the crucial years between 1899 and 1902) that came close to splitting the denomination in two.

Daniells, Kellogg, and Jones got along quite well for a time, but that began to change during the first half of 1902. For one thing, on February 18 the massive Battle Creek Sanitarium burned to the ground. Its reconstruction soon became a bone of contention. The General Conference leaders, backed by Ellen White, wanted a modest rebuilding program, whereas Kellogg schemed from the start to construct a grander institution than the one destroyed. In a church of scarce resources that problem became a constant irritant.[36]

Even more serious, however, was the conflict between Kellogg and Daniells over the establishment of a sanitarium in Great Britain. Both men wanted to erect the institution, but Daniells insisted that it involve no deficit spending. All new enterprises, he held, must be on a pay-as-you-go basis. Their confrontation infuriated Kellogg, who had been used to getting his way with the two previous General Conference administrators. In Daniells he had finally met his match.[37]

The solution, Kellogg was quick to recognize, was to replace Daniells with a General Conference Executive Committee chairman more in harmony with his plans. That could easily be done, since, according to the 1901 constitution, the chairman had no stated term of office. The Executive Committee could replace him at any of their meetings. A coup d'état by Kellogg was not out of the question. After all, his medical organization had nearly 25 percent of the votes and a great deal of sympathy among the other committee members.

As a result, November 1902 saw the Kellogg forces make a drive to elect Jones in place of Daniells as chairman of the denomination's Executive Committee. Daniells rose to the occasion, declaring, according to Jones, "I'm not a foot-ball: to be kicked into the ring, and then kicked out again." Even though the attempt to overthrow Daniells failed, its meaning was not lost on Jones. He had come to see that his hope for denominational power lay in aligning himself with Kellogg. Later he would date that month as the exact time that he made his decision to cast his lot with the doctor.[38]

The publication of Kellogg's *The Living Temple,* which he had written for Adventists to sell widely across the nation, further complicated the political situation. The profits were to go to rebuild the Battle Creek Sanitarium. *The Living Temple* turned out to be a problem, since it contained certain types of pantheistic teachings that made God a force within, rather than above, nature. As such, it undermined aspects of Adventist theology. Kellogg rightly pointed out that he was merely repeating what he thought Waggoner, Prescott, and others had been teaching in the 1890s. Denominational leaders widely critiqued the book. Daniells, W. A. Spicer (secretary of the Foreign Mission Board), Prescott (who had backed away from his earlier pantheistic expressions), and others condemned it. Jones, on the other hand, found its theology to be quite acceptable.[39] *The Living Temple* controversy brewed throughout the period from 1901 to 1903.

Another subject of dispute during this period, especially to Jones, was that Daniells had begun to sign his papers as "president" rather than "chairman" soon after the 1901 General Conference session. Daniells explained the shift as one of necessity. If he was to sign certain legal documents, he argued, he had to use an accepted title so that people did not become confused as to his actual position. He and most of the committee agreed that "the meaning of the expression in the Testimony was not that the General Conference should have no president, but that the president of the General Conference should not be the one person to whom the details in the various parts of the field should be referred." W. C. White agreed with Daniells' interpretation, claiming that he never expected the title to be deleted. Prescott concurred with Daniells and White, even though he had ardently opposed the title earlier. When Daniells had flatly presented him with the problems involved in the 1901 change, he recanted. By the spring of 1902, Prescott was even willing to be elected as vice president of the General Conference Committee.[40]

Jones, on the other hand, remained violently opposed to both the title and the concept of a president. His bitterness on the topic finally would erupt in grand style in 1906.

Other issues also tended to separate the Daniells-Prescott forces in the period between the 1901 and 1903 General Conference sessions from the developing Kellogg-Jones alliance. One was Daniells' desire to make the medical program a department of the church. A second was Kellogg's plan to reopen Battle Creek College in 1903 in the face of counsel from Ellen White to the contrary.[41] The college had moved to Berrien Springs as

Emmanuel Missionary College in 1901 to keep Adventist young people out of problem-filled Battle Creek. Jones would play an important role in the reopening.

The burning of the Review and Herald publishing plant on December 30, 1902, added to the complexity of the situation in Battle Creek. The fire totally destroyed the building. Its loss led to discussions early in 1903 regarding the transfer of both the General Conference offices and the publishing establishment to another location.

DOING BATTLE AT THE 1903 GENERAL CONFERENCE SESSION

The leadership on both sides of the denominational struggle approached the 1903 General Conference session with great forebodings. In late January Prescott reported to Daniells that Kellogg was claiming that he and his cohorts would make "every possible effort . . . to overthrow the present administration" at the meetings. He had good reason to believe that there would be "a combining of all other interests to make Brother A. T. Jones the President of the General Conference."[42]

Daniells also expected trouble. "I have learned," he wrote to W. C. White just before the session, "that the corruption that we were called upon two years ago to cleanse from this denomination was much greater than I had any idea, and it exists in ranks where it is not supposed to exist." A few days later Kellogg expressed his fears: "I have no hope for the future of this work unless the Daniells-Evans-Prescott ring can be broken up."[43] All parties approached the meetings in the spirit of war. The issue at stake was control of the denomination and its institutions.

The conflict came out in the open on April 9 at the reading of the majority report on a revised denominational constitution. Several weaknesses in the 1901 constitution had become evident. Two of the proposed changes received hot debate: (1) the provision for the General Conference in session to elect its president (not chairman) and other officers, rather than entrusting that task to the Executive Committee; and (2) provisions for transacting business when the full Executive Committee was not in session.

Those modifications obviously sought to stabilize the church's administrative officers on the one hand, and at making a coup d'état, such as was attempted in the fall of 1902, impossible on the other hand. The consideration of the new constitution set off a massive debate, with Jones, Waggoner, Dr. David Paulson, and P. T. Magan as the major opponents of the changes. All the old arguments for radical individualism with each member under the direct guidance of the Holy Spirit surfaced again. Anything more than that, Jones and his allies claimed, was both papalism and a return to pre-1901 church government with its presidential king and small decision-making committees.[44]

Their arguments, of course, were not valid, even though they contained an element of truth. They were true in the sense that the denomination would once again have an official president and that a small part of the large Executive Committee could make important decisions. Nevertheless, their arguments were false in that much of the previous authority of the General Conference had been dispersed through the creation of union conferences with regional authority.

Despite the impassioned arguments against the 1903 constitution, a majority vote accepted it even though Jones made a last-ditch attempt to block it. The next day a few asked him if he had slept after the constitution's adoption. He claimed to the delegates that he had no axe to grind, that it was his constitution now that it had been adopted, and that no matter who became president he would have no more faithful follower than A. T. Jones. Having said this, he added that he felt comforted by the fact that "even though Israel started back to Egypt a number of times, they never got there. . . . The Lord was with them all the time, and kept them out of Egypt; so I am not afraid."[45]

In spite of those conciliatory words, Jones never came to terms with the reinstitution of the presidency of the General Conference. In 1906 he pilloried the 1903 constitution as a backsliding step that he would always oppose.[46] His resistance to it lasted, as we shall see, until his death. Unfortunately, his bitterness over the issue increased with time.

Both his program and his person had experienced public rejection in 1903. That is always a bitter pill. It is doubly bitter to someone who has a sensitive ego. Such was the case with A. T. Jones. The 1903 constitutional decision definitely thrust him toward the Kellogg camp. In addition, the fact that the delegates had reelected Daniells as president did not help his attitude.

Kellogg, meanwhile, also received his setbacks at the 1903 General Conference session. Especially galling was the approval of a recommendation that all denominationally operated institutions come under direct denominational ownership. He defiantly vowed before the delegates that he would never be bound by the regulation.[47] By early 1903 he had definitely set his course in direct opposition to that of Daniells.

In the succeeding months Jones and Kellogg would solidify their alliance. Their formal split with the denomination would not take place until 1906 and 1907, but from the conclusion of the 1903 meetings, despite a couple periods of repentance, they were headed in a direction that had but one outcome. Kellogg and Jones had met Daniells and Prescott in a power struggle and had lost. They eventually united their forces, even though they had large areas of disagreement with each other. One major aspect involved Jones's principles of organization. Kellogg was convinced that Jones's principles "would be beautiful when we got to heaven, but [that] we have to have some kind of organization" here on earth.[48]

Their disagreements, coupled with their aggressive personalities, would eventually force them apart. Before their separation, however, they would work together for several years (a topic that we will cover in chapter 15).

In the meantime, we will examine Jones's last substantial position in the Adventist Church in the next chapter. It is astounding, given his strongly held views, that he took the presidency of the California Conference in 1901. That acceptance, for whatever reasons, leaves one with the suspicion that he would have found some justification to assume the General Conference presidency in 1903 had the church offered it to him. Unfortunately, Jones, like most, did not thrive on a diet of sour grapes.

THE CHARISMATIC CONTEXT OF JONES'S ECCLESIOLOGY

From a wider perspective, Jones's theories on church organization should, like so many aspects of his theology, be seen within the larger context of the developing holiness movement that would explode into Pentecostalism in the earliest years of the twentieth century. For example, in the Keswick movement, which began in the 1870s and developed throughout the rest of the nineteenth century, the Holy Spirit was "practically regarded as the *presiding officer* and *chief administrator* in all truly holy assemblies." The Spirit was the "true Archbishop, the Supreme Teacher, the Divine Guide and Governor."[49]

Early Pentecostalism had the same organizational flavor. Thus Frank Bartleman, an early leader in the movement, could write that some of those who were becoming Pentecostals "had become ambitious for a church and organization. It seemed hard to them not to be 'like the other nations (churches)' round about them." "We had," he penned, "no pope or hierarchy. We were 'brethren.' We had no human programme. The Lord Himself was leading. We had no priest class, nor priest craft. . . . All were on a level." Again, one William Durham warned that organization will "kill the work" because "no religious awakening . . . has ever been able to retain its spiritual life and power after man organized it and gotten it under his control."[50]

But in spite of such utterances most Pentecostals by the second decade of the twentieth century realized that they would benefit from organization and began to explore the topic. Due to the needs of the real world, they in the next few years began to organize the various Pentecostal and Assembly of God denominations. It was that fact that would so frustrate Jones in 1922 when the group of seventh-day Pentecostals with whom he was fellowshipping decided to organize.[51]

While Jones was obviously in harmony with holiness/Pentecostal ecclesiology, his anti-organizational impulses were undoubtedly heightened by the high-handed and kingly-power treatment he had received at the hands of Butler and Smith in the late 1880s. But the anti-organizational core of Jones's ecclesiology predate his experiences at that time. They seem, as we noted earlier, to have developed in the late 1870s and early 1880s when he worked in the Pacific Northwest with W. L. Raymond.

---

[1] For treatments of the development of SDA organization, see Andrew G. Mustard, *James White and SDA Organization* (Berrien Springs, Mich., 1988); Barry David Oliver, *SDA Organizational Structure* (Berrien Springs, Mich., 1989); George R. Knight, *Organizing for Mission and Growth* (Hagerstown, Md., 2006).

[2] *RH*, Sept. 11, 1888, p. 590.

[3] Topeka *Daily Capital*, May 8, 1889, p. 4; May 10, 1889, p. 4. (Ital. sup.)

[4] 1 Cor. 12:28; 1 Tim. 3:5; Heb. 13:17; Acts 20:28.

[5] *RH*, Apr. 2, 1889, p. 224; cf. 1895 *GCB*, pp. 52, 346.

[6] EGW to SNH, c. June 10, 1884; *ST*, July 3, 17, 1884, pp. 408, 424.

[7] EGW to ATJ, Jan. 14, 1894; GAI to AGD, Nov. 3, 1903.

[8] JHK to WCW, Aug. 7, 1895.

[9] 1897 *GCB*, p. 4.

[10] EGW to Conference Presidents and Counselors, August 1896. (Ital. sup.)

[11] 1897 *GCB*, pp. 215, 229, 255; ATJ, *The Final Word and a Confession* ([Battle Creek, Mich., 1906]), p. 39.

[12] WCW to AGD, May 24, 1901.

[13] 1897 *GCB*, pp. 279-285; 1897 *GCQB*, 1st Qtr., pp. 14-54.

[14] 1897 *GCQB*, 1st Qtr., pp. 28, 29, 34, 35. (Ital. sup.)

[15] *Ibid.*, pp. 35, 37, 40, 47.

[16] 1899 *GCB*, pp. 74, 75-77; cf. *RH*, Mar. 7, Apr. 4, 1899, pp. 160, 217, 218. The EGW quotation is from EGW to Brother and Sister EJW, Aug. 26, 1898. (Ital. sup.)

[17] 1899 *GCB*, pp. 85-96.

[18] *Ibid.*, p. 86. (Ital. sup.)

[19] *Ibid.*, p. 87.

[20] *Ibid.*, pp. 90, 91.

[21] *Ibid.*, p. 91.

[22] *Ibid.*, pp. 91, 92.

[23] *Ibid.*, pp. 92-94.

[24] *RH*, Dec. 6, 1853, p. 173; July 21, 1859, p. 68; Knight, *Organizing*, pp. 28-47.

[25] *Ibid.*, pp. 178, 179. (Ital. sup.)

[26] GAI to EGW, Jan. 20, 1899.

[27] EGW, MS 43a, Apr. 1, 1901.

[28] *Ibid.*

[29] 1901 *GCB*, pp. 23-27, 33.

[30] *Ibid.*, pp. 37-42.

[31] *Ibid.*, pp. 38, 41.

[32] ATJ, *Some History, Some Experience, and Some Facts* ([Battle Creek, Mich., 1906]), pp. 18, 22; AGD to WCW, June 12, 1901.

[33] 1901 *GCB*, pp. 69, 70, 89, 101-105, 265; ATJ, *The Divine Right of Individuality in Religion or Religious Liberty Complete* ([Battle Creek, Mich.], 1908); ATJ, *Religious Liberty* ([Battle Creek, Mich., 1906]).

[34] 1901 *GCB*, p. 464; ATJ, *Some History*, pp. 17-24.

[35] GCC Min, Apr. 18, 1901.

[36] *RH*, Feb. 25, 1902, p. 125; "Report of a Portion of a Council Meeting Held at Mrs. E. G. White's Home, . . . Oct. 19, 1902," unpub. MS.

[37] "Report of a Portion of a Council Meeting . . ." Oct. 19, 1902, unpub. MS.; WWP to FMW, Dec. 7, 1902; AGD, "Statement," unpub. MS, Mar. 3, 1903; GCC Min, Nov. 16, 20, 1902.

[38] GCC Min, Nov. 15, 1902; AGD to C. C. Nicola, July 30, 1906; *AS* (2), July 1922, p. 6; ATJ, *Some History*, pp. 24-27.

[39] GCC Min, Nov. 20, 22, 1902; GIB to JHK, Oct. 18, 1903; JHK to Colleagues and Friends, c. Oct. 24, 1903; AGD to WCW, Sept. 29, 1903; JHK to ATJ, Aug. 27, 1903.

[40] AGD to WCW, May 31, July 1, 1901; AGD to C. C. Nicola, July 30, 1906; WCW to AGD, June 19, 1901; Aug. 13, 1906; GCC Min, Feb. 15, 1902.

[41] GCC Min, Nov. 13, 1902; EGW to ATJ, Aug. 2, 1903; AGD to WCW, Aug. 9, 1903; *RH*, Aug. 27, 1903, pp. 4, 5, 11, 12.

[42] WWP to AGD, Jan. 25, 26, 1903; JHK to GIB, Feb. 8, 1903.

[43] AGD to WCW, Mar. 11, 1903; JHK to WCW, Mar. 18, 1903.

[44] 1903 *GCB*, pp. 145-173.

[45] AGD to GAI, Oct. 5, 1904; 1903 *GCB*, p. 177.

[46] ATJ, *Some History,* pp. 22, 23.

[47] 1903 *GCB,* pp. 67, 73-82.

[48] "Interview at Dr. J. H. Kellogg's Home," unpub. MS, Oct. 7, 1907.

[49] Arthur T. Pierson, quoted in Oliver, *SDA Organizational Structure*, p. 233.

[50] Frank Bartleman, *Azusa Street* (Plainfield, N. J., 1980), p. 31; F. Bartleman, quoted in R. Laurence Moore, *Religious Outsiders and the Making of Americans* (New York, 1986), p. 140; W. Durham, quoted in Edith L. Blumhofer, *Restoring the Faith: The Assemblies of God, Pentecostalism, and American Culture* (Urbana, Ill., 1993), p. 116.

[51] Blumhofer, *Restoring the Faith*, p. 116; *AS* (2), October 1922, pp. 3, 4.

CHAPTER XIV
A CONFERENCE PRESIDENT ANYWAY

One of the most remarkable occurrences in Jones's eventful career was his assuming the presidency of the California Conference of Seventh-day Adventists in June 1901. He had been relieved of the editorship of the *Review and Herald* in April so that he would be "free to engage in evangelistic work in the field." The reasons given for the change, interestingly enough, were just the opposite of those offered for putting him in as editor four years earlier. Denominational administration had placed him in the editorial post so that he could bless all with his pen rather than a fewer number with his voice and personal presence.[1] On the other hand, the church removed him from the editorship so that he could bless Adventist gatherings by his presence. The implication is clear: Jones had not worked out as editor of the denomination's foremost periodical. As a result, the leadership was putting him out to pasture.

Ellen White undoubtedly had a hand in the change. His place, she opined, "is not in the editorial chair. He has a message to bear and power with which to bear this message, and he should enter the fields where the need is greatest and open the truths of the word of God to the people." Editorial work had been hard on his health. He was a "man who must not be confined to mental work, with no exercise of his physical powers." She wept and thanked God when Uriah Smith again became editor in chief of the *Review.*[2]

It was fine and good to have Jones as a minister for the church at large, but just what was he supposed to do? That question undoubtedly posed a problem for the infant Daniells administration. As a first step, the General Conference Committee appointed Jones as chairman of the newly created Religious Liberty Department of the General Conference and gave him back his old job as editor of the *Sentinel*.[3] That, however, seemed to be only a stopgap measure, since the religious liberty front was quiet and the journal was barely surviving. The position was hardly one to challenge a high-powered individual like Jones.

Jones, of course, could speak at general meetings of the church as a minister at large, and that is apparently what leadership planned for him during the summer of 1901. In that capacity in May he had helped reorganize the Upper Columbia Conference. There, W. C. White complained, Jones had made "strong utterances" in favor of "discarding . . . the office and title of president. He tells our people that the General Conference has no president any more, that our state conferences are not to have presidents, and that the office of president of the Union Conference will soon be done away." Jones was entirely successful in the Upper Columbia Conference. The conference reorganized without anyone bearing the title of president.[4]

JONES ELECTED PRESIDENT

It was one month after the Upper Columbia meetings that he attended the California camp meeting. Presumably, he had the same reorganizational goals in mind, but his plans would get turned on their head. Before the meetings ended he had accepted the conference presidency. His decision, however, did not come without some serious heart searching.

When he arrived at the camp meeting, he told the constituents in his pre-election speech that "all the committees and all the conferences on this earth could not get me to be president of a conference, that is [sic] settled long ago; but when God speaks then it is all settled with me." The change came about through a series of interviews with Ellen White. In the first she told him that God had a mission for him to reform the institutions on the Pacific Coast, especially in California. Sometime later, members of the conference committee began to ask if he would take the presidency. Their inquiries inspired him to return to Ellen White's house to query her directly regarding the position. "Then I asked her[,] should I be president of this conference?' She asked a question or two, which I answered: and then she said 'Do it.'" "That," Jones added, "is the only way it could possibly have come about."[5]

He reasoned that if he was president he would have an easier time reforming the conference's institutions, even though he continued to claim that "position does not give authority" and that he would have no more authority after an election than before. Ellen White's support of the plan clinched it in his mind. For A. T. Jones in 1901, her approval was still that of God.[6]

Not all the constituents wanted Jones as president. His candidacy met fairly stiff resistance, and he openly confessed his faults before the delegates. Three problems particularly concerned his enemies. First, he preached too long—often from two to three hours. That he promised to correct: "I confess it, and I quit." Second, they worried about his "lack of executive ability." He admitted the truth of the accusation, claiming that it was really a virtue, since it would lead him to delegate authority. Third, he received criticism for his "directness and plainness of speech," because "it hurt folks." Jones had a hard time with that accusation. While he could acknowledge it, he claimed, he could not repent of it, "because it is simple christianity [sic]." One of the conference committee members said that it was not his plainness that was the problem, but his harsh manner. After that explanation, Jones promised to overcome, but it is evident that he continued to confuse directness with harshness.[7] That confusion became a major source of his failure as a conference president.

His confessions, along with Ellen White's encouragement, must have been enough to quiet his detractors. The conference elected him president in mid-June. His acceptance was a surprise to Adventist leadership across the country. The president of the Pacific Union Conference wrote to Daniells that the conversation with Ellen White had put Jones's mind to rest on the issue of the presidency. W. C. White hoped that the election would silence Jones in his attack on both the position and the title of president. White wrote to A. G. Daniells, the General Conference president, "that Eld. A. T. Jones has been elected to the presidency without any protest to the use of the title." Time would demonstrate, however, that Jones's cessation of criticism would only be temporary.[8]

That same day Daniells noted that he was "astonished to receive a telegram from California . . . stating that Elder Jones had been elected president of the California Conference." "Brother Jones," he stated, "is a mighty man in the Scriptures and in history; but he is a queer fellow in business affairs. . . . We had been counting on Brother Jones for a lot of fine field work during the coming year. What on earth he will do with a Conference, is more than anybody can tell. Of course he will be a strong man to travel over the State, but he will need a whole committee to keep business affairs in proper shape." Daniells assumed that the election was to get Jones on the west coast and once that was accomplished he would be replaced as president so that he could be given "a roving commission over the Pacific Union Conference."[9] Such a presumption was far from reality. Jones definitely had his eye on the presidential role.

But unfortunately for the California Conference, Jones was more interested in reforming its institutions than he was in running the conference itself. Of particular importance was the mandate from Ellen White to deal with the St. Helena Sanitarium, the Pacific Press Publishing Association, and Healdsburg College. When he had finished with those tasks, he wrote Daniells, he would gladly give up the presidency.[10] One result of Jones's focus was that his administration suffered from a lack of guidance in many areas outside the realm of his reform program.

REFORMING CALIFORNIA'S ADVENTISTS

Jones first turned his attention to the area of education. He labored with the college teachers, the church school teachers, and the Healdsburg College board for two weeks in September 1901, endeavoring to establish the changes in the California college that he had stimulated with E. A. Sutherland's aid at Battle Creek College. The board, under Jones's leadership, voted that "the college should be conducted strictly upon Christian principles." After all, he noted, if the college did not meet the goals for which it was established, the church did not need it and it was a waste of means. A program of useful work for every student was a central feature in his reform package. As a result, the board voted: (1) to bring in every appropriate trade as soon as possible, (2) that there would be no distinction between work and education, and (3) that all teachers would work with the students daily. The college board also voted, for both student convenience and continuity in the labor programs, to abolish long vacations. As Jones put it, "the school year goes on forever."[11]

At the elementary level, he sought to expand the number of church schools, and to ensure their support through a system of second tithes. The Jones administration also sponsored the establishment of three "intermediate schools" for young people who had finished elementary school but were either not planning to go to college or were too young to attend the Healdsburg school. It was his goal to build these schools as much as possible with student labor.[12]

A. T. Jones was a definite friend of Christian education. Periodically throughout his presidency he spent significant periods of time on the Healdsburg campus in efforts of reform and revival. In the area of educational reform he found a great deal of sympathy among the teachers and educational administrators. The going would be much more difficult in his attempt to transform the medical program.

Jones's efforts to reorganize Adventism's medical institutions in California followed several lines. The first involved the denomination's most important West Coast medical institution—the St. Helena Sanitarium in northern California. He spent six intense weeks at the sanitarium in October and November 1901. When he went there he found "not a single principle for which the institution stands" being practiced in its daily operations. It was more of a "general hotel" with bathing rooms than it was a true sanitarium, he reported to Daniells. "The patients instead of the doctors have run it: that is they could have whatever they required—tea, coffee, flesh meats, and all, and all these three times a day if they choose." Beyond that, the institution's leading physician practiced hypnotism and mind cure. All agreed that the spiritual condition of the institution was poor indeed.[13]

Working and praying day and night, he met the problems of the hospital with his usual enthusiasm. His goal was to clear its atmosphere of the "spiritual malaria" that filled it, and to place the institution "firmly upon the clear-cut principles of the Third Angel's Message."[14]

His goal was undoubtedly worthy, but, as usual, his methods left something to be desired. That was particularly true in the case of Dr. Sanderson, the sanitarium's medical superintendent. Ellen White was quite aware of the doctor's infatuation with hypnotism, but she had been patiently laboring with him while he worked through his difficulty. Unfortunately, she told Jones of the problem, and in his zeal to cleanse the camp he challenged Sanderson before the board of directors either to resign or change his views. Much to the disappointment of Ellen White, he resigned. She felt that the proper approach could have saved him for the institution. A few days later she appealed to Jones not to manifest an authoritative and "masterly spirit, as if seeking to drive matters. Christ does not say, 'My sheep see and feel my whip and go before me.'" Her appeal to him, as usual, was to speak in love and tenderness, even in correcting the erring.[15]

In spite of his harsh methods, Jones made good progress at St. Helena. By late 1901 he could report that nearly all shared a spirit of confession and reform. Besides the six weeks in the autumn of 1901, Jones spent a significant amount of time at the institution during the next year. Ellen White could later report that there had been "a decided change for the better" in the sanitarium's spirituality, and that many reforms had been instituted in the face of stout resistance.[16]

A second line in the medical area that Jones fostered with great interest was the establishment of treatment rooms and a health restaurant in San Francisco. Such efforts, under his leadership, were linked with more traditional methods of evangelism. Jones's goal in medical reform and reorganization was to keep the medical and evangelical branches united.[17]

The third prong of his labor in the medical field was the organization of the Pacific Union Medical Missionary Association. Ellen White wanted to make sure that the California medical institutions and programs did not come under the direct administration of Kellogg's International Medical Missionary and Benevolent Association. She urged local control. Jones, with his emphasis on self-control and local control, was much in harmony with her sentiment.[18] As a result, in the summer of 1902 he was instrumental in developing a legal structure for medical institutions in the Pacific Union Conference based on local ownership and administration.[19]

Subsequently Jones presented his plan for medical organization to the General Conference Committee during its autumn 1902 meetings. Kellogg, possibly sensing that local control and ownership would be to his advantage, since it was easier to dominate a local board than the General Conference, made a motion that the denomination adopt the principle for its burgeoning medical program.[20] Thus he willingly traded possible control of all Adventist medical institutions for almost certain control of the Battle Creek Sanitarium. A beneficial result of his choice was that when Kellogg left the church and wrested the Battle Creek institution from the denomination, he did not take much other medical property with him. His power play might have been much more disastrous if Jones's principle of local ownership had not become a part of the reorganization policy.

By the beginning of 1902 Jones had his educational and medical reforms well under way. Early in the year, therefore, he trained his guns on the revival of spiritual vigor among the employees and management of the Pacific Press in Oakland. For five weeks he worked with them, achieving much, but claiming much more was yet to be done.[21]

Concurrent with his activities at the Pacific Press, Jones held a five-week workers' convention across the bay in San Francisco. His usual emphases in reform and reorganization received full exposure. The last 10 days gave special attention to the medical program, with Drs. Paulson and Kellogg spending nearly the entire time at the convention.[22]

One of the most remarkable features of the convention was Jones's aggressive plan to send church employees and money outside the state into more needy fields in the United States and abroad. After demonstrating that California had more denominational employees and members than other areas of the world field, he urged the acceptance of a program that had five essential points: 1. Unfruitful laborers were to be released from the payroll to free up funds for fields outside California. By February 25 he could announce that the California Conference had cut its working force by approximately 33 percent. 2. The best of the conference employees were to be sent to needy fields, especially overseas and to the American South. By October Jones could report that about 30 percent of the California staff had accepted such calls, while others were looking for opportunities abroad. 3. To fill the gap in the working force made by those laid off and those leaving for missions, every laymember would have to become active in spreading the Adventist message. 4. The California Conference would financially support the ministers it sent to needy fields. 5. A second tithe system would be implemented to help defray the costs of this program and the conference's elementary schools.[23]

Jones's mission expansion program had many merits. He pushed it for the remainder of his tenure as conference president. It was built upon the belief that the Adventist work is one work, and that conference lines should not stop the flow of means and personnel. The church can still learn from some of his ideas in this area in the early twenty-first century.

RESCUED BY ELLEN WHITE

Notwithstanding his successes, everyone seemed to be unhappy with Jones's presidency. As the time for his first annual reelection approached, the pressure began to mount for his removal.

W. T. Knox, the president of the Pacific Union Conference, was quite worried over the problem. He admitted that Jones had done a great deal of good, but despite the glowing reports of his reforms and his many talents, Knox claimed that "the real conference work of California is in a most decidedly unorganized condition and things are drifting." The conference committee was dissatisfied, and its members were no longer cooperating with each other. Everyone except W. C. White, Knox claimed, wanted a change, but they were all but hopeless that it could be accomplished, on account of White's power and Jones's forcefulness. He pleaded with Daniells to give Jones a call to the General Conference, believing that such an offer "is the only thing that will cause him to relinquish his position" in California.[24]

M. H. Brown, the California Conference secretary, also urged Daniells to bring Jones to the General Conference, claiming that their fears of him before the election had all come true. "He promulgates great principles and presents grand thoughts, but when he comes to practical work in conference affairs, he is utterly impractical because of lack of executive ability, judgment and wisdom. While theoretically he desires counsel and asks for it, yet so strong and masterful is his personality and his convictions, that he brushes aside the views of others unless they agree with his views, so that his committeemen are obliged to yield or have a battle, and they avoid an issue whenever they think it advisable to do so for the sake of peace." Brown ominously declared that Jones's reelection would be hotly contested, and that if he was not returned to office, given the circumstances, he would "be discredited, and his influence greatly injured."[25]

Even W. C. White, Jones's staunchest supporter in California and a praiser of his reform efforts, recognized his weaknesses. While applauding his reforms as being of "untold value," White could also see that Jones's "enthusiasm and energy lead him to carry some lines of instruction so far and in such an emphatic way that our brethren feel that he is trying to force something down their throats without giving them time to chew and swallow."[26] Both Jones's manner and his extremes turned people off.

Ellen White also felt troubled over Jones. She claimed that, in spite of his confession on the day of his election, the very next day he "spoke in a magisterial manner, as a commanding officer." He was committing, she complained to him, the same error that he had made at the Review and Herald. Writing to Daniells, she lamented that Jones was exercising "kingly authority."[27] Strangely enough, that was the very thing that he had fought so hard against and would condemn Daniells for until the day of his death. It is a sad anomaly that he never managed to conquer the problem in his own life. On the other hand, he may have hated it so much in others because of his own struggle with it.

Ellen White would counsel him against his abuse of power for the rest of his tenure, noting that he had a natural "desire to rule" and a "dictatorial spirit" that had increased in his efforts to correct "the evils which have come in since the Minneapolis meeting." As on similar occasions, she pointed him consistently to the loving manner of Jesus. Jones acknowledged his appreciation of her counsel, but as usual, he found it next to impossible to abide by it.[28]

Deeply concerned with his reelection in the fall of 1902, she plainly explained to him that if he was not reelected others would regard his work as a failure. Wanting to save the man, she frankly warned him that he did not understand the job of a conference president, that he was not to be a ruler, and that he must let God soften his spirit. In short, he needed a "genuine conversion."[29]

At the Fresno camp meeting on October 6, 1902, Ellen White told the assembled ministers of the California Conference that it was "the pleasure of God" for Jones to serve the conference for another year. On the other hand, it was also "His pleasure that A. T. Jones should put away all appearance of a magisterial, domineering, authoritative manner." She endorsed his physical and mental capabilities for the job, but claimed that he needed the Holy Spirit if he was to succeed. Also she predicted that he would be "reconverted."[30]

Jones responded with a humble confession of his wrongs before the assembled ministers. After he and J. O. Corliss—his second in command—both made heartfelt prayers of surrender, they "fell upon each other's necks, and with many tears confessed their shortcomings." That scene, Ellen White claimed, changed the mood of the meeting, and the influence of the Holy Spirit came into it in a marked manner. Although at first she believed that Jones had been reconverted, his actions in the subsequent year led her to question her initial judgment. During the next 10 years, as he drifted further and further from the church, she would repeatedly hold his 1902 experience up to him and others as an example of what he needed to become. Eventually she would feel compelled to warn him of a public exposure of all the facts of his problems at the Fresno meeting if he continued to sabotage the church.[31]

One of Jones's difficulties that he at least partially solved at Fresno was his relationship to his wife. Frances Jones had been a talented young woman at the time of their marriage, but his extremely dominating and opinionated personality undoubtedly weighed heavy upon her independence and individuality. Coupled with those factors was his total dedication to his work—an obsession that led him to work long days without holidays or vacations and that sometimes took him away from home for weeks and months at a time. Such problems did not make marriage easy, but the real crisis of their family life was that their first child had been born mentally incompetent and needed constant attention for her entire life.[32] That calamity placed an extra burden of care, frustration, and perhaps guilt on both parents and on the relationship itself.

Surviving records indicate little regarding Jones's personal life. We do know, however, that he was the up-front man who was "doing the Lord's work," while his wife seemed to vegetate unnoticed at home.

Their marriage appears to have had little intimacy. Its condition had reached crisis proportions by the time Jones became president in California. He moved to California without Frances and their two daughters during the summer of 1901. While he kept up a fairly healthy correspondence with his fellow church employees, he failed on that count with his wife. According to Daniells, she desired his presence, but he had not even kept her informed if he would return to Battle Creek for the General Conference Committee meetings at the end of October. She had to get that information from Daniells at church on Sabbath. The General Conference president wrote to Jones of the visit in a manner that indicated a definite concern.[33]

Both W. C. White and his mother were also apprehensive over Jones's family life. W. C. White wrote to Frances on April 25, 1902, urging her to move to California. We do not know if his appeal was instrumental in the decision, but we do know that a month later he was able to write to Jones expressing joy that Mrs. Jones was heading west.[34]

Part of their anxiety undoubtedly resulted from Jones's indiscretions with certain women belonging to his California constituency. Ellen White flatly told him that he had no business playing the detective in inspecting the private rooms of the nurses in his work in reforming the St. Helena Sanitarium. That, she noted, had made him look ridiculous, but her major concern related to the attentions he had shown to a young female physician as her "counselor." Separated from her husband, she had fastened her affections on Jones. Justifying his actions on the premise that as conference president he needed to watch over his flock and help them with their problems, Jones took care of the young woman as though, Ellen White wrote, she was his wife. That had put him in a dangerous position. He had confused, Ellen White intimated, his personal problems with the Lord's work.[35]

Jones's indiscretions and his family difficulties loomed large as the time for his reelection approached in October 1902. In September Ellen White informed him that she was aware that he had had the problem of showing special attention to young women back in his teaching days at Healdsburg College in the late 1880s. With that in mind, she noted, it was not strange that his wife wore a sad countenance. She advised him to keep his sympathy for his wife, who needed all the love and care he could give, and to point his physician friend to a woman counselor.[36]

The work of the Whites for the Jones family bore some fruit. In the fall of 1902, for example, we find the unprecedented information that Jones was taking his wife with him to a meeting in southern California. Ellen White undoubtedly pressed him hard on the family issue at his reelection at Fresno. Soon after his confession at that camp meeting he made things right with his wife. He later reported to Ellen White that Frances was happier than he had ever seen her, and that they were both determined to maintain their new relationship.[37]

After Ellen White's successful face-saving attempt to get him reelected, the General Conference Committee did its best to rescue California from his administrative ineptitude. On December 23, 1902, it offered him the secretaryship of the General Conference Religious Liberty Department. W. T. Knox, president of the Pacific Union Conference, believed the change would be good for both California and the religious liberty program. He was also convinced that Jones was quite pleased with the opportunity. Jones, however, turned the offer down.[38] He would remain in California until late 1903, when he would join forces with J. H. Kellogg as president of the reestablished Battle Creek College.

[1] RH, May 14, 1901, p. 320; Oct. 5, 1897, p. 640.

[2] EGW, MS 37, c. April 1901; EGW to AGD, June 24, 1901; EGW to Brother and Sister SNH, Feb. 5, 1902.

[3] GCC Min, Apr. 19, 29, 1901.

[4] WCW to AGD, May 24, 1901.

[5] [Confession of A. T. Jones], unpub. MS, June 13, 1901; cf. WTK to AGD, July, 8, 1901.

[6] [Confession of A. T. Jones], unpub. MS, June 13, 1901.

[7] *Ibid.*

[8] *RH,* July 9, 1901, pp. 450, 461; WTK to AGD, July 8, 1901; WCW to AGD, June 19, 1901.

[9] AGD to E. R. Palmer, June 19, 1901.

[10] WCW to AGD, Sept. 26, 1901; ATJ to AGD, Sept. 8, 1901.

[11] ATJ to the People of the California SDA Conference, Feb. 25, 1902; ATJ to WCW, Nov. 13, 1901; ATJ to AGD, Sept. 8, 1901.

[12] *RH,* Nov. 25, 1902, p. 18; ATJ to the People of the California SDA Conference, c. fall 1902.

[13] ATJ to the People of the California SDA Conference, Feb. 25, 1902; ATJ to AGD, Oct. 22, 1901; EGW to JHK, Oct. 9, 1901; ATJ to EGW, Nov. 22, 1901.

[14] ATJ to the People of the California SDA Conference, Feb. 25, 1902; ATJ to AGD, Oct. 22, 1901.

[15] EGW to JHK, Oct. 9, 1901; ATJ, "Talk to the Helpers of the St. Helena Sanitarium, St. Helena, California, Oct. 27, 1901," unpub. MS; EGW to ATJ, Oct. 19, 1901.

[16] ATJ to EGW, Nov. 14, 1901; EGW to Brother and Sister Burden, Feb. 5, July 23, 1902.

[17] ATJ to WCW, Nov. 13, 1901; ATJ, "Talk on the Principles Underlying the Reorganization of Our Medical Institutions, Given Before the Medical Missionary Council, Sanitarium, St. Helena, California, June 19, 1902," unpub. MS.

[18] WCW to ATJ, July 19, 1901; ATJ to WCW, July 25, 1901.

[19] ATJ, "Talk on the Principles Underlying the Reorganization of Our Medical Institutions . . . , June 19, 1902," unpub. MS; cf. *RH,* Feb. 24, 1903, pp. 9, 10; Mar. 3, 1903, pp. 9. 10.

[20] GCC Min, Nov. 13, Oct. 18, 1902.

[21] ATJ to WCW, Dec. 27, 1901; ATJ to the People of the California SDA Conference, Feb. 25, 1902.

[22] *RH,* Feb. 18, 1902, p. 109; ATJ to the People of the California SDA Conference, Feb. 25, 1902.

[23] ATJ to the People of the California SDA Conference, Feb. 25, 1902; ATJ to the People of the California SDA Conference, c. October 1902; *RH,* Nov. 25, 1902, p. 18; ATJ to Brethren and Sisters of the Sabbath Schools, Jan. 29, 1903. Cf. AGD to E. A. Sutherland, Mar. 6, 1902.

[24] WTK to AGD, July 13, 1902.

[25] M. H. Brown to AGD, Aug. 8, Sept. 3, 1902.

[26] WCW to AGD, July 12, Feb. 7, 1902.

[27] EGW to AGD, June 1901 (letter 63, 1901), June 24, 1901.

[28] EGW to ATJ, June 30, 1901; ATJ to EGW, July 25, 1901; cf. EGW to ATJ, Oct. 19, 1901, September 1902 (letter 164, 1902).

[29] EGW to ATJ, September 1902 (letter 164, 1902); cf. EGW to ATJ, May 7, 1902.

[30] "Report of a Ministers' Meeting Held on the SDA Campground, Fresno, California, Oct. 6, 1902," unpub. MS.

[31] Ibid.; EGW to GIB, Apr. 11, 1906; EGW to Brother Whitelock, Oct. 6, 1902; EGW to P. T. Magan and E. A. Sutherland, July 23, 1904; EGW to ATJ, Mar. 23, Apr. 9, July 3, Oct. 26, 1906; Nov. 19, 1911; EGW to the Elders of the Battle Creek Church, July 17, 1906.

[32] FEJ to Department of Interior, Bureau of Pensions, c. 1944, c. 1945; W. D. Upton to Whom It Concerns, Sept. 16, 1940; A. B. Olsen to Whom It May Concern, Sept. 10, 1940; 1893 GCB, p. 515.

[33] AGD to ATJ, Oct. 8, 1901.

[34] WCW to Mrs. ATJ, Apr. 25, 1902; WCW to ATJ, May 25, 1902.

[35] EGW to ATJ, n.d. (letter 207, 1901). Written sometime between late 1901 and October 1902.

[36] EGW to ATJ, September 1902 (letter 164, 1902); cf. EGW to ATJ, Mar. 23, Oct. 26, 1906.

[37] ATJ to WCW, Sept. 2, 1902; EGW to GIB, Apr. 11, 1906; cf. EGW to ATJ, Apr. 9, 1906.

[38] GCC Min, Dec. 23, 1902; WTK to AGD, Dec. 31, 1902; AGD to ATJ, Jan. 9, 1903.

CHAPTER XV

THE DRIFT TOWARD APOSTASY

The General Conference session in April 1903 was a major turning point in Jones's life. He attended the Oakland meetings expecting never to resume his presidency of the California Conference. Even though he later claimed that he had intended to link up with Kellogg as a teacher in the sanitarium after the session, we have good evidence to believe, given his strong reaction to the results of the conference, that he had more grandiose expectations. If he did not, however, Kellogg did. The doctor definitely hoped to overthrow the Daniells-Prescott regime politically, and he was supporting Jones as Daniells' replacement. Daniells and Prescott, in turn, surmised that Kellogg's candidate for the denomination's top post in the General Conference would be Jones, as it had been in the attempted coup the previous November.[1]

As noted in chapter 13, however, the Jones-Kellogg forces suffered a major setback at the 1903 meetings. Not only had the General Conference approved a resolution recommending that all denominationally operated institutions (including sanitariums) come under direct denominational ownership, but it had adopted an amended constitution that officially reinstated the office of president and elected Daniells to that post. Jones made a last-ditch attempt to block the acceptance of the new constitution by declaring that it would take a three-fourths vote to pass it, but it passed anyway. That was one of the low points of his career. Daniells, on the other hand, declared that Jones's defeat on the vote "was a supreme moment in my life."[2]

Jones left the 1903 General Conference session a defeated and bitter man. His rejection especially hurt because he was sensitive and proud, and had been used to being on the winning side since 1888. Unfortunately, he let his bitterness fester in his heart and mind. He would publicly work to discredit Daniells until his own death in 1923.

The defeated Jones, however, was not powerless, despite his failures in Battle Creek and California. In 1903 he was still a person to reckon with in Adventist circles. His reputation would carry him along for some years to come. After all, was not this the man, Ellen White had repeatedly claimed, sent by God with a message from heaven? In mid-1903 he may still have been the most influential thought leader among large sectors of Adventism's laity and clergy. That would all change by the summer of 1906. By then he had discredited himself to most Seventh-day Adventists. In the meanwhile, it took time for him to clarify his position and make it publicly evident.

Immediately following the 1903 General Conference session Jones performed the valuable task of mediating a peace between Kellogg and Daniells at the legal meetings of the Medical Missionary and Benevolent Association. In April Ellen White sent Jones several testimonies for the leaders of both the General Conference and the medical program and instructed him to read them to the assembled group at the opportune time. She particularly admonished him to work for Dr. Kellogg as "a friend of the medical missionary work," to do all he could "to save Dr. Kellogg and his associates," and to "talk and pray with him."[3] Jones took those admonitions as a commission from the Lord, one that should not be treated lightly.

In late April he read the testimonies to the General Conference Committee and appealed to them to open their hearts. The next evening he delivered them to the medical group, tactfully reading those addressed to the General Conference leaders first. After the meeting he spoke privately with Kellogg in the doctor's residence until three in the morning. During that meeting, Jones read a special testimony to the doctor, pleaded with him to surrender, and earnestly prayed with him. The doctor, Jones reported, fell "on the rock and was broken," and made a thorough confession.

The next day Kellogg repeated his confession before the General Conference Committee. "Brother Daniells and Brother Prescott," Jones related, "immediately responded with heartfelt confessions, and these were followed by all the brethren in [the] Committee." "There was a breaking down all around. With tears of contrition and joy, brethren embraced one another in Christian love." After that three-hour meeting the General Conference Committee met with the Medical Missionary Association in the Tabernacle, where Kellogg and Daniells unitedly announced that "peace has come and unity is established; that Christ has triumphed, and His was the victory, and His the glory."[4]

That episode was not only a victory for the church at large, but also a personal triumph for A. T. Jones, who once again found himself at the center of action as the mediator between the denomination's leading powers. The victories, however, were not permanent. In a matter of weeks the medical and evangelical leaders would again be at odds, and Jones would continue to drift toward alliance with Kellogg in a power struggle that eventually would carry both men out of the church.

THE YEAR OF DECISION, 1903

War clouds continued to form over Adventism's contending forces throughout the summer of 1903. July saw the publication of Jones's tract One-Man Power by the Pacific Press, with its obvious implications for the role of the president of the General Conference. Somewhat in the antimonopolistic, trust-busting spirit of the times, he berated the "universal spirit of combine" and proclaimed the certainty that a one-person power will always develop into a "despotism." The ideal, he would later clarify, was that one individual should never "rule within a given territory." Thus in 1903 Jones was still actively advocating his pet theories on church organization, even though he was yet serving as the California Conference president and would bitterly complain to his conference committee after resigning that his rights as conference president had not been respected.[5]

Meanwhile, his ties with the medical forces continued to strengthen throughout the summer of 1903. In June he participated in the dedication of the rebuilt Battle Creek Sanitarium, and by August he had accepted the presidency of Kellogg's reopened Battle Creek College. On August 27 the doctor wrote him a flattering letter, thanking "the Lord that he has given us you for our champion." He contrasted Jones's course with that of Prescott, Spicer, and Daniells, who "have evidently gotten into a state of mind in which they see spooks. They are sure there is a devil in the wood pile, and if there is not one they will make one." "The contrast between the course you have pursued during our trials and perplexities, and the course of Daniells and Prescott is as great as between midnight and the noon-day sunshine."[6]

Not everybody, of course, was sure that Jones's course in accepting the presidency of Battle Creek College was toward the sunshine. That group included Ellen White. On August 2 she appealed to him in straightforward language. "I have a caution for you," she wrote. "I know that you are in danger of encouraging plans that ought not to be encouraged. . . . The Lord plainly called the school out of Battle Creek, and it is not wise to build up a school there, and call people back again. Brother Jones, . . . do not lend your influence to the building up of anything like a college in Battle Creek. This should not be done under any consideration."[7]

Two weeks later, he had an extended visit with her. She pleaded with him not to go to Battle Creek to "establish . . . something that the Lord has forbidden." To her, such a move was equivalent to turning back to Egypt. She told him that Kellogg was "controlled by the spirit of the devil" and that he was chuckling that Jones had fallen into his trap.

Although for years he had been respectful of her counsel, even when he did not understand it, now he argued with her the whole way. Having made up his mind, he was not going to let anyone change it. His will was set, and he justified his decision on the ground that his mission was to convert Kellogg and to help the students in the school to find the correct way. Ellen White countered him by claiming that Adventist young people should not even be attracted to Battle Creek to attend the school.[8]

The August 15 meeting was the first of several conferences that he and Ellen White had together on the topic, but all, from her perspective, were unsuccessful. By early September Jones refused to talk further on the topic, claiming that it was God's will for him to go. After all, had not Ellen White herself told him in April to work for Kellogg's conversion, and had she not in their recent meetings claimed that there was nothing wrong with his "burden" for Kellogg and the Battle Creek Sanitarium? Insisting that it was his duty to accept the position, despite the many warnings, he promised that he would not work for long in Battle Creek and that he would be on his guard. In their final meeting, just before he left for Battle Creek, Ellen White "told him that in vision I had seen him under the influence of Dr. Kellogg. Fine threads were being woven around him, till he was being

bound hand and foot, and his mind and his senses were becoming capti-
vated." The future would plainly show the truth of that prediction.[9]

The developing problem went public to the Adventist constituency on
August 27, 1903, when the *Review* (now located in Washington, D.C.)
published two articles on the reopening of Battle Creek College. The first
was an editorial by Prescott that condemned it on the basis of Ellen
White's counsels. The second article sought to justify the reopening and
was signed by A. T. Jones, E. A. Sutherland, P. T. Magan, E. D. Kirby, and
J. H. Kellogg.[10]

The battle over the college had begun, and the issue was now in the
open. Adventists, of course, had viewed Battle Creek for years as the center of the denomination's most prestigious educational opportunities. It
still contained the American Medical Missionary College and the massive
sanitarium. Thus it had great drawing power. The struggle that was developing involved the church's most important treasure—its youth. Both
Kellogg and the General Conference sought their allegiance. After all, the
future of the church rested in their hands. Jones's role, needless to say,
perplexed many staunch Adventists, who had long looked upon him as a
reforming light in their midst.[11]

What had been a smoldering ember in the heart of Adventism was about
to burst into flame. Both sides used warlike talk. Daniells related that "the
survival of this whole movement is at stake. . . . If we surrender to this
thing, our cause is ruined." Kellogg was much of the same mind. "It
looks," he wrote on August 31, "as tho *[sic]* a line of battle was *[sic]* being
formed. . . . The conference men are determined to run the Sanitarium
and the medical missionary work." Appealing to Dr. David Paulson—
head of the medical program in Hinsdale, Illinois—to stand with him,
Kellogg noted that Jones, Waggoner, Sutherland, and Magan had already
"crossed the Rubicon."[12]

Ellen White, out in California, also recognized the atmosphere of war.
In October she penned that "*the time has come to take decided action*" in
meeting the *Living Temple* theology with its "spiritualistic sentiments," and
in countering the move to bring the cream of the denomination's youth
under the influence of Battle Creek.[13]

The leaders on both sides recognized that the central issue in the struggle was administrative control rather than theology. Theology, on the

other hand, played an active part, as we have seen in chapter 13 and will see again in the discussion of the Berrien Springs meeting in 1904. The role and authority of Ellen White also became a major factor in the hostilities, particularly since she finally had to take sides openly.[14] She had put that move off as long as possible, hoping to draw the two factions together, but by October 1903 she was ready to come out publicly against Kellogg and his allies. The opening of Battle Creek College and the struggle for the church's youth had forced her to speak out. The Kellogg forces interpreted her decision to mean that W. C. White and the General Conference leadership were manipulating her—a charge they never tired of making.

One of the great paradoxes of the reopening of Battle Creek College is that it was Jones who, as president of the Seventh-day Adventist Educational Society, had stimulated the transfer of the original college from Battle Creek in 1901 on the basis of Ellen White's testimony concerning the problems there. Those problems, of course, had not altered. But Jones had changed. Between the spring of 1901 and the summer of 1903 he had nursed his wounded pride and hurt feelings to the place where he was now ready to oppose what he had once stood for. Both Ellen White and Kellogg knew that when Jones chose to go to Battle Creek College he had made one of the major decisions of his life. As Kellogg put it, Jones "crossed the Rubicon . . . when he left Oakland and came to Battle Creek."[15]

THE SIDES HARDEN, 1904

The denomination entered the year 1904 in a running battle, with Kellogg firmly believing that the General Conference leaders had a "settled determination to crush" him and to drive him out of the denomination with their "rule or ruin" policy.[16]

The high point in the year, as far as the denominational crisis was concerned, was the Lake Union Conference session, which met at Berrien Springs, Michigan, in May. The meetings were fraught with potential for both good and evil. Kellogg had decided to make his stand at the session. Ellen White, on the other hand, saw the meetings as an opportunity "to save Dr. Kellogg." By that, however, she did not mean that the General Conference should back down in the face of either Kellogg's philosophical errors in The Living Temple or his demand for administrative autonomy. The doctor, to her way of thinking, was to be saved *from* his errors, not *in* them. During her first message at the session she addressed the problems of pantheism in *The Living Temple*.[17]

Prescott was slated for the Friday evening sermon. He also intended to talk on pantheism. Ellen White had advised him to go ahead with his presentation, but on Friday morning she wrote him not to do it, since she did not want it to appear that Kellogg was "receiving a threshing." She handed her letter to W. C. White to deliver to Prescott, but her son never passed it along to him. White had apparently convinced his mother that her first judgment was correct. As a result, she gave him permission to hold the letter.[18] The upshot was that on Friday evening the audience, including Kellogg, heard a vivid presentation on the evils of pantheism. Prescott's sermon resulted in what Ellen White had feared—it brought others to Kellogg's defense.

The most significant defender was Jones, who had been harboring resentment against Prescott on the subject of pantheism for some time. Prescott quoted part of Jones's *Revelation of God,* published by Kellogg's organization in 1902, and earlier he had used the quotations at several union conference sessions in a way that inferred that the author was a pantheist. As one could expect, such treatment raised Jones's blood pressure considerably. He had come to the Lake Union Conference meetings prepared to do combat if Prescott raised the issue.[19]

Jones got his chance at the 5:45 meeting on Monday morning. After the prayer, he requested the floor, then entered into a two- to three-hour tirade against Prescott. In it he strived to show that "Prescott was the responsible party for introducing among us pantheistic teachings." He endeavored to demonstrate, from Prescott's *Review* editorials of 1902, "that Dr. Kellogg had obtained his theology from Professor Prescott." Kellogg then stood up and said that it was all true—"that he simply adapted Professor Prescott's teaching to his physiological work."[20]

The attack provided a difficult moment for the General Conference officials. However, I. H. Evans, the General Conference treasurer, soon arose, inquiring of Jones if he might ask some questions. Evans wanted him to explain how *The Living Temple* could derive from Prescott's *Review* articles, since the book had been completed in February 1902, whereas the editorials quoted by Jones were not published until between June and

December of that year. "Brother Jones," Daniells reported, "looked into blank space, and said nothing." Kellogg, meanwhile, who was still walking back to his seat, "cleared his throat a number of times, and then stated that perhaps there had been a mistake on this point." Perhaps it had been some of Prescott's earlier editorials or his teaching in the sanitarium.[21]

Evans' well-aimed question gave the General Conference leaders a short breather, but the meeting continued for six hours with Jones leading a bloodletting attack on Prescott that neither Prescott nor Daniells would ever forget. Daniells reported that "we left the meeting sick at heart, and hoping that we would never be obliged to pass through another like experience."[22]

Ellen White pleaded and preached for unity throughout the session, but needless to say, she made little headway. Even though both sides made confessions, the real result was the hardening of lines. Kellogg resigned from the Medical Missionary Association, while Sutherland and Magan—his sympathizers—resigned from the leadership of Emmanuel Missionary College.[23]

The Kellogg forces at first thought that they had won quite a victory at Berrien Springs in 1904, but in actual fact they had suffered another major defeat. Ellen White wrote in July that the meetings, contrary to their promise, had confirmed Kellogg in his course. She later pointed out to Jones that at the Berrien Springs session he also had reached a negative turning point in his relation to the Holy Spirit. The Berrien Springs meetings were the last really significant attempt to unite the two sides in the struggle that had rent the denomination's leadership in twain. Both elements subsequently continued to grow further apart. After the meeting Ellen White sided more and more openly with Daniells and Prescott, writing to Sutherland and Magan in July that the General Conference leaders were God's chosen men in the struggle.[24] Her words were sadly reminiscent of those she had repeatedly written about Jones, Waggoner, and Prescott a decade earlier.

Perhaps at this point we should say something about Jones's personal belief in, and relationship to, pantheism. Even though he does not appear to have been a pantheist in the same sense as Kellogg and Waggoner, he certainly used language and symbolism in harmony with *The Living Temple* theology. While he had not abandoned the traditional Adventist teaching on the sanctuary and its cleansing during this period, he did confound the indwelling of God in the living human temple and the cleansing of the body temple with the doctrine of the heavenly sanctuary and its cleansing. The problem showed up in his public presentations to the medical personnel on the subject of the heavenly sanctuary and the human (living) temple in early 1902 and in his *Consecrated Way to Christian Perfection.* Pacific Press published the book in 1905, but they did not market it. By April 1907 they had sold only some 70 copies, even though they had printed 3,000. The denomination also pulled other books during this period off the market that were too close to *The Living Temple* theology. A case in point was *The Abiding Spirit,* by Mrs. S.M.I. Henry, a close associate of Jones in the "Receive Ye the Holy Ghost" emphasis until her death in 1899.[25]

To put it mildly, the Adventist air was quite heavy with ideas that one could interpret as pantheistic in the late nineties and early 1900s. Some of them undoubtedly grew out of exaggerated and overly literalized views of the indwelling Christ. The concept of the indwelling power of Christ was inherent in the 1888 message, but when pushed too far it easily crosses the border into pantheism. It was certainly so in the case of Waggoner, as Woodrow Whidden has forcefully demonstrated.[26]

It is probably no accident that the three foremost ministerial proponents of righteousness by faith in the 1890s—Jones, Waggoner, and Prescott—all got entangled in pantheistic language and sentiments. Waggoner had fully accepted pantheism by 1897. Prescott had used terminology that one could interpret as pantheistic, but definitely rejected pantheism when he saw its implications. Jones had used language and concepts compatible with pantheism, but never rejected them when the pantheistic implications of *The Living Temple* became evident. That both Jones and Waggoner endorsed *The Living Temple* is clear from the volume's preface, which lists them as approving readers. It seemed evident to Jones's contemporaries on both sides of the struggle that he never did have much problem with the ideas in the book.[27]

ATTEMPTS TO RECLAIM JONES, 1905

The year 1905 saw two attempts to arrest Jones's drift toward apostasy. Ellen White was the prime mover in both efforts.

Her first tactic to rescue Jones was to get him to move from Battle Creek to Washington, D.C., to assist in religious liberty activities. Agitation for Sunday legislation had been quiescent for several years, but it revived in

1904, the year after the General Conference headquarters had moved to the capital. Two bills introduced that year attempted to pass Sunday legislation for the District of Columbia. Unlike the Sunday legislation of the 1890s, which labor unions had opposed, labor had now united with the Sunday forces. That made the situation even more critical. The battle for Sunday legislation carried over into 1905.[28]

Ellen White saw that crisis as a good excuse to get Jones out of Battle Creek. On January 16, 1905, she wrote to the General Conference leaders, asking them if they could take him into the religious liberty program. W. A. Colcord, secretary of the Religious Liberty Bureau, was all for the idea, but the suggestion astounded Daniells and Prescott. After all, was not Jones the leading spokesman in the enemy camp? Had not he done everything he could to destroy the influence of the General Conference leaders? How could they possibly work together with him?[29]

Their understandable reticence did not seem to discourage Ellen White. On February 13 she informed Jones that it had been presented to her that he should join Daniells and Prescott in Washington. She sent a copy of the letter to Daniells, who replied that it was impossible for him to harmonize Jones's course with her instruction. Nevertheless, Daniells claimed that he was willing to bow to what he considered to be the Lord's revealed will, even though he did not understand it. He would give Jones a "hearty welcome." That evening he wrote to Jones, extending to him a call to join them. But he added that he did not comprehend how they could work together unless Jones changed his views, though he was willing to follow God's voice as revealed through Ellen White.[30]

Jones informed her that he was going to accept the offer, even though he also was somewhat perplexed over it. Kellogg, meanwhile, urged him to take it. "He ought to go," Kellogg wrote, "and let a little light shine into that dark place." Daniells, on the other hand, was not sure he wanted Jones's brand of light. Someone had reported to him that Jones had boasted on the West Coast and in Battle Creek that he was being called to headquarters "to correct us, to set us straight, and to put things in proper shape." Understandably, the General Conference president wanted no part of that.[31]

The General Conference leadership attempted to siphon Jones off into the task of fighting the pending Sunday legislation in Wisconsin before he reached Washington, D.C., probably with the hope that something unforeseen would rescue them from the problem. Jones was quite content with that solution.[32]

At that point, however, events in Washington, D.C., took a rapid move in an unexpected direction. A new crisis had developed over the teaching of religion in the public schools. On March 9 Jones received a telegram that read: "Important developments. You should come Sunday. Letter follows. A. G. Daniells."[33]

Jones went to Washington as directed. The immediate Sunday law crisis had passed with the end of the congressional session, but he did participate effectively and unitedly with Prescott and other denominational leaders in squelching the move to teach religion in the public schools.[34] It looked as if there might be some hope for a revival of the Jones-Prescott team of the previous decade.

Then, in the first week of April, Jones summoned the leaders together to tell them that he was returning to Battle Creek. His wife, he told them, needed his help with their older daughter, who was violent at times. That plea, interestingly enough, is the only recorded instance I have discovered in which Jones indicates that family concerns made an impact on his planning. The General Conference leaders suggested that he should move his family to Washington. At that point, his real reason surfaced: Jones had never planned to leave his work in Battle Creek from the beginning, except for a few weeks. Daniells wrote to W. C. White that "we are all greatly disappointed that the effort . . . to get Bro. Jones under different influences, has failed." For his part, Jones was glad to be gone: "I would rather *have* religious liberty, without *preaching* it," he noted a few months later, "than to try to *preach* it without *having* it." His definition of freedom was that of not being "hedged in and bound about by conditions and limitations" that the denomination's leaders might feel were important.[35]

Ellen White's second attempt to rescue Jones from Battle Creek came during the 1905 General Conference session. Unlike previous sessions, Jones hardly participated in the meetings. He made no formal presentations, and Daniells had purposefully arranged the meetings so that the uncontrolled discussions that had dominated much of the 1899, 1901, and 1903 sessions could not get a foothold. That meant deliberately restricting the mentality inculcated earlier by Jones and his friends that suggested that instead of planned business meetings, every meeting should be "principally a devotional and revival meeting, with the belief that if we get the Spirit we shall not need to plan very much." Outside of offering a couple prayers, the delegates seldom heard Jones's voice during the conference. However, the special *Review* numbers that had taken the place of the *General Conference Bulletin* advertised his books, and the session renewed his ministerial credentials. In spite of the fact that Jones did not get placed on any important committees, the session selected him to be a member of a group that presented a copy of the conference's stand on civil government and religious liberty to President Roosevelt in a White House ceremony.[36]

May 30 saw the closest thing that Jones made to a speech during the 1905 meetings. Following a talk by Ellen White, in which she came down hard on Kellogg and *The Living Temple,* Jones attempted to justify his work in Battle Creek. "I know," he claimed, "that the third angel's message, as I preach it, can, and will, before the Lord comes, redeem the Battle Creek Sanitarium." He went on to speak of the great things he was accomplishing. When pushed to give his position on *The Living Temple,* he refused to repudiate its teachings. Many, including Ellen White, were surprised by his boasting concerning his great triumphs in Battle Creek. A few weeks later she would confide to her diary that Jones had eagerly sought to exalt himself, and needed to be converted.[37]

During the session Ellen White had a three-hour conference with him in which she pleaded with him to abandon his proud ways. He kept his face turned from her, she reported, as much as possible. Their meeting failed to accomplish its goal. Jones went back to Battle Creek to convert Kellogg and the sanitarium.[38]

Arriving in Battle Creek, Jones penned a report of the 1905 General Conference session. He was, as we might expect, quite critical, noting particularly the lack of sermons on righteousness by faith. "Almost wholly the sermons were devoted to guarding 'the pillars of the faith,' the 'pins' and the 'pegs,' and 'planks' of the 'platform' of the message." Beyond that, he ridiculed the "'new era'" Medical Missionary Department of the General Conference that had replaced Kellogg's Medical Missionary and Benevolent Association. He lamented that the reformers in the areas of medical, educational, religious liberty, and righteousness by faith lines had been eliminated from denominational employment. Stating that he had been forced out of the "'organized' work," he claimed that, despite their machinations, he was still active in the mission of the third angel. Jones closed his evaluation with a tirade against the Adventist bureaucracy as opposed to true republican forms of government. There were, he pointed out, two strands of Adventism. "The question for consideration and careful study therefore is—which of these two orders of work will be found in the long run to be the true organized work of God in the work of the Third Angel's Message? Will it be the machine form, restricting and confining? or shall it be the free, open, living, growing form?"[39]

His answer to his questions should be obvious. He was still the foe of any church organization other than the headship of Christ working through the Holy Spirit in the individual life. That alone was organization—that alone was freedom.

ALL-OUT WAR ON BOTH SIDES, 1906

Upon his return to Michigan and his presidency of Battle Creek College, Jones worked with characteristic vigor to transform the institution into a university. The September *Medical Missionary* advertised the upgraded system as "The Battle Creek Schools, Professional, Scientific, Literary, Biblical, Technical, Industrial. Forty courses leading to diplomas and degrees." "Hundreds and thousands of worthy youth," the article pointed out, "are now facing the problem of how to obtain the necessary education for work in Christ's vineyard. The Battle Creek Schools have undertaken to solve that problem."[40]

The proposed solution put Daniells into a dither. He perceived the upgraded institution to be "a great drag-net with which to catch our young people. . . . Unless something decided is done to counteract the movement, we shall lose hundreds of the very flower of our young people." He appealed to Ellen White to make her counsels regarding the evils of Battle Creek more widely known through publishing her testimonies on the topic. "*Has not the time come,*" he queried, "*for the ship to strike the iceberg?*" The next day he flatly declared that "*a war is on.*" The issues in the conflict, as he saw them, were "undermining confidence in the Spirit of Prophecy, prejudicing minds against our general management, and drawing our young people to Battle Creek."[41]

In December Daniells and his associates in Washington, D.C., took the war into the very camp of the enemy in an attempt to persuade faithful

Adventist students and employees to abandon the Battle Creek institutions. The General Conference leaders went supplied with an armload of testimonies, which they read to the church and various other groups in Battle Creek. Their days and nights were full of activity, motivated by the conviction that they were in a life-and-death struggle.[42]

The Kellogg forces, predictably, did not sit quietly. On the evening of December 25 Kellogg gave a six-hour talk to his department heads in which he claimed that he believed Ellen White was inspired by God, while, at the same time, illustrating that not all of her communications could be trusted or relied upon. As a result, many of his listeners found themselves filled with fresh doubts.[43]

The next morning, Daniells received a testimony in the mail dated January 1, 1904. Ellen White had written it in her diary nearly two years before, but, not feeling the time was right, she had never sent it. On the morning of December 21, 1905, she felt impressed to have the message copied and sent to Battle Creek. It arrived on December 26. Daniells read it to the Battle Creek church that same day. Afterward, three men who had been in Kellogg's six-hour meeting the night before came up and told Daniells that "the meeting . . . had been clearly described by the testimony" he had read. The General Conference president interpreted the experience as an evidence of God's providential working.[44]

On December 28 Kellogg held a meeting with the sanitarium "family" on the topic of the ownership of the Battle Creek Sanitarium. He took the position that the denomination did not own it, but rather the stockholders.[45]

The real fireworks from the Kellogg camp, however, came from the ever-vocal A. T. Jones. On January 2 he turned his artillery on the General Conference in a public meeting in the Tabernacle. In his extensive address, soon published as a 60-page booklet, he reiterated his well-worn theme of Israel's choosing a king, and related that apostasy to their destruction. He then gave an extended defense of his return to Battle Creek that he based on two principles: (1) that God works for lost people in His love, rather than deserting them; and (2) that the testimonies of Ellen White had given him no choice but to come to Battle Creek.

His second argument was quite ingenious, since she had labored hard with him to convince him not to go to Battle Creek. In order to make his argument he obviously had to twist her counsel around 180 degrees. He did that by selecting only those testimonies or parts of testimonies that suited his purpose, and by ignoring their context or intended meaning. For example, in part of his argument he used counsels written while Ellen White still held out some hope for Kellogg. Jones completely ignored messages subsequently composed under changed circumstances, when she had come to believe that it no longer would be helpful to work for the doctor. Time and place of a testimony, he suggested, were not interpretive factors. By such techniques he managed to make her say just the opposite of what she was teaching in 1906.

Jones concluded his talk with an extensive discussion of the ownership of the college property and a justification for calling young people to Battle Creek in the face of Ellen White's warnings to the contrary. Technically picking at her language, he pointed out that the college wanted mature people as students, not immature children who still needed parental guidance. Thus, by providing his own definitions and by focusing on certain elements of the letter of her argument, he managed to frustrate its spirit.[46]

His talk delighted the Battle Creek *Daily Journal*. In its headline, front-page article it claimed that his defense of Kellogg showed "that the more intelligent and wiser portion of the Advent community are not carried away by the unreasonable fears and advice of those who . . . are trying to persuade the friends of the Sanitarium to forsake it."[47]

Daniells and his allies, meanwhile, were busy meeting individually with hundreds of persons who had questions about remaining in Battle Creek in the face of Ellen White's writings on the topic. They also spent much of their time helping people regain confidence in Ellen White, who had become the storm center of the controversy ever since she had disagreed with Kellogg's plans and ideas and had openly sided with Daniells and Prescott. Jones and several others, on the other hand, talked with each individual who desired to leave the sanitarium, attempting to persuade them to remain on its working force. He was doing just the opposite of what he had attempted in 1892-1893 when he had precipitated an exodus from Battle Creek on the basis of Ellen White's counsel. Meanwhile, Kellogg was in a panic over the threatened labor shortage. The doctor did his best to convince the faithful Adventists not to leave by claiming belief in Ellen White's messages and confessing that things needed to change at the sanitarium.[48]

The Adventist sector of Battle Creek in January 1906 rapidly was approaching the explosive stage. Insight into the spiritual atmosphere comes from the remarks of and responses to "Railroad Jack," a popular entertainer who performed for the sanitarium family in the gymnasium early in the month. One of the faithful Adventists wrote to Daniells that Railroad Jack had "said he would tell them about anyone whose name they would hand in. He said about a dozen had handed in Sister White's name. He said she was in her dotage, too old to be of any use; he hoped the bombshells she had thrown at B.C. would act like a boomerang and come back on her own head. He closed his remarks by saying that for further particulars they could go to A. T. Jones." His remarks split the audience, many leaving in disgust. Others undoubtedly doubled up in knots of laughter over his treatment of a contemporary issue.[49]

Evaluations of Daniells' Battle Creek crusade varied. Jones, near its beginning, told the packed Tabernacle "that he would rather be sunk ten thousand fathoms deep" than to do what the General Conference leaders were attempting. Daniells, on the other hand, was quite happy with their accomplishments, noting that they had won many over.[50]

On February 4 Jones resumed his public attack on the General Conference and the work of Ellen White in the regular monthly meeting of the sanitarium family. His basic theme was the religious liberty of every individual. "No man," he asserted, "is ever answerable to any man or set of men for his *belief* on any question whatever." While he was correct in the ultimate sense of salvation, he failed to distinguish between God's salvation and membership in a church. His argument harmonized perfectly with his view that churches had no right to discipline their members or clergy. In essence, he was protesting any official action against himself or Kellogg and their associates. The bulk of his talk he aimed at Daniells' use of Ellen White's writings to rebuke the Battle Creek leaders in December and January. The best way to achieve his goal was to discredit the testimonies, while proclaiming individual freedom from discipline at the same time. Jones's message soon saw publication as *Religious Liberty*.[51]

But his most deadly "bomb," according to the Battle Creek *Daily Moon*, was "hurled into the camp of the enemy" at the March 4 meeting of the sanitarium family. Claiming full belief in the third angel's message and the testimonies, he did his best to prove that it was W. C. White and the

General Conference leaders who did not believe Ellen White's counsels, since they did not always, from his distorted and limited perspective, carry them out in just the way he thought they should. As a result, he accused them of picking and choosing among the testimonies because they really did not believe them. His line of argument led him to conclude "that not everything is Testimony that is issued as Testimony."[52]

Thus Jones justified the position that he and Kellogg had already accepted: that every individual had to choose for himself which of Ellen White's counsels were inspired and which were not. That, he inferred, he and Kellogg could do as well as W. C. White, Daniells, or Prescott. Furthermore, he accused W. C. White and the General Conference leaders of influencing the content of her counsel. Beyond that charge, he also distorted her statement in which she had publicly claimed that "I am not a prophet." In addition to his extensive criticism of her authority and role, Jones developed major offensives on the concept of a president, the 1903 reversal of the 1901 General Conference position on the presidency with its papal tendencies, and the denomination's unfair attack on Kellogg. He later printed his talk as *Some History, Some Experience, and Some Facts,* a 72-page tract. Jones and his supporters had 20,000 copies printed. The booklet soon spread throughout Adventism.[53]

The Battle Creek newspapers once again trumpeted Jones's accomplishment. The *Daily Moon* proclaimed that "Elder Jones is proving himself the Moses in drawing together the misguided followers of those who are striving for temporal power, and in leading them into a plain path of duty."[54]

His March 4 thrust put the General Conference forces in a defensive posture. One of the first things Daniells did was to ask W. C. White to forward copies of the original testimonies from which Jones had quoted. Fortunately for the General Conference leaders, Jones had misused much of his material, and the complete documents did not support his arguments. He had wrested many quotations from both their literary and historical contexts. Thus his arguments lost much of their point upon further examination.

Jones's widely-scattered March 4 pamphlet had created doubt among Adventists across the nation, especially since many still looked to him as God's special messenger. In addition, his arguments seemed to be particularly forceful because they dealt with minor details that he authoritatively set forth as the truth.[55]

The public response of Daniells and his allies was twofold. First, they read the statements that Jones had used in their full context to large gatherings of church employees and believers. That tended to discredit him wherever it was done. Unfortunately, the leaders could not hold as many meetings as necessary, since the tract had spread everywhere. They therefore published a 96-page rebuttal in May entitled *A Statement Refuting Charges Made by A. T. Jones Against the Spirit of Prophecy and the Plan of Organization of the Seventh-day Adventist Denomination.* Printing 25,000 copies, they distributed them, with no charge, throughout the church.[56]

Meanwhile, Jones still held credentials as an ordained Adventist minister. On May 16 he met with the church leaders at the Lake Union Conference biennial session. They read a large portion of their *Statement* against him, giving Jones a chance to reply. He did so, claiming that he still believed in Ellen White's testimonies, that he had never changed his theological teachings, and that he did not intend to leave the denomination. The delegates, hoping and praying, in light of the facts, that he would repent of his duplicity, "were terribly disappointed with his talk." Near the close of the meetings the Indiana Conference leaders presented a statement censuring Jones's course. The delegates accepted it as their consensus.[57]

The General Conference's *Statement* did much to break his tenacious hold on the minds of both clergy and laity throughout the denomination. It exposed his blatant misuse of documents and his unfair methods of combat. Never again would A. T. Jones prove to be the threat to the church that he had been in early 1906.[58]

Jones published an answer to the *Statement* in July as *The Final Word and a Confession.* He attempted to discredit the *Statement* and reemphasize the papal tendencies of the church, but he merely rehashed his previously stated position. Being unable to prove satisfactorily his arguments, *The Final Word* fell flat on its face. The General Conference leadership decided not even to make a formal reply to it, although they did cover the points it raised in the *Review* without mentioning either the tract or Jones's name. Some dissidents, of course, were willing to grasp any straw available in order to discredit Ellen White and the church organization, but the events of 1906 had largely shattered Jones's influence.[59]

Daniells and Prescott clearly saw the conclusion of the war as a victory for their side. The General Conference president pointed out that the

struggle had united the conferences for concerted action. By early July
Prescott was suggesting that it was time to shift their energy from Battle
Creek "to aggressive moves in the field."[60]

The victory, Ellen White claimed, had come because the General
Conference leaders had followed her counsel not to press the battle too
early. Some had urged immediate action years earlier, but she had cautioned them repeatedly to "make no move until Dr. Kellogg and his associates had taken a decided position to repudiate the Testimonies." In 1906
Jones had made those very moves. According to her understanding, he
"had lifted the lid too soon, and spoiled their game." Had the Battle Creek
group waited a longer time before making their position evident, she indicated, they would have had many of the churches on their side.[61] For
once she could be thankful for Jones's ever-impulsive nature.

During the battle of 1906 Jones had rapidly moved from the center of
controversy to the periphery. Ellen White chose not to do combat with
him, noting that he created straw men. If you destroyed one, he would
raise up another. She saw no merit in that form of dialogue. However, she
did answer his charge that she had claimed that she was not a prophet,
explaining: "My commission embraces the work of a prophet, but it does
not end there." Also she accused him of being Kellogg's mouthpiece and
of being dishonest in saying he still believed in her work and the Adventist
message when he did not. In October she bluntly told him: "You have
apostatized, and it becomes necessary to warn our people not to be influenced by your representations."[62]

A. T. Jones had come full circle from his privileged position of 1888. His
drift had not been rapid, but it had been certain. Bitterness toward the denomination that he had done so much to build up would fill the last 20
years of his life. Before moving to that topic, however, we first need to examine his relationship to Ellen White—the person who would be the target of so much of his animosity in his latter days, just as she had been the
object of his admiration in happier times. His attitude toward her we can
best describe as one of love and hate.

[1] ATJ to California Conference Committee, Oct. 1, 1903; ATJ, *Some History,* p. 37; JHK
to WCW, Jan. 21, Mar. 18, 1903; WWP to AGD, Jan. 26, 1903; JHK to GIB, Feb. 8, 1903.

[2] AGD to GAI, Oct. 5, 1904.

[3] EGW to ATJ, Apr. 19, 22, 1903. (The letters of both dates are found in the Apr. 19 letter.)

[4] ATJ to EGW, Apr. 29, 1903; AGD to WCW, Apr. 29, 1903; JHK to EGW, Apr. 28, 1903.

[5] ATJ, *One-Man Power* (Oakland, 1903), pp. 1, 3, 4; GCC Min, Oct. 19, 1903; ATJ to California Conference Committee, Oct. 1, 1903.

[6] *RH,* June 9, 1903, p. 19; JHK to ATJ, Aug. 27, 1903.

[7] EGW to ATJ, Aug. 2, 1903.

[8] "Report of the Interview Held Between Mrs. E. G. White and Elder A. T. Jones, Aug. 15, 1903," unpub. MS.

[9] EGW to WCW, Aug. 18, 1903; EGW to AGD, Aug. 27, 1903; ATJ to WCW, Sept. 7, 1903; EGW to the Elders of the Battle Creek Church, July 17, 1906; EGW, MS 9, Apr. 11, 1906; EGW to Brother and Sister DP, Apr. 2, 1906.

[10] *RH,* Aug. 27, 1903, pp. 4, 5, 11, 12.

[11] A. G. Haughey to AGD, Aug. 5, 1903; AGD to WCW, Aug. 9, 30, 1903.

[12] AGD to WCW, Oct. 8, 1903; JHK to DP, Aug. 31, 1903.

[13] EGW, MS 117a, October 1903.

[14] GAI to AGD, Aug. 28, 1904; AGD to GAI, Oct. 5, 1904; WWP to CLT, Feb. 5, 1905.

[15] 1901 *GCB,* p. 219; JHK to GIB, Feb. 28, 1905; EGW, diary 17, pp. 353-360, c. July 1908.

[16] JHK to GIB, Feb. 21, Mar. 14, 1904.

[17] JHK to GIB, [May 1904]; EGW to AGD and WWP, May 20, 1904; EGW, MS 46, May 18, 1904.

[18] EGW to WWP and AGD, May 20, 1904; WCW to W. S. Sadler, July 13, 1906.

[19] ATJ to EGW, Apr. 26, 1909.

[20] AGD to GAI, July 8, 1904.

[21] *Ibid.*

[22] *Ibid.*; AGD to I. H. Evans, June 9, 1904.

[23] EGW, MS 52, May 22, 1904; MSS 54, 56, May 23, 1904; A. Spaulding to his mother, May 26, 1904.

[24] A. Spaulding to his mother, May 26, 1904; GIB and SNH to JHK, May 27, 1904; JHK to GIB, June 15, 27, 1904; EGW, MS 74, July 25, 1904; EGW to ATJ, Apr. 9, July 3, 1906; EGW to P. T. Magan and E. A. Sutherland, July 23, 1904.

[25] *RH,* Feb. 18, 1902, p. 109; ATJ, *Consecrated Way,* pp. 62, 67, 68, 70, 73, 74, 113; WAC to EWF, Apr. 25, 1907; JHK to SNH, Feb. 10, 1904.

[26] Whidden, *E. J. Waggoner,* pp. 305, 306, 363, 364, passim.

[27] WWP to EJW, Nov. 14, 1904; JHK, *The Living Temple* (Battle Creek, 1903), p. 6; GIB to JHK, Aug. 12, 1904; AGD to WCW, Sept. 29, 1903; GCC Min, Nov. 14, 17, 1902.

[28] *RH,* May 18, June 1, 1905, pp. 9, 28, 29; GCC Min, Sept. 19, 1904.

[29] EGW to WWP and WAC, Jan. 16, 1905; WAC to EGW, Feb. 3, 1905; WAC to WCW, Feb. 17, 1905; WWP to EGW, Feb. 6, 16, 1905; WWP to WCW, Feb. 16, 1905.

[30] EGW to ATJ, Feb. 13, 1905; AGD to EGW, Feb. 22, 1905; AGD to ATJ, Feb. 22, 1905.

[31] ATJ to EGW, Mar. 3, 1905; JHK to GIB, Feb. 28, 1905; AGD to WCW, Feb. 23, 1905.

[32] ATJ to EGW, Mar. 3, 1905; WAC to WCW, Mar. 3, 1905; WAC to ATJ, Mar. 3, 1905.

[33] AGD to WCW, Feb. 23, 26, 1905; Telegram, AGD to ATJ, Mar. 9, 1905; cf. letter from AGD to ATJ on same date.

[34] AGD to WCW, Mar. 10, 14, 21, 1905.

[35] AGD to WCW, Apr. 14, 1905; *MM*, April 1905, p. 111; May 1905, p. 139; ATJ, *Elder A. T. Jones at the Tabernacle, Jan. 2, 1906* (Battle Creek, 1906), p. 14.

[36] AGD to EGW, Mar. 15, 1909; *RH*, May 11, p. 30, May 25, p. 20, June 1, pp. 7, 20, 32, June 8, p. 21, 1905.

[37] EGW, "Remarks to the Delegates of the General Conference, May 30, 1905," unpub. MS; ATJ, "Remarks to the Delegates of the General Conference, May 30, 1905," unpub. MS; EGW to Brother and Sister Amadon, June 26, 1906; EGW, diary 55, pp. 79, 80, c. August 1905.

[38] EGW to ATJ, Apr. 9, 1906; EGW to Brother and Sister Amadon, June 26, 1906; EGW to Brother and Sister DP, Apr. 2, 1906.

[39] ATJ to Brother ___, June 8, 1905.

[40] *MM*, September 1905, pp. 282, 283.

[41] AGD to EGW, Oct. 11, 1905; AGD to WCW, Oct. 11, 12, 1905. (Ital. sup.)

[42] AGD to Dear Friends, Dec. 17, 1905.

[43] AGD to GAI, Dec. 27, 1905.

[44] *Ibid.*; EGW, MS 120, diary entry for Jan. 1, 1904.

[45] JHK, "Report of the Work of the Sanitarium, Dec. 28, 1905," unpub. MS; *MM*, February 1906, pp. 40-48.

[46] ATJ, *Elder A. T. Jones at the Tabernacle*.

[47] Battle Creek *Daily Journal*, Jan. 3, 1906, p. 1.

[48] AGD to EGW, Jan. 26, 1906; AGD to WCW, Jan. 10, 1906; CLT to EGW, Jan. 24, 1906.

[49] Unknown author to AGD, Jan. 12, 1906.

[50] AGD to EGW, Jan. 26, 1906; AGD to WCW, Jan. 24, 1906.

[51] ATJ, *Religious Liberty*, p. 5.

[52] Battle Creek *Daily Moon*, Mar. 5, 1906; ATJ, *Some History*, p. 59.

[53] ATJ, *Some History*, pp. 52-69; AGD to WCW, Apr. 12, May 17, 1906.

[54] Battle Creek *Daily Moon*, Mar. 5, 1906; cf. Battle Creek *Daily Journal*, Mar. 5, 1906.

[55] AGD to WCW, May 17, 23, 22, 1906.

[56] AGD to WCW, Mar. 29, May 17, 1906; WWP to WCW, Apr. 17, 1906; WCW to DP, Apr. 11, 1906; WCW to AGD, GAI, and WWP, Apr. 11, 1906; *RH*, May 17, 1906, p. 24; AGD to Dear Brother, May 16, 1906.

[57] *RH*, May 24, 1906, pp. 5, 6; ATJ, "Talk Given at Berrien Springs, May 16, 1906," unpub. MS; AGD to GAI, May 18, 1906.

[58] WCW to AGD, May 25, 1906.

[59] AGD to WCW, June 15, July 26, 1906; WCW to AGD, June 24, 1906.

[60] AGD to WCW, June 15, 1906; WWP to WCW, July 19, 1906.

[61] EGW to Brother and Sister Kress, Aug. 1, 1906.

[62] EGW to the Elders of the Battle Creek Church, July 17, 1906; EGW to Brother and Sister DP, Apr. 2, 1906; EGW to N. Druillard, Mar. 25, 1906; EGW, MS 34, Mar. 23, 1906; EGW to ATJ, Oct. 26, 1906.

CHAPTER XVI

CHARISMATIC CONFUSION:
A. T. JONES'S LOVE/HATE RELATIONSHIP
TO ELLEN WHITE

It should be evident to anyone who has read this far that Jones's relationship to Ellen White was central to his entire ministry.

WORKING TOGETHER[1]

Jones first met Ellen White in 1878, soon after his baptism. Later, she played an important role in encouraging him in his early ministry in the Washington Territory, and was probably instrumental in pointing out his potential to those who invited him to the editorial and college teaching fields in 1884. More important, she was almost singly responsible for thrusting Jones to the forefront of denominational activity at the Minneapolis General Conference session in 1888. He and E. J. Waggoner, she asserted, were "God's men" with a special message for the Advent people. Proud of that endorsement, Jones mentioned it publicly when he felt he needed it to bolster his authority.[2]

In the period from the 1888 General Conference session through the summer of 1891, Jones, Waggoner, and Ellen White campaigned on behalf of righteousness by faith across North America. They fought together on the same side in hard times. By late 1891, with Waggoner in England and Ellen White in Australia, Jones had surfaced as the leading figure in progressive Adventism in the United States. From a nobody in 1888, he had risen to prominence in his church through both his own forcefulness and talents and through the mentorship of Ellen White.

Jones returned her favor by becoming in nearly every way her spokesperson to American Adventism throughout the 1890s. He relished that position, and by 1899 nearly the entire denominational leadership recognized his unique place as a zealous expounder of the testimonies and an undaunted crusader for the reforms they called for, a fact evidenced in particular by his role in the General Conference sessions of 1897 and 1899. The delegates respectfully treated him during those meetings as the acknowledged authority on the testimonies and the public "reader" of weighty messages from Ellen White. During those sessions he several times led the delegates to their knees in response to testimonies from Australia.

Ellen White was anything but adverse to him playing that role, even though she had warned him again and again against harshness, being overbearing, and mixing too much of himself into her counsels. Even with those acknowledged weaknesses, however, she repeatedly sent him testimonies for individuals and institutions. After all, he was willing to read her communications to their intended recipients and to urge them to make a positive response. O. A. Olsen and G. A. Irwin, the two General Conference presidents of the 1890s, lacked that courage. By way of contrast, Jones was more than happy to undertake those confrontational tasks. In all his 73 years, the records suggest, he never once turned his back on a battle.

THE ROOTS OF ALIENATION

Jones himself was the recipient of a fair number of testimonies during the nineties. Many were not complimentary to his personality, his methods of labor, or his strong ideological beliefs. Nevertheless, he always claimed to accept them—even when he did not understand them—and he nearly always promised to change. Unfortunately, however, he never did let God soften his personality and methods of labor, and, too often, he never really accepted Ellen White's messages in the sense that if they were right, then he must be wrong. Instead, he often merely remained quiet on the topic of disagreement and wrote and spoke in ways that avoided the point of difference. Examples of such behavior are his positions on not laboring on Sunday, reading the Bible in the schools, receiving the African land grant, and tax-exempt status for churches.

Because Jones frequently did not really believe he was wrong when reproved, his differences with Ellen White festered in the subterranean compartments of his mind. Some of them would surface in ways hostile to her after he became disaffected from the Seventh-day Adventist Church.

Perhaps the root of the difficulty between Jones and Ellen White was that he was an ideological extremist, while she was quite pragmatic. For Jones, the truth on a point and logical consistency meant everything. A person must, according to him, push the pure truth in its absolute, black or white form to its logical conclusion no matter what the human consequences, a point illustrated in his advocacy of not paying fines for Sunday labor to the point of bringing on the death penalty. For Jones, truth was truth—period. There were no other factors to consider. Every issue was either totally white or totally black, without extenuating circumstances or shades of gray. For him the ideological end justified the means—however harsh or confrontational they might be. The shortest way between two points in his mind was always a straight line. He had no use for rational explanations in matters of faith, except to extend his conclusions to their furthest extremities or to harmonize what appeared to him to be contradictory data. In the latter situation he could be an ingenious logical contortionist, but always to prove the ideological point with which he had begun.

Ellen White, on the other hand, was quite pragmatic in her approach to problems. That is not to say that she was not confrontational or a firm believer in truth. She was both of those, but she realized that not everything was black or white, that extenuating circumstances did exist, and that one needed to consider contextual factors in making decisions. As seen in chapter 10, she was willing to accept Bible reading in the public schools— even though it was not ideal—since Adventists probably could not defeat it and God would be able to use Bible reading to enlighten schoolchildren. She defended tax exemptions and the acceptance of certain government favors. And she certainly held that human flexibility was more important than ideological rigidity. For her it was spiritual, rather than ideological, ends that justified the means used. In addition, she advocated, contrary to Jones, rational thought in the application of Christian principles. Ellen White was quite flexible in applying principles in varying contexts, whereas Jones was a classic case of one who had swallowed the "myth of the inflexible prophet" in its entirety.[3]

With their basic differences in outlook and attitude it was only a matter of time before the two of them would come into open conflict. Her stay in

Australia had probably postponed their confrontation, but that buffer disappeared in 1900 when she returned to the United States. She could now speak for herself and explain her positions. Since they often contradicted his interpretations, a showdown was inevitable unless one of them changed. That proved to be an increasingly unlikely prospect as time went on.

The probability of conflict between Jones and Ellen White had also been heightened by the fact that he had somewhat discredited himself as her spokesperson by his pushy methods and extremism in the late nineties. On top of that, she had returned from Australia with a spokesperson who was more in harmony with her flexible approach than Jones—one who was a moderate and who was certainly more politically astute. That man was A. G. Daniells, who had spent the nineties in Australia in close relationship to her. Becoming General Conference president in 1901, he took over the reforming role where less forceful presidents had failed in the 1890s. Thus he inherited both of Jones's roles—spokesperson for Ellen White and chief denominational reformer—long before Jones was ready to retire. It is no accident that he became alienated from both Daniells and Ellen White early in the new century.

His disaffection surfaced in 1903, but as seen in previous chapters, it was not until 1906 that it boiled over into open warfare against Ellen White. His 180-degree turnabout caught the denomination's leadership by surprise. G. A. Irwin wrote in 1903 that "I am more surprised at the position that A. T. Jones has taken than almost any other man connected with that movement [to reopen Battle Creek College]. In the past Jones has been so loyal to the Testimonies. Whenever they spoke condemning a certain thing, he was almost the first one to right up; but it seems now as though he was taking the bit in his teeth and running according to his own mind." Later Daniells referred to Jones in the same light, when he characterized him as the one who in the 1890s "took a strong position regarding the Testimonies, and used them with great force to wheel men and policies into line."[4]

Daniells, like Irwin and most of the church, found it almost impossible to understand the new Jones. Jones, of course, probably did not understand himself, but he did not need to in order to respond. He lashed out at his supposed enemies in his bitterness. Ellen White, having rejected his interpretation of her writings, was one of his primary targets. It is to an analysis of his problem with her writings and work that we now turn. Such study is relevant for two reasons: (1) his understanding and misunderstanding of Ellen White led him to reject her work; and, (2) many Adventists are still confused on the same issues that perplexed him.

AN ANATOMY OF JONES'S ALIENATION

The most basic error in Jones's adherence to Ellen White's writings in the 1890s was his position on their relationship to the Bible. At the 1893 General Conference session he used passages from her works as "texts" to base some of his sermons on, a practice he approved of when "preaching to our own people" but not when addressing non-Adventists. Four years later he would refer to her writings as the "Word." The 1893 General Conference session saw a great deal of preaching from the writings of Ellen White. Haskell observed that they had heard more from her in her absence than if she had been there in person. That would all change at the 1895 session. In the wake of the Anna Rice crisis in 1894, Ellen White had counseled Jones and others not to rely so much on the gifts, but to get back to the Bible. As a result, the 1895 *General Conference Bulletin* is notable for the absence of uses of Ellen White as an authority, especially during the first half of the meetings.[5]

Quite repentant for his blunder in the Rice affair, Jones did everything he could to rectify his mistake by pointing Adventism back to the Bible. That was particularly evident in his Week of Prayer reading for 1894, titled "The Gifts: Their Presence and Object." In discussing the gift of prophecy in general, he pointed out that the Holy Spirit is the only interpreter of the Bible and that the Spirit's "interpretation is infallible." From that proposition he moved to the role of Ellen White's testimonies, correctly using her statements that the purpose of her writings was not to provide new information, but to lead her readers to the Bible itself.[6]

Up to that point his argument seemed to be solid enough, but then he veered off into a line of thought that contradicted both biblical principles and Adventism's historic position on the relation between Ellen White's gift and the Bible. Jones wrote that "the right use of the *Testimonies*, therefore, is not to use them *as they are in themselves,* as though they were apart from the word of God in the Bible; but to study the Bible *through them,* so that the things brought forth in them we shall see and know for ourselves *are in the Bible;* and then present those things to others *not from the Testimonies* themselves, but *from the Bible itself*. . . . This and this alone is the right use of the *Testimonies,* whether used privately or publicly. . . . This of itself will make us all 'mighty in the Scriptures.'"[7]

His argument, while intended to maintain the primacy of the Bible, actually subordinated it to Ellen White's writings. Thus Jones and those sharing his logic came to view her writings as a divine, infallible commentary on the Bible. That, of course, was not the position she had taken on the subject. A little thought on the topic would have led him to see that it was the exact position that she had opposed in 1888 when Jones and Waggoner's enemies had argued that because of her testimonies, the law in Galatians could not be the moral law. She flatly rejected their argument, and implied that they would have to solve the problem through Bible study.[8]

While Ellen White's writings ever pointed her readers to the Bible, she never claimed that they were an infallible commentary on it. Rather, her works shed light on the application of biblical principles in her day. As such, contrary to Jones's erroneous view, they needed to be studied "*as they are in themselves*" in the same way that one should approach the Bible. The reader must examine them in relation to their literary and historical contexts.

Adventism has too often taught Jones's approach to the relationship between the Bible and the writings of Ellen White. Unfortunately, his concept of her "infallibility" and his failure to consider fully the contexts of her writings helped set him up for disaster.

By 1905, when he had become disillusioned regarding both Adventism and Ellen White, he began to lay renewed emphasis on the place of the Bible in the Christian's life. A definite downplaying of her gifts accompanied the emphasis. "Sister White," he remarked to a sanitarium audience in the explosive month of December 1905, "is getting old. She may die sometime. If she should die what would we do for Testimonies[?] What we need is to study our Bibles. If we lived close enough to the Lord and studied our Bibles as we ought to we would not need the Testimonies."[9]

In 1906 Jones still held his old position on their relationship to the Bible, but he had become much more interested in moving people away from her writings altogether. He was particularly incensed because others had employed them to combat him and Kellogg, when, as he continued to claim, their *only* correct use was to help people understand the Bible. Their public use in rebuking contemporary situations, Jones asserted, was "a *perverse use* of the testimonies."[10] Thus he still maintained his 1894 position that Ellen White's writings should not be studied "*as they are in themselves.*"

His nearly total misunderstanding of the purpose of the testimonies led to his rejection of them. Coupled with that problem was his concept of their verbal inspiration and their infallibility or inerrancy. Those beliefs also contributed to his disaffection, especially when he found that those positions did not hold up in the light of the facts.

Concepts of Ellen White being verbally inspired were quite prevalent among Adventists early in the twentieth century. Many of the problems associated with that view came to light in relationship to the Jones-Kellogg attack on her early in 1906. Their onslaught led to a virtual hornet's nest of criticism and questioning regarding her work. Early in 1906 she wrote to several leaders connected with Kellogg who were perplexed about her role, asking them to send her their questions so that she could answer them.

Dr. David Paulson replied to her on April 19. One of his queries had to do with verbal inspiration. It typified much Seventh-day Adventist belief. "I was led to conclude and most firmly believe," he wrote, "that *every* word that you ever spoke in public or private, that *every* letter you wrote under *any* and *all* circumstances, was as inspired as the ten commandments. I held that view with *absolute* tenacity against innumerable objections raised to it by many who were occupying prominent positions in the cause." He wanted to know if he should continue to hold that position.[11]

"My brother," she answered, "you have studied my writings diligently, and you have never found that I have made any such claims. Neither will you find that the pioneers in our cause have made such claims." She went on to explain to him that there were both divine and human elements in inspiration, and that the testimony of the Holy Spirit is "conveyed through the imperfect expression of human language."[12]

Being the extremist that he was, Jones believed that inspiration was all divine. As a result, he held for verbal inspiration. Kellogg wrote of him in 1904 that he had "always stood very stiffly for the verbal inspiration of the Testimonies" and still did. In the summer of 1906 Jones claimed in his *Final Word* that he was not a verbal inspirationist, but his argument in the rest of the pamphlet demonstrates that he was having trouble with Ellen White's writings because he still was a verbalist at heart.[13]

Jones found it next to impossible to disentangle his incorrect belief in verbal inspiration from her work. As a result, when he felt compelled to surrender his erroneous belief in her verbal inspiration, he saw no alternative but to deny that she was divinely inspired at all. In his mind the two went together. He was truly an all-or-nothing person in all he touched.[14]

Closely related to the issue of verbal inspiration in his thinking was the problem of infallibility or inerrancy. For most of his ministry he had firmly believed that it was impossible for Ellen White to make an error in her written work. "I thought," he stated in 1906, "that we *must not* recognize that there were mistakes in the matter that was written and sent out from the source of the Testimonies: and I acted strictly according to that view." When faced with the fact that inspiration did not guarantee inerrant information in every detail, his faith in Ellen White shattered.[15] (He apparently never applied his fundamentalist rule of thumb to the factual problems in the Bible.)

Ellen White, of course, had never claimed infallibility or inerrancy. To the contrary, she had plainly stated that "God and heaven alone are infallible." That truth, however, proved in those days (and still does so today) to be almost impossible for the fundamentalist mind to grasp. The discovery of any factual errors destroys such misinformed faith. Such was the case with Jones. It shocked him when he discovered that a certain General Conference department head could still claim belief in Ellen White's gift while asserting that he did not believe she was infallible. Jones could not harmonize what appeared to him to be a contradiction.[16]

The real problem, however, was not in either Ellen White or the Bible, but in the fact that he and his allies in belief had assumed an a priori concept of inspiration and then used it to reject anything that did not conform to their humanly devised standards. They determined the rules, and demanded that God act accordingly. To take that course, however, is not the way to develop faith, as Jones's experience demonstrates. His faith wavered because of unwarranted beliefs in Ellen White's verbal inspiration and infallibility or inerrancy.

His extremist notion that one should never attempt to explain an inspired statement compounded his problem of rigidity on inspiration and infallibility. He claimed many times throughout his career that inspired statements needed no explanation. At the 1897 General Conference session, for example, Kellogg, in the midst of his presentation, publicly queried Jones on an interpretation that he was building on Ellen White's counsel, noting that he was asking Jones because he was the resident authority on her writings. Jones replied: "I am not an authority on the Testimonies. All I can do is to just believe what they say, and that is all we can know about it. Just what they say is so." He took the same position in 1909, when he finally (three years after Ellen White made the request) received word that she had asked him and others to write to her regarding their perplexities concerning her work so that she could clarify them. He replied to her that if her writings were really a word from God "they need no explanation."[17]

On the surface, his approach to Ellen White's writings looks like simple, accepting faith. Unfortunately, he failed to realize that his understanding of them was not perfectly objective. He was not cognizant of the fact that he interpreted her writings in the light of his own perspective. As a result, when using them he often mixed his words with hers, a practice she had rebuked him for in 1899.[18]

Not recognizing the subjectivity he shared with other mortals, Jones was adamant in his position that inspired writings never needed to be explained—they must only be believed and accepted. Thus in 1905 he could take an 1899 testimony out of context to "prove" to the sanitarium family that Ellen White believed that the institution was undenominational and did not belong to the Adventist Church. That, of course, was just the opposite of her view, but Jones had found some words that, when wrested from their context, said what he wanted her to say. When urged to interpret the passage, he answered: "I never explain the Testimonies. I believe them." Kellogg was of the same mind. "I don't know that it needs explanation," he stated. "There is just the statement there."[19]

Jones had adopted a legalistic use of language that emphasized the exact words a person used, while it excluded any interpretation of what they may have meant. By that technique he could isolate words and sentences and make Ellen White and others say just the opposite of what they intended. He employed this approach to Ellen White's claim that her role encompassed more than that of a prophet. Jones picked up on the words "I am not a prophet" and made a big to-do over them. He told audiences: "As for what she *meant* other than what she said, they would have to ask her. But as for what she had *said,* that was plain enough. She said, 'I am not a prophet.' I believe it." With Daniells he used the same tactic. Writing to him on a controverted point, he argued, "Whatever you *meant,* the words as given above are what you *said.*"[20]

Using that technique, Jones could pick and choose isolated quotations from the writings of Ellen White and drive them home on anyone who would listen, even though she did not mean what he implied. It was so with his use of Ellen White's 1897 statement that "it is not wise to choose one man as president of the General Conference," which he interpreted to mean that there should be no General Conference president at all. He held rigidly to his position, even though the letter he quoted from proved the opposite point and she repeatedly denied his interpretation in her subsequent writings. After all, he had her words and she could never change nor recall them. When challenged, therefore, on not reading all of a testimony in its complete context, he shot back that neither the context nor subsequent counsel could "destroy or make of none effect" the words he had selected to read.[21]

Closely coupled to his ignoring a document's literary context was his rejection of explanations based on time, place, or changed circumstances. Thus Jones held in 1906 that he was being faithful to the testimonies by living in Battle Creek and working for Dr. Kellogg, because he had a quotation from an earlier period that said that the denomination should do all it could to save the doctor. The fact that Ellen White now claimed that Kellogg had moved beyond reach through his attitudes and actions made no difference to Jones. Refusing to "explain away" the testimonies, he told the Tabernacle's congregation in January 1906 that "I have not a cent's worth of respect for any such plea as is made too often and especially of late years on [sic] 'Testimonies up-to-date;' as if a Testimony up-to-date is to take the place of all that ever went before it. . . . God's revelation is not that way. God's revelation is truth, and is just as good to-day as it was a thousand years ago. It never gets out of date; and the last one that comes is not going to contradict, or vitiate, or set aside, or annihilate any that went before it."[22]

Ellen White was diametrically opposed to his principles of interpretation. Just two years before she had noted to others, who were misusing her writings in the same manner, that "God wants us all to have common sense, and He wants us to reason from common sense. Circumstances alter conditions. Circumstances change the relation of things." She regularly admonished her readers to take time, place, and other contextual factors into consideration in understanding her writings.[23]

Her principles of interpretation were completely out of harmony with those of Jones, yet he claimed the morally superior position. Just believe, he implied, just have faith in the words of inspiration. Mindless faith without understanding and common sense, however, is far from God's ideal. In Jones's case, his false hermeneutical theory provided the justification for him to take a giant step down the road to apostasy.

Prescott claimed that a selective use of the testimonies, that chose to accept some while ignoring others, did not impress him as the course of one who was really seeking "to know and to follow the instruction which is now being given for the guidance of God's people."[24] That thought brings us to the reminder that we cannot separate Jones's use of the testimonies from his bitterness toward Daniells, Ellen White, and a denomination that he believed had wrongly rejected him. He had let his own hurt pride affect his relationship to what he had earlier believed was God's inspired counsel.

Bert Haloviak has indicated that Jones and Kellogg's position on the inspiration of the writings of Ellen White "that minimized context and interpretation seemed to place them in a situation where a choice between only two alternatives was possible. They could totally reject the messages that they had been following for years or they could find some explanation that could deal with seemingly inconsistent messages."[25]

They chose the latter course, claiming that not everything that Ellen White had written was inspired. As Jones put it, not all that she sent out as a testimony was in reality a testimony. His rejection of his previous position resulted from his mistaken conceptions of the nature, function, and purpose of her gift, as discussed above, and by the political necessities of his battle with Daniells and the General Conference. The problem was that Ellen White had taken the side of the General Conference administration against Jones and Kellogg. Rather than believing that God had guided her to select the side closest to His will, Jones and his colleagues developed and published the thesis that Daniells, Prescott, W. C. White, and their kind were influencing the content of her messages to the detriment of the sanitarium forces. Thus not all she wrote was inspired.[26]

That position left Jones and those who believed like him with the task of sorting out which of her ideas were inspired and which were not. They were more than happy to take that responsibility. As Jones put it, "*every* [*individual*] *testimony should be tested by the Scriptures and by the Spirit,* to know *whether it is so.*" From that posture the Jones-Kellogg coalition could reject any counsels from Ellen White that rebuked their course of action, while accepting those that were "correct." As a result, they could go on claiming to believe that the Spirit of God spoke through her, while ignoring much of what she wrote.[27]

The duplistic stance of the Jones-Kellogg camp, as we might expect, confused the church members, and made it nearly impossible for Ellen White and the church leaders to communicate with the leaders in Battle Creek. By 1907 the two strands of Adventism had reached the breaking point in their relationship. The complete separation was now a mere formality that would occur between 1907 and 1909.

Meanwhile, one claim of Ellen White that Jones rejoiced in was her statement that she was not a prophet. By his often repetition of it, he hoped to impale both her and the Daniells forces on one or the other of two horns. If they said she was inspired, they would have to admit she had prophetically invalidated her testimony to divine inspiration by even making the statement. On the other hand, if they said that it was not an inspired statement, then they had taken his own position that individuals had to pick and choose as to which of her statements were inspired. Jones, true to his logic, would listen to no explanations regarding her comment, but she did clarify her intended meaning to those who had ears to hear. In the *Review* of July 26, 1906, she answered his charge. "Some," she wrote, referring particularly to Jones, "have stumbled over the fact that I said I did not claim to be a prophet; and they have asked, Why is this? I have had no claims to make, only that *I am instructed that I am the Lord's messenger;* that He called me in my youth to be His messenger, to receive His word, and to give a clear and decided message in the name of the Lord Jesus. Early in my youth I was asked several times, Are you a prophet? I have ever responded, I am the Lord's messenger. . . .

"Why have I not claimed to be a prophet?—Because in these days many who boldly claim that they are prophets are a reproach to the cause of Christ; and because my work includes much more than the word 'prophet' signifies. . . . If others call me by that name, I have no controversy with them. . . . When I was last in Battle Creek, I said before a large congregation that I did not claim to be a prophetess. Twice I referred to this matter, intending each time to make the statement, 'I do not claim to be a prophetess.' If I spoke otherwise than this, let all now understand that what I had in mind to say was that I did not claim the title of prophet or prophetess."[28]

Jones did not deny that Ellen White had the Spirit of prophecy. She had it, he suggested, even though she was not a prophet. That gift, however, was not of any special advantage to her, since, according to his interpretation of Revelation 12:17 and 19:10, all of God's remnant people would have the Spirit of prophecy, just as all would keep the commandments of God. That was essentially the same message that he and Prescott had preached at the time of the Anna Rice excitement in 1894, and that Waggoner had taught at the 1899 General Conference session. Jones's old charismatic self was still alive and well.[29]

In summary, a major problem that led to Jones's apostasy was his rigidity in interpreting Ellen White's role and message. He possessed an all-or-nothing doctrinaire mind that would brook no ifs, ands, or buts. She did not fit neatly into his theory of inspiration, nor did she always agree with his interpretation of her writings. Furthermore, her explanations and solutions tended toward the pragmatic and conditional, whereas his were doctrinaire and black or white. With all those problems she certainly could not be God's prophet. Then again, he could hear the voice of God as well as the next person. Hadn't he demonstrated that in his dealings with Anna Rice? From his viewpoint, he was right and Ellen White was wrong, so he rejected her. In the long run, Jones was a victim of both the "myth of the inflexible prophet" and his own injured ego. His bitterness would continue to the day of his death.

---

[1] The discussion in this section and the next one are based upon material treated earlier in this book. Footnotes, therefore, are not included except where I have introduced new material.

[2] 1893 GCB, p. 184; RH, Jan. 9, 1900, p. 24.

[3] See Knight, Myths in Adventism, pp. 17-25.

[4] GAI to AGD, Nov. 3, 1903; ATJ to AGD, Jan. 26, 1906; ATJ, Some History, p. 35.

[5] 1893 GCB, pp. 39, 69, 358; 1897 GCB, p. 3; SNH to EGW, Feb. 23, 1893; EGW to ATJ, Apr. 16, 1894.

[6] *HM* Extra, December 1894, p. 12.

[7] *Ibid.*; cf. 1893 *GCB*, p. 358; 1899 *GCB*, p. 46.

[8] See chapter 2. For a helpful study on the relationship of Ellen White to the Bible, see Tim Poirier, "Contemporary Prophecy and Scripture: The Relationship of Ellen G. White's Writings to the Bible in the Seventh-day Adventist Church, 1845-1915" (research paper, Wesley Theological Seminary, March 1986).

[9] "Substance of Remarks by A. T. Jones, c. Dec. 10, 1905," unpub. MS.

[10] ATJ, *Final Word*, pp. 5, 6; ATJ, *Religious Liberty*, pp. 10, passim; "Talk Given by Elder A. T. Jones at Berrien Springs, May 16, 1906," unpub. MS.

[11] DP to EGW, Apr. 19, 1906.

[12] EGW to DP, June 14, 1906.

[13] JHK to GIB, Jan. 8, 1904; ATJ, *Final Word*, pp. 4, 7-9, 11, 14, 20, 21, 25.

[14] ATJ, *Final Word*, pp. 4, 7-9, 11, 14, 20, 21, 25.

[15] *Ibid.*, pp. 26, 21.

[16] *RH*, July 26, 1892, p. 465; EGW to Nephew, June 9, 1895; ATJ, *An Appeal for Evangelical Christianity* ([Battle Creek], 1909), pp. 60-62, 67.

[17] 1897 *GCB*, p. 311; *RH*, Sept. 20, 1898, p. 606; ATJ to EGW, Apr. 26, 1909; cf. 1897 *GCQB*, 1st Qtr., p. 24.

[18] EGW to ATJ, May 1, 1899.

[19] "Report of the Work of the Sanitarium by Dr. Kellogg, Dec. 28, 1905," unpub. MS.

[20] ATJ, *Some History*, pp. 62, 26.

[21] ATJ, *Final Word*, pp. 38, 39; GCC, *A Statement Refuting the Charges Made by A. T. Jones Against the Spirit of Prophecy and the Plan of Organization of the Seventh-day Adventist Denomination* (Washington D.C., 1906), pp. 29-31; ATJ, *Elder A. T. Jones at the Tabernacle*, pp. 24, 25.

[22] ATJ, *Elder A. T. Jones at the Tabernacle*, pp. 18, 19, 24, 25.

[23] EGW, MS 7, Jan. 14, 1904; "Report of an Interview Held Between Mrs. E. G. White and Elder A. T. Jones, Aug. 15, 1903," unpub. MS; EGW, *Counsels to Parents, Teachers, and Students*, p. 531; for more on this topic see Knight, *Myths in Adventism*, pp. 17-25; George R. Knight, *Reading Ellen White*, (Hagerstown, Md., 1997), pp. 58-118.

[24] WWP to CLT, Feb. 5, 1905.

[25] Bert Haloviak, "In the Shadow of the 'Daily': Background and Aftermath of the 1919 Bible and History Teachers' Conference," unpub. MS, Nov. 14, 1979, p. 16.

[26] ATJ, *Some History*, pp. 53-66, 70; ATJ to EGW, Aug. 9, 1908; ATJ, *Final Word*, pp. 27-31.

[27] ATJ, *Appeal for Evangelical Christianity*, pp. 60, 61; ATJ, "The Testimonies," unpub. MS, Aug. 31, 1906; WAC to EWF, Apr. 25, 1907; ATJ, *Final Word*, pp. 3, 4.

[28] *RH*, Jan. 26, 1905, p. 9; July 26, 1906, pp. 8-9; "Substance of Remarks by A. T. Jones," c. Dec. 10, 1905, unpub. MS; ATJ to ___, Jan. 27, 1907; ATJ, *Some History*, pp. 61-64; GCC, *A Statement Refuting the Charges Made by A. T. Jones*, pp. 81-85.

[29] ATJ, *Appeal for Evangelical Christianity*, pp. 68, 69; ATJ to ___, Jan. 27, 1907; EGW to Brethren and Sisters, Mar. 16, 1894; 1899 *GCB*, p. 14.

CHAPTER XVII
CHARISMATIC UNTIL THE END: THE BITTER YEARS

The war between Jones and the denomination did not cease with his loss in the Battle Creek struggle of 1906, even though the Daniells administration viewed him as less of a threat after that time. Jones, however, still had a great deal of influence with the Adventist public, and he was more than happy to create doubts and to widen the gap between the denomination and those among its members who felt discontented for one reason or another.

RAIDING THE CHURCHES

He had a fruitful turf in which to work. In proportion to the size of the church, Adventism in the first decade of the twentieth century probably had more disaffected elements than it has had at any time in its history. Beside the major split in the denomination over the Kellogg-Battle Creek crisis, there was A. F. Ballenger (an old colleague of Jones in the Adventist holiness movement and the religious liberty work), who had been "cast out" of the church because of his teachings on the sanctuary doctrine early in the new century; L. C. Sheafe (Black pastor of the People's Seventh-day Adventist Church in Washington, D.C.), who in 1907 was in the process of leading his local congregation out of the denomination because of alleged racial discrimination; and E. E. Franke (one of Adventism's most innovative and successful evangelists), who had become estranged from the denomination's leadership. These individuals, of course, were merely the leaders of the disaffected.[1]

A symbiotic relationship existed between Jones and the various alienated elements at the edges of Adventism. On the one hand, the Battle Creek rebellion and Jones's 1906 pamphlet war undoubtedly emboldened those factions. On the other hand, the presence of their disaffection provided Jones with a core population for his message against both church organization and Ellen White. They also offered him potential sources of funds and associates for his activities.

The publication of *Gospel Simplicity*, by W. L. Winner, an Adventist dentist, in December 1906 aided Jones in his disorganizing effort. According to Daniells, Winner's thesis was: "Let every church be supreme in its field, and the sole custodian of its interests, and the administrator of all its funds." His message was an obvious repudiation of all conference organization. Winner, Daniells reported, had taken Jones's doctrine and made it more dangerous because Winner's tract was much better written than Jones's work on the topic. "The meaning of all this is plain," Daniells wrote. "In the beginning of our controversy the sanitarium leaders thought that they were strong enough to defeat the General Conference. They have found that they were mistaken. Now what they failed to do by firing a broad-side, they are attempting to do piece-meal. Their aim is to sow disaffection among the separate churches; wherever they can find a church that is out of joint with the body, they will fan the disaffection to a flame, and if possible, induce them to separate from the general organization. This I am sure was one of the objects A. T. had in his lecturing tour."[2]

The General Conference president's prediction was quite accurate. During the next few months, Jones was instrumental in helping both Sheafe in Washington, D.C., and Franke in Newark, New Jersey, take their congregations out of the denomination. Daniells imagined that those at the Battle Creek Sanitarium must have greatly rejoiced "over the fact that right here at headquarters we have lost one of our churches." Jones, of course, pleaded innocence in both cases, claiming that he just happened to be present when the congregations made separatist decisions, but that he had had nothing to do with them.[3]

What the Jones forces hoped for, and what the denominational leaders feared, was that the congregational exodus would become a general movement. Kellogg's Good Health Publishing Company had published *Gospel Simplicity*, and most of the initial printing of 10,000 copies had gone to Jones for mass distribution to the churches across the country. By late January 1907 at least one conference treasurer had reported that "some of our people [are] already withholding their tithes . . . as a result of reading this tract."[4]

Preaching to the People's Church in Washington, D.C., in April, Jones claimed that the General Conference had no real future. "He thought," W. A. Colcord reported, "there was going to be such a complete smash and break-up of that thing, that there would be nothing left of it."

Colcord challenged him twice during his Washington meetings. After Jones had "ridiculed the idea of having 'committees' and 'presidents' in religious work, and made some bold assertions in regard to each individual being absolutely independent of every other individual in all religious matters," Colcord invited him to publicly explain Hebrews 13:17: "Obey them that have the rule over you, and submit yourselves." Jones ignored the question, even though Colcord raised it twice. His failure to respond "made quite a little flurry over the congregation," Colcord said, "and I think quite a good many persons really saw that he was teaching unsound doctrine—something that would not harmonize with the Bible." Further, Colcord asked him how long it had been since he had been president of anything. That query also put Jones on the spot, since he was still president of Battle Creek College, even though he regularly preached against both the title and office of president.[5] His own wounded pride and bitterness had apparently blinded him to some of his personal contradictions.

The battle for the churches, meanwhile, moved ahead as fast as Franke, Sheafe, Winner, and Jones could push it. For a time it looked as though the Eighth Street Church in Washington, D.C., would be lost. Sheafe, meanwhile, was busy seeking to alienate Black congregations in other parts of the country from church administration.[6]

By the spring of 1907, however, the General Conference forces had thoroughly organized to combat the trend toward congregationalism. Through weekly articles in the Review, by meeting the people at camp meetings and other gatherings, and by the publication of J. N. Loughborough's *The Church: Its Organization, Order and Discipline*, Daniells and his men did their best to educate the people. Beyond those efforts, *Testimonies for the Church*, volume 9 (1909), had a section on stewardship and organization.[7]

Jones and others continued to travel and speak at various places in an attempt to "free" Adventists from General Conference domination, but they never made much headway, except to drain off some tithe to support their efforts. Adventist congregations, meanwhile, had received warnings not to open their churches to him.[8]

Beyond his efforts to split off independent congregations from the conferences during this period, Jones continued to level accusations of papalism in Adventist organization, to question openly the authority of Ellen White, and to find fault with the denomination's theology. As in 1906, he often distorted his evidence and based his conclusions on false premises. He had become quite aggressive toward his Adventist brothers and sisters and he made every effort to battle them publicly, even though—strangely enough—he was quite cordial to them when he met them on the street or at social gatherings.[9]

THE DEFROCKING OF JONES AND THE APOSTASY OF ADVENTISM

Surprisingly, up through the middle of 1907 Jones retained credentials as an ordained Seventh-day Adventist minister, even though he had warred against the denomination for nearly two years. That would change in 1907. On October 4, 1906, the General Conference Committee set up a special subcommittee to examine "the propriety of Elder A. T. Jones holding credentials from the General Conference."[10]

As one could expect, the special subcommittee found "that Alonzo T. Jones' work and influence have ceased to be helpful to the denomination from which he received his credentials; that his public utterances and published statements which have been widely circulated, show his attitude to be antagonistic to the organized work of the denomination which granted him his credentials." As a result, after discussing the efforts made to reclaim him, the General Conference Committee voted unanimously on May 22, 1907, to ask Jones to turn in his credentials as an ordained Seventh-day Adventist minister.[11]

He replied that they did not need to make such a big fuss about it, because he cared "nothing for such credentials, and never had a care for them." Jones claimed he would continue to preach the third angel's message with or without official credentials.[12]

That statement, however, was not the end of the matter. The committee had made the decision to remove his credentials while meeting in Gland, Switzerland, without giving him a public hearing. He would demand and receive one at the 1909 General Conference session.

In the meantime, Jones was still a member of the church in good and regular standing. The Battle Creek Tabernacle, however, had disfellowshipped Kellogg on November 10, 1907. The same fate had befallen several of his Battle Creek colleagues. Jones's membership had undoubtedly escaped being purged from the Battle Creek church records because he had never transferred it from California where he had served as conference president from 1901 through 1903.

In protest to the predictable purging of the church rolls, and with an eye on the probable fate of his own membership, he published *The Christian Church and Church Federation* in 1907, in which he argued that no church ever had the right to disfellowship anyone. "In the Church of Christ, in dealing with any who are in fault," Jones asserted, "the only procedure prescribed, is for the gaining and restoring of them and the keeping of them in the Church if possible. In the New Testament there is no provision made for turning people out of the church." Ellen White had reprimanded him for holding that nonbiblical position on church discipline when he was president of the California Conference, but like most of her counsel to him, he had ignored it while remaining quiet on the topic.[13]

The year 1908 saw two major developments in the Jones case. The first began in July when S. N. Haskell, once again president of the California Conference, persuaded the Berkeley Adventist Church to form a committee to consider the status of Jones's membership in their congregation. Not yet convinced of his apostasy, the church made no charges, but on August 15 passed a resolution of censure, committing itself to formalize charges at the end of three months.[14]

To complicate matters, Jones made a visit to California. On August 22 he met with several of the leaders of the Berkeley congregation, claiming that their censure was contrary to the Bible. "He spoke at length on Christ as the sole head of the church and exhorted" the church to place "no man or set of men in Christ's place." The censure, he claimed, was really an unjust move by the presidents of the California and Pacific Union conferences and should therefore be removed by the church. Jones further

claimed that he was preaching the same doctrines he had always presented and "that he was *not* doing a work of tearing down our churches."
And, remarkably, given the facts of the case, "he stated that he had never
been labored with by any one" regarding his problems.[15]

The ever forceful Jones managed to split the congregation, with Dr.
Arthur Hickox moving on August 29, 1908, to remove the church's censure. It was only prompt and decisive action by Haskell and H. W.
Cottrell, president of the Pacific Union Conference, that reunited the
members behind their original resolution of censure. A vote of the
California Conference executive committee to restrict Jones from preaching in the conference's churches followed up the action of censure.[16]

The second 1908 development in Jones's relation to the denomination also took place in California. His purpose in touring the state
was to preach the third angel's message wherever he could get a hearing. One of his stops was Calistoga, a few miles from the homes of Ellen
and W. C. White. Elder White, hearing that Jones was speaking nearby,
went with Daniells, who was visiting in California, to hear him. They
found Jones, street preaching on contemporary issues, in front of the
local hotel with a large world map stretched between the hotel pillars.
He had about 30 listeners who came and went as they pleased. White
and Daniells had to leave before Jones finished, but they left a note for
him to visit them.

The next day Jones met with Ellen White, Daniells, and W. C. White in
her home. He then spent an hour alone with the aged prophetess. "She
talked with him very plainly and kindly about his position and his work,"
W. C. White reported, "and pleaded with him to break the spell which
was over him." She also read a testimony to him that she had penned a
few days before. Part of it was a request to republish his talks in the 1893
and 1897 *General Conference Bulletins*. Those messages contained "strong
arguments regarding the validity of the Testimonies, and which substantiate the gift of prophecy among us." Reprinting the articles, she asserted,
would strengthen the faith of many, including their author.[17]

After his private meeting with Ellen White, her son reported that Jones
proposed that the entire group "pray for that work to be done for him
which she had spoken of; and we knelt down and had an earnest season
of prayer. Mother prayed very earnestly, and in a way that I thought

would touch his heart. Elder Jones prayed earnestly, expressing, among other things, his thankfulness for the light and liberty which the Lord was giving him."[18]

Soon after prayer he left for the nearby St. Helena Sanitarium, where he underwent treatment for a severe boil. He rested at the sanitarium for several days. On Sabbath he went to church and heard Daniells preach. Two days later he and Daniells had an extended talk together.[19]

To some it appeared that there still might be hope for Jones. Ellen White, however, was not optimistic. She noted that he had little sense of his true condition and that she saw nothing to encourage hope that he was coming out of his spiritual darkness. Any potential chances for reconciliation soon vanished, since the Whites and Daniells did not feel that Jones should have access to the pulpit of the San Francisco church. That hurt the ever-sensitive Jones. He fired off a letter to Ellen White, disparaging her motives for wanting to republish his articles from the *General Conference Bulletin* and telling her that he had no desire to use the San Francisco church. He was happy, he claimed, to preach on the streets. Thus ended the 1908 attempt at reconciliation. If there ever had been any hope—which is extremely doubtful—it had gone up in a puff of smoke. Jones would continue his tour of California, extolling his version of religious liberty (which included freedom from the conference organization) and accepting tithe money wherever offered.[20]

The final strands of Jones's formal connection to the Adventist Church severed in 1909. April 26 was a busy day for him. He posted two important letters. The first was a 19-page critical letter to Ellen White that informed her as to why he did not have confidence in her work. His second letter was an appeal to the General Conference requesting a public hearing before the full session of that body that would be meeting in May.[21]

Daniells was quite willing to grant him a hearing, but he insisted that it would be before a committee rather than before the entire body of delegates. Jones received more than two hours to make his case. In the course of his remarks he pointed out that even the Papacy had provided hearings for Huss, Jerome, and Luther, but that "organized" Adventism had not done the same for him when it removed his credentials in 1907. The obvious implication was that the Adventist leaders were more papal than the Papacy, an idea that Jones firmly believed by 1909. He did not appeal to the General Conference to have his credentials returned, because "no true credential was taken away: all that was taken away was a piece of paper." Nor did he request the reversal of any action taken against him. His entreaty, he stated, was a petition to be heard as an act of Christian justice. He later published his talk as a 76-page booklet entitled *An Appeal for Evangelical Christianity.*[22]

The grievance committee met three times with him over a period of four days. On May 31, before the committee took final action, Daniells made a statement of appreciation to the committee concerning Jones's many years of faithful service. "Then turning to Brother Jones," reports a participant, "he made a very tender and touching appeal for him to forget the past and to come back to stand shoulder to shoulder with his brethren in the service of the Lord. He assured him that we all loved him and that we wanted him to go with us in the march toward the kingdom of God. Extending his hand across the table, he said, in a choking voice, 'Come, Brother Jones, come.' At this, Brother Jones arose, started to reach his hand across the table, only to draw it back. Several times, as Brother Daniells continued to plead, saying, with tears in his voice, 'Come, Brother Jones, come!' Brother Jones would hesitatingly reach out his hand part way across the table, and pull it back again. The last time he almost clasped the hand outstretched from the other side, then, suddenly, pulled it back, and cried out, 'No! No!' and sat down." Following that moving incident, the grievance committee unanimously voted to reaffirm the 1907 decision of the General Conference Committee.[23]

The Washington newspapers treated the meeting in a sensational manner. The Washington *Post,* for example, devoted half of an illustrated page to the topic. The large headlines read: "IS ANOTHER RELIGION TO COME OUT OF WASHINGTON—A RIVAL TO THE SEVENTH DAY [sic] ADVENTISTS?" The article characterized Jones as "one of the ablest thinkers" of the denomination. In the face of Ellen White's reprimanding attitude toward him, the *Post* noted that "he has proved as intractable as John Knox with Scotland's fascinating Queen Mary."[24]

The "hero" of the episode, however, did not split the church or start a new denomination. On the other hand, the Berkeley, California, church formally disfellowshipped him on August 21, 1909. Unfortunately, his loss of membership did not end his war against Adventism. In many ways it only intensified the struggle.[25]

The stimulus was the publication of the ninth volume of *Testimonies for the Church*. Ellen White had included in it a section on religious liberty, which counseled Seventh-day Adventists not to challenge Sunday laws by working on Sunday where such laws were in force. Rather, they should "show their wisdom by refraining from their ordinary work on that day, devoting it to missionary work." Her position radically disagreed with Jones's that Adventists should oppose Sunday laws in the same way that the three Hebrew worthies challenged Nebuchadnezzar by refusing to bow to his image on the plain of Dura. As a result, Jones published a rabid attack on the denomination in December 1909 in his *Ten Commandments for Sunday Observance,* inferring that both Ellen White and the Seventh-day Adventist leadership had apostatized, gone over to Rome, and were advocating acceptance of the mark of the beast.[26]

Interestingly, Ellen White had never advocated the breaking of Sunday laws, even though the denomination had officially espoused that position in 1885. Carrying out that decision had caused the arrest of numerous Adventists in Tennessee and other states during the late 1880s and early 1890s. It was Jones and his colleagues in the religious liberty work who had continually fostered the extremist position on the issue. When the depth of the problem became evident to Ellen White in 1895, she immediately wrote to Jones and others that it was best to obey the laws and do missionary work on Sunday—the same counsel she later published in volume 9. As shown in chapter 6, however, Jones never did accept her advice. It contradicted his views.[27] As a result, her stand on the topic had festered in his mind for 14 years, finally breaking out in 1909 as the apostasy of Ellen White and the church. A. T. Jones had a difficult time accepting the fact that truth could ever be different from his own opinion.

In years to come, when some appealed to him to come back into the "grand old message," he would invariably reply that *he was in the message, while the denomination had left its old teachings.* His key example was the decision to compromise with the devil by not working on Sunday. That, he publicly claimed, made the denomination an apostate from its former position, and a church that was no longer able to defend God's truth or to preach the third angel's message. Neither, he retorted, had he left the denomination: he was *"driven out* by the would-be-head of the family."[28]

A NEW BRAND OF "RELIGIOUS LIBERTY"

Just because Jones differed from his former Adventist colleagues did not mean that he could not or would not work with them. For example, on at least three different occasions in 1909 and 1910 he teamed up with Adventists to work against pending Sunday legislation before congressional committees. In February 1909 Jones, W. W. Prescott, and W. A. Colcord testified before the House Committee for the District of Columbia. Jones spoke on the rights of the individual. His talk, according to Daniells, "was one of the best addresses made." The next month the head of the Adventist Religious Liberty Association once more called on Jones to testify. The year 1910 again found him going before a congressional committee with Colcord and Prescott. On that occasion the Religious Liberty Association published their speeches. It was probably the last time an Adventist press printed one of his presentations during his lifetime.[29]

Jones not only yoked up with Adventists—he also enjoyed attending their gatherings. In October 1911, for instance, he held meetings in an empty store about a block from the Battle Creek Tabernacle. The first night he had an audience of about 25. About half that many attended the next night, and a few the third. Then, on the evening that Daniells opened a ministerial institute in the Tabernacle, Jones and his assistant had not a single person present. They finally turned out the lights and went to the Adventist meeting. After that, Jones daily sat in on some of the institute sessions, not "to engage in argument or discussion" but just to be there. "I can not help but pity poor A. T.," Daniells wrote near the end of the institute. "When I think of the times he has stood in the Tabernacle, holding thousands of people spellbound with the mighty truth he was preaching, and then see the poor old man trying to hold meetings in a poor, dingy, dirty store-room, unable to get a baker's half dozen, I certainly feel sorry for him. It is strange he can not be brought to his senses, and be led to see the terrible mistake he is making."[30]

A humorous event took place during the Battle Creek institute. One woman, on the basis of her belief that Jones and Daniells would not speak to each other, invited both men to dinner without telling either one about the other. It caught them both off guard. "We had," Daniells claimed, "a good laugh about the surprise party, and made the best of it. We had an enjoyable visit through dinner, and a little while after. Nothing was said about the controversies that have separated us."[31]

In spite of Jones's occasional working together with Adventists and almost "fraternizing" with them in their meetings, he consistently claimed that he was glad to be free from denominational control. That freedom, in fact, became the basis for his new emphasis on religious liberty.

"Liberty," he stated, is "'the state of being exempt from the domination of others, or from restricting circumstances.'" That same freedom, he asserted, is true for religious liberty. He characterized churches as having absolutely no authority or jurisdiction over individuals. It is only the Holy Spirit who has any authority. Self-government is the goal to be reached. The divine right of "*individuality*" is an "eternal principle" that should guide all human relationships. Jones was particularly upset with organized denominations, claiming that when a person held membership in a church he belonged to a local congregation, not a "hierarchy." According to his logic, however, even the local congregation would not have any jurisdiction over its individual members.[32]

It is plain that his new brand of religious liberty stemmed directly from both his theory of church organization and the mistreatment he believed he had received at the hands of religious authorities. In his usual manner, he had taken part of the truth too far, while neglecting other elements of it. He had captured the concepts of the priesthood of each believer and the headship of Christ over the church, but had completely missed the fact that the New Testament described it as a corporate body with each believer as a person-in-community and not as an isolated individual. His own course of action showed how desperately he needed the corrective influence of the larger body of the church. If anybody was an individual it was Jones, but it was that very individualism, coupled with his view that he was always right (presumably because he was under the direct guidance of the Holy Spirit), that led him down the path of his own destruction.

Jones had a second thread to his new message on religious liberty during this period. That was his war against the Federal Council of Churches. He had attended the interchurch meeting that recommended the federation in 1905, and he had fought it from its inception, viewing it as a superdenomination that would destroy individualism and promote Sunday laws. Between 1906 and 1910 he wrote at least three books against the federation. Those books, as well as his preaching on religious liberty during this period, combined the themes of the divine right of individuality and the crisis of federation with traditional religious liberty issues such as opposition to Sunday laws. Adventism, he was quick to point out, was not free from the problems inherent in federation. In fact, the Adventist Church could hardly hope to stand against the evils of the Federal Council or the Catholic Church, since it was more federated than either of them.[33]

CLOSING LABORS[34]

The Berkeley Seventh-day Adventist Church disfellowshipped Jones in 1909. Subsequently he associated with the People's Church in Washington, D.C. He moved to the capital in 1915, at which time he founded a private journal entitled the *American Sentinel of Religious Liberty* (not to be confused with the earlier denominational journal with the same title). At first he did not join the People's Church because it had reentered the Seventh-day Adventist denomination in 1913. But he did take part in their services. The congregation and pastor eventually asked him to become a member. Jones replied that he would never unite with an organized denomination. At that point they made arrangements for him to connect with the local church without joining the denomination. In response to their offer, he told them to count the cost, since the conference would not be happy with the arrangement. They voted to accept him anyway. The upshot was that the People's Church withdrew from the Seventh-day Adventist denomination a second time in 1916. Soon after, they published a tract on their experience that wholeheartedly expounded Jones's organizational theory. He, in fact, was probably the ghostwriter behind the tract, even though his name does not appear as one of the authors.[35]

His main function from 1915 until the beginning of 1923 was to edit the *Sentinel*. Beyond that, he was still an active speaker on topics related to religious liberty. In 1916 he took time out to preach the funeral sermon of E. J. Waggoner, his *"blood-brother* in 'the blood of the everlasting covenant.'"[36] They had teamed up together in 1888, both had split off with Kellogg in 1903, and now the first of them was gone. Jones would outlive his friend by nearly seven years.

His *American Sentinel* not only opposed religious legislation, but spoke out against church federation and organization, and never lost an opportunity to take a public shot at Seventh-day Adventists. On the positive side, it uplifted the Holy Spirit and Jones's interpretation of the gospel.

A sampling of its contents indicates that Jones was still playing the same tunes that he had played earlier in his work. In April 1921, for example, he wrote that "there has never been a system of what is called 'church organization' that has not demonstrated itself to be as cruel as the devil." Then in May he rebuked the Adventist Church for calling itself the remnant church, whereas Revelation 12:17 spoke of the remnant of the church. The July and August issues found him taking the Adventists to task for giving a positive word on behalf of the recently deceased Cardinal Gibbons and doing business with a Catholic lawyer.[37] In short, the *Sentinel* had much of a muckraking quality that expressed the aggressive side of Jones's personality—a characteristic that had complicated matters in 1888 and had proved to be a detriment to his work throughout the nineties.

Perhaps the apex of his bitterness occurred when the denomination elected W. A. Spicer in place of Daniells as president of the General Conference in 1922. The San Francisco newspapers featured articles that clearly indicated that a political struggle had taken place on the part of those who wanted Daniells out, and that he had objected to their methods as a betrayal. Jones published photocopies of the newspaper articles in the *Sentinel* and analyzed Daniells' role in a critical light. His personal animosity toward the man rose to the surface when he asked how it was "that for *twenty-two years* Elder Daniells could be the master politician in a world-campaign of this same kind of ecclesiastical politics, and then kick so like a wild-ass when the thing *struck him.*"[38] Though he had written so much about the Holy Spirit through the years, Jones still had not surrendered his tongue or his pen to the Spirit in his seventy-second year.

During his final years he continued to hold most of the extreme positions he had taught in the nineties. During World War I, for example, when the United States struggled with the problem of how to determine the true conscientious objectors to war, Jones published the final test: "*Do You Vote?*" From his perspective, anyone who voted was a citizen of the United States and not of heaven. Since a person could not hold citizenship in both, the solution was simple. Anyone who voted must fight to support what he voted for. Jones was still an absolute separationist who had not yet come to a realistic position on "rendering unto Caesar." His ideological argument, however, did not hinder him from requesting a military pension for his part in the Modoc War. He went after his governmental pension with gusto and perseverance within a few months of the first publication of his article on conscientious objectors.[39]

Also insightful into Jones's experience was his attitude toward the Pentecostal movement that had swept the nation since the turn of the century. It elated him to discover a group of Pentecostals who believed in the Seventh-day Sabbath. He wrote that speaking in tongues and Sabbathkeeping belonged together. "*Now*," Jones exuded, "in His good Providence and by His good Spirit, the Lord is blending *in one blessed people* the Pentecostal truth and the Sabbath truth that always ought to have been so blended, and that now will be forevermore."[40]

With the rise of this new group, Jones's charismatic self—which had been evident at his baptism and throughout his ministry—glimpsed a chance at fulfillment. Here at last was a group he could truly feel at home with. He preached at their camp meetings and fellowshiped with their clergy.

His euphoria, however, was short-lived. In the next issue of the *Sentinel* the crestfallen editor proclaimed that the Pentecostal Sabbath observers had committed the ultimate sin—they had begun to organize a denomination. Was not that, he howled, the very thing that had "spoiled the Lord's Sabbath-keeping movement of the latter time" and "is spoiling the Lord's Pentecostal movement of the latter time." To him that was the ultimate failure. It was the act of driving away the Spirit. Jones was destined to remain spiritually frustrated to the very end of his active life.[41]

"MORTEM" AND POSTMORTEM

The January 1923 issue of the *American Sentinel* failed to meet its publication deadline. The reason: its editor in chief had been struck with "sudden and severe illness" and had been taken to the Adventists' Washington Sanitarium and Hospital for treatment. After spending a month in the Washington hospital, Jones transferred to the Battle Creek Sanitarium. "My sickness," he wrote on March 4, "has not been of suffering from pain but from the weariness of utter exhaustion." As usual, however, he was optimistic. Both he and his physicians recognized that he was making good progress in recovering. The 72-year-old Jones committed himself to slow but steady progress. "It took fifty years to get down to where I was, and I am not going to be impatient or rebellious if it takes fifty *days* or even more to get back again to where I belong."[42]

By early May his condition had improved to such an extent that it appeared that he would soon be going home. In anticipation, he and his wife had recently purchased a house in Battle Creek. At 6:30 in the morning on May 12, however, he suffered a cerebral hemorrhage and passed to his rest.[43]

Despite his animosity toward the organized church, Jones seemed to long for Adventist companionship until his end. When he was seriously ill in Washington, Clifton L. Taylor went to visit him at the sanitarium, but Mrs. Jones turned him away at the door. Jones, however, heard that Taylor—his former student and colleague—was there, and invited him in, greeting him warmly and pleading with Taylor never to forget that "I have never given up the faith of Seventh-day Adventists. There was never a time in my life when I loved the Message more than I do today." He wept and spoke, Taylor noted, "with emotions, such as I had never seen him display before." Taylor's opinion harmonizes with that of Jones's daughter (Mrs. Desi Stevens), who also testified that he had never departed from Seventh-day Adventist beliefs. On the other hand, we should not forget that Jones had developed a sort of double talk regarding his beliefs in Adventism and Ellen White. We always need to interpret his statements in the light of his personal definitions and language usage.[44]

On another occasion, when Jones was well enough to sit in the hospital lobby, Daniells passed by him without recognizing him in his weakened condition. Jones, claimed his attendant, was terribly disappointed that Daniells did not stop and talk with him. Both Taylor and Daniells (as well as Jones's hospital attendant, who was an Adventist) expressed the opinion that they expected to see Jones in the kingdom despite his bitterness, discouragement, and differences with the church.[45] That decision, of course, will be made by a higher tribunal than human opinion, but human opinion is still of interest as we seek to understand the complexity of the man.

Frances Jones survived her husband by 23 years, passing away on March 5, 1946, at the age of 91. In spite of her husband's disaffection from the denomination, his widow received sustentation benefits from May 1924 until her death. Beyond that, the Battle Creek pastor and the

Michigan Conference president managed to obtain special General Conference funds for her in time of illness. To most people that seemed to be a generous gesture, but some of Jones's former colleagues in his war against the denomination saw it as a device to "padlock" her mouth.[46] The war had continued, even though one of its leaders had fallen.

Mrs. Jones remained a member of the Battle Creek Seventh-day Adventist Church until the end of her life. Her pastor for the final few years was Taylor G. Bunch, whose father had witnessed Jones's baptism in 1874, had heard his first sermon shortly thereafter, and had corresponded with him until his death. Bunch, upon the death of Mrs. Jones, inherited a black trunk containing Jones's private papers. Interestingly enough, he had kept "all of Sister White's letters to him and many to others."[47]

The *American Sentinel* continued under the editorship of H. M. Lawson, but the new editor faced a peculiar frustration as he sought to carry on Jones's work. Lawson penned his discouragement to E. S. Ballenger in 1928: "I have tried hard for six years to find three or five good men that will tell the truth to take hold with me and organize, but they stand back and cry, Brother Jones advised us never to tie up to anything again." Nine years later, Lawson had still not been able to organize a body of believers. "From the time that A. T. Jones first flew the track on the subject of Church Organization," Lawson complained, "his friends have refused to listen to anything that does not hold to his teaching."[48] Such was the lasting fruit of Jones's labor.

In concluding our study of Jones, perhaps it will be helpful to go back to a thought expressed in this book's preface. Having studied his life for several years, I find it almost impossible to believe that the mighty Jones of the early 1890s could have shipwrecked his faith. On the other hand, it seems almost impossible—given his pride, headstrong opinions, and extremism—for him to have done anything else. The key to his future lay in the message that was so close to his heart—to let the power of the Holy Spirit transform his life through faith. It was on that point that he failed. He had a correct theory of the truth, but he failed in its practice.

A. T. Jones's message still speaks to each of us today. Each of us can learn from the triumphs and tragedies of his life. Like him, each of us has more than one way to live our life. Jones would say that the choice is "individually" up to us.

[1] On A. F. Ballenger, see Edwards and Land, *Seeker After Light;* on L. C. Sheafe, see Douglas Morgan, *Lewis C. Sheafe: Apostle to Black America* (Hagerstown, Md., 2010).

[2] AGD to HWC, Jan. 20, 1907; AGD to WWP, Jan. 20, 1907; cf. AGD to WCW, Jan. 18, 1907.

[3] AGD to WCW, Mar. 18, 1907; AGD to HWC, Apr. 3, Jan. 20, 1907; ATJ to Dear Brother, July 3, 1907.

[4] AGD to WCW, Jan. 23, Feb. 20, 1907.

[5] WAC to EWF, Apr. 25, 1907.

[6] AGD to HWC, Jan. 20, 1907.

[7] AGD to WCW, Jan. 23, 1907; WCW to AGD, Feb. 14, 1907.

[8] AGD to WCW, June 23, 24, 1908; Mar. 22, Apr. 4, 1909; AGD to L. R. Conradi, Feb. 23, 1909; W. B. White to WCW, July 26, 1908; WCW to W. B. White, Aug. 18, 1908; EGW to SNH, Nov. 11, 1908.

[9] ATJ, *An Appeal for Evangelical Christianity*, pp. 34, 45, 60-76; ATJ, *God's Everlasting Covenant* (Battle Creek, 1907); ATJ to AGD, Aug. 20, 1907; AGD to ATJ, Aug. 15, 1907; AGD to WCW, Nov. 17, 1911; C. H. Edwards to ESB, Nov. 6, 1922; WAC to EGW, Apr. 25, 1907; J. H. Morrison, *A Straight Talk to Old Brethren* ([n.p.], c. 1914), pp. 162, 163.

[10] GCC Min, Oct. 4, 1906.

[11] GCC Min, May 22, 1907; WAS to ATJ, June 17, 1907; *RH*, June 27, 1907, pp. 5, 6.

[12] ATJ to GCC, June 21, 1907.

[13] ATJ, *The Christian Church and Church Federation* ([Battle Creek], 1907), pp. 99-107; EGW to ATJ, May 7, 1902.

[14] SNH to EGW, July 17, 1908; SNH to WCW, July 19, 26, 1908; WCW to SNH, July 21, 1908; Minutes, Berkeley, California, SDA Church, Aug. 15, 1908.

[15] Minutes, Berkeley, California, SDA Church, Aug. 22, 1908.

[16] *Ibid.*, Aug. 29, Oct. 7, 1908; SNH to WCW, Aug. 19, 1908; SNH to EGW, Aug. 23, Sept. 30, 1908; HWC to AGD, Sept. 12, Oct, 5, 1908; SNH to AGD, Oct. 8, 1908.

[17] WCW to WWP, Aug. 20, 1908; WCW to SNH, July 31, 1908; EGW to ATJ, July 25, 1908; EGW to SNH, Aug. 3, 1908.

[18] WCW to WWP, Aug. 20, 1908.

[19] *Ibid.*

[20] EGW to SNH, Aug. 3, 1908; WCW to WWP, Aug. 20, 1908; ATJ to EGW, Aug. 9, 1908; WCW to E. R. Palmer, Aug. 3, 1908; SNH to AGD, Oct. 6, 1908.

[21] ATJ to EGW, Apr. 26, 1909; ATJ to the General Conference of SDA, Apr. 26, 1909.

[22] AGD to EGW, Mar. 15, 1909; 1909 *GCB*, pp. 270, 271; ATJ, *An Appeal for Evangelical Christianity*, pp. 9, 69.

[23] A. V. Olson, "Experience of A. T. Jones at 1909 General Conference," unpub. MS, n.d.; C. H. Edwards to ESB, Nov. 6, 1922; 1909 *GCB*, pp. 270, 271; WAS to ATJ, June 7, 1909.

[24] Washington *Post*, July 18, 1909, p. 4.

[25] Membership records of Berkeley, California, SDA Church.

[26] EGW, *Testimonies for the Church*, vol. 9, p. 232; D. E. Robinson to J. O. Corliss, Jan. 6, 1911; ATJ, *The Ten Commandments for Sunday Observance* ([Battle Creek], 1909).

[27] *RH*, Feb. 10, 1910, pp. 5, 6; Dec. 1, 1885, pp. 744, 745; J. H. Morrison, *Straight Talk*, pp. 150, 151; EGW to ATJ, Nov. 21, 1895; EGW, MS 22a, Nov. 20, 1895; CPB to OAO, Dec. 9, 1896.

[28] ATJ to A. Moon, Jan. 13, 1910; ATJ to [M. C.] Wilcox, Jan. 7, 1912; ATJ, *That*

Debate: Why Is It? What Is It? (n.p., [1911]); ATJ to GCC, Mar. 15, 1912; ATJ, *The Story of Two Days Rest in Seven* (Washington, D.C., [1917]).

²⁹ AGD to WCW, Feb. 19, 1909; ATJ, *Church Federation and the Kingdom of God* ([Battle Creek], 1910), p. 76; WWP, ATJ, and WAC, *Partial Report of Hearing on Johnston Sunday Bill* (Washington, D.C., [1910]).

³⁰ AGD to WCW, Nov. 17, 1911; AGD to EWF, Nov. 20, 1911.

³¹ AGD to EWF, Nov. 20, 1911; AGD to WCW, Nov. 17, 1911.

³² ATJ, *The Divine Right of Individuality*, pp. 5, 79, 112; ATJ, *The Christian Church and Church Federation*, pp. 56, 72, 106.

³³ *MM*, December 1905, p. 399; ATJ, *The World's Greatest Issues* ([Battle Creek], 1906); ATJ, *The Christian Church and Church Federation*; ATJ, *Church Federation and the Kingdom of God*; Battle Creek *Daily Enquirer*, Jan. 14, 1913; ATJ, *An Appeal for Evangelical Christianity*, p. 59.

³⁴ In *From 1888 to Apostasy* I erroneously claimed that Jones had ministered for the Seventh-day Adventist Reform Movement after leaving mainline Adventism. Since that publication I have concluded that the minister in question was E. B. Jones rather than A. T. Jones. See Oscar Kramer to Editor, Aug. 12, 1991.

³⁵ 1913 GCB, pp. 212, 213; J. W. Allison et al., *Experience of the People's S.D.A. Church* ([Washington, D.C., c. 1917]), pp. 1-17. See also, Morgan, *L. C. Sheafe*, chapter 35.

³⁶ *The Gathering Call*, November 1916, pp. 5-7.

³⁷ *AS* (2), April 1921, p. 4; May 1921, p. 8; July 1921, pp. 7, 8; August 1921, pp. 5, 6.

³⁸ San Francisco *Chronicle*, May 22, 23, 1922; San Francisco *Examiner*, May 23, 1922; *AS* (2), July 1922, pp. 2-7.

³⁹ *AS* (2), October 1922, pp. 7, 8 (this article was first published in the *Sentinel* in June and July 1917); ATJ to the Commissioner of Pensions, May 10, 1916.

⁴⁰ *AS* (2), September 1922, pp. 7, 8.

⁴¹ *Ibid.*, October 1922, pp. 3, 4; cf. November 1922, pp. 4-6; December 1922, pp. 3, 4.

⁴² *Ibid.*, January 1923, p. 8.

⁴³ Certificate of death, state of Michigan, city of Battle Creek, May 12, 1923; *AS* (2), July 1923, pp. 1-7; *RH*, June 28, 1923, p. 22; Battle Creek *Moon-Journal*, May 12, 1923, p. 12.

⁴⁴ CLT to LEF, Oct. 26, 1960; LEF to TGB, Oct. 24, 1961.

⁴⁵ LEF to TGB, June 27, 1967; TGB to LEF, Nov. 1, 1961; Mar. 12, 1967; CLT to LEF, Oct. 26, Nov. 9, 1960.

⁴⁶ *RH*, Apr. 25, 1946, p. 20; HHC to FEJ, May 27, 1924; TGB to HHC, May 31, 1938; C. B. Haynes to HHC, May 9, 1938; HHC to FEJ, June 2, 1938; ESB to W. P. Faulkner, Apr. 26, 1945.

⁴⁷ TGB to ALW, Nov. 25, 1964; TGB to LEF, Nov. l, 1961, Mar. 12, 1967. I have not been able to locate that "black trunk" or its contents in spite of a diligent search.

⁴⁸ H. M. Lawson to [ESB], Aug. 14, 1928, June 22, 1937.

INDEX

136, 139, 156, 185, 186, 189, 199, 221;
against Jones's interpretation of prophecy,
93-95; attitude toward Ellen White's in-
spiration, 55; editorial policy of, 94;
Jones's associate editor of the *Review*, 190;
on Daniel 7, 32, 33, 38, 39; on righteous-
ness by faith, 58
Solusi, 159-164, 186, 188
Some History, Some Experience, and Some Facts,
250
South Lancaster, Mass., 52, 134
Spalding, Arthur, 18
Spicer, W. A., 85, 117, 214, 281
Spirit of Christ, 75
Spirit of Minneapolis, 46, 47, 56, 75-77, 94,
124, 166-169
St. Helena Sanitarium, 225, 226, 231, 275
Statement Refuting Charges Made by A. T. Jones,
251
Stevens, Desi, see Jones, Desi
Stokes, Anson Phelps, 92
Strong, Josiah, 30
Sunday, a papal institution, 151, 152
Sunday laws, 20, 45, 83-86, 93, 95, 115, 122,
151, 155, 158, 161, 163, 242-244, 277,
278, 280; Arkansas, 31, 45, 83; national,
30-32; Tennessee, 83
Sutherland, E. A., 199, 200, 224, 238, 241

T

Tait, O. A., 189
Tax exemption for church property, 158-160
Taylor, Clifton L., 283
Ten kingdoms, see Daniel 7
Ten Commandments for Sunday Observance, 92,
277
Testimonies, relationship to Bible, 259, 260
Third angel's message, 72-75, 80, 122
Thoughts on Daniel and the Revelation, 24, 32
Turkey, 186
Two Republics, 152, 156, 158

U

Unions, labor, 243
Upper Columbia Conference, 20, 222
User-Friendly Guide to the 1888 Message, 11

V

Valentine, Gilbert, 11
Van Horn, Issac, 18, 19, 20, 199
Vande Vere, E. K., 35
Verbal inspiration, 261

W

Waggoner, E. J., 130, 195, 196, 216, 280; biog-
raphy of, 11; E. White did not always
agree with his theology, 41, 77, 78, 179;
essential contribution to Adventist theology, 42; on health reform extremes, 112;
on human nature of Christ, 166, 167,
169, 171-178; on law in Galatians, 26-30;
on righteousness by faith, 41; shared
Jones's ecclesiology, 205-218
Waggoner, J. H., 23
Wahlen, Clinton, 11
Walla Walla, Wash., 17, 135
Walla Walla College, 199
Warren, Luther, 194
Washington, 18, 19
Whidden, Woodrow, 11
White, Ellen G., 18, 19, 20, 28, 35, 51, 52, 58,
62, 63, 94, 119, 221, 222, 226, 235, 238,
240, 241, 246, 252, 255, 272-277; a
moderate, 257; attempts to reclaim Jones
for the church, 242-245; cautions Jones to
less abrasiveness, 191, 198, 225, 226,
229; cautions Jones not to align with
Kellogg, 237; Christ-centered writing after
1888, 54; conflict with Butler, 34-36, 40,
41; counseled Jones not to create excessive feeling in preaching, 193; counseled
Jones not to mix his words with hers,
198; did not always agree with
Waggoner's theology, 41, 77, 78, 179; extent of endorsement of Jones and
Waggoner, 77-79; held that her role was
not to settle theological controversies,
180, 181; Jones's early support of, 20, 21;
later relationship with Jones, 255-267;
moderate on church-state issues, 157,
160, 163, 164; not concerned with failure
in 1893, 125; on acceptance of 1888 message, 68; on Anna Rice, 134-138; on authority of General Conference, 198, 206,
208; on essence of 1888 message, 71-73;
on faith healing, 106-108; on government
aid, 162-164; on justification, 73, 74; on
law in Galatians, 28, 43, 45, 76; on "not
being a prophet," 266, 267; on Sunday
labor, 91, 92; on third angel's message,
72-74; practical rather than doctrinaire,
181, 182; rejection of at Minneapolis, 47,
48; rescues Jones's conference presidency,
228-232; sparks 1901 organizational reform, 210; supports Jones and Waggoner,
41
Ellen G. White 1888 Materials, 70
White, James, 19, 27

White, J. Edson, 166
White, W. C., 21, 22, 23, 34-36, 40, 42, 46,
        51, 68, 69, 78, 89, 101, 163, 185, 187,
        214, 215, 222, 228, 230, 239, 240, 249,
        250, 265, 274
Wilcox, F. M., 79, 111, 130, 136, 138, 161
Winner, W. L., 270, 271
Women's Christian Temperance Union, 30, 191

Z
Zimbabwe, 160-164

Take the Tour

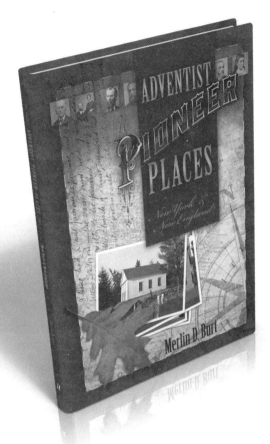

Visit the sites where the Adventist faith began: the pioneers' homes and churches, the sites of births and deaths, the special places where visions descended and revival arose.

Adventist Pioneer Places includes:

- maps • current, color photographs of landmarks • historic photographs
- stories that illuminate the lives of the pioneers • GPS coordinates

Merlin D. Burt's handbook serves as an invaluable guide for a trip in the family car or for a virtual tour taken in the comfort of your favorite reading chair. You will feel inspired as you walk in the footsteps of people who, though weak and fallible, were used by God in remarkable ways to establish a global community of believers and begin a series of events that would eventually touch your own life. 978-0-8280-2568-3

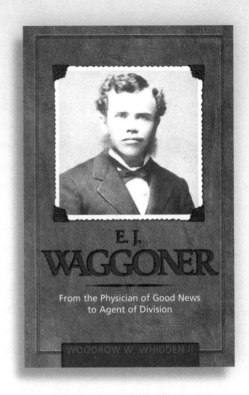

Lest We Forget ...

"We have nothing to fear for the future, except as we shall forget the way the Lord has led us, and His teaching in our past history." —ELLEN G. WHITE.

JOHN HARVEY KELLOGG

Pioneering Health Reformer

A surgeon, dietitian, inventor, administrator, religious leader, and author, Kellogg packed the accomplishments of many men into one lifetime. In this engrossing biography Richard Schwarz probes Kellogg's complicated, controversial, and unforgettable life. Hardcover, 240 pages. 978-0-8280-1939-2

SHOP **YOUR** WAY

- Visit your local ABC
- Call 1-800-765-6955
- www.AdventistBookCenter.com

Availability subject to change.

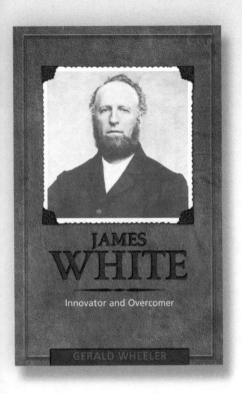

Ellen White Series

by George R. Knight

Discover the life, times, and counsel of Ellen G. White as well as the lady herself.

978-0-8280-1089-4

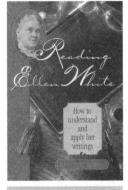

978-0-8280-1263-8

978-0-8280-1356-7

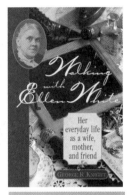

978-0-8280-1429-8

Adventist Heritage Series

by George R. Knight

A fascinating look at the development, beliefs, and structure of the Seventh-day Adventist church.

978-0-8280-1430-4

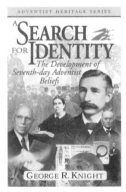

978-0-8280-1541-7

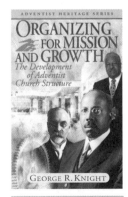

978-0-8280-1980-4